TALMUDIC LAW AND THE MODERN STATE

by Moshe Silberg, Dr. jur.

*Former Deputy President of the Supreme Court of
Israel*
*Professor Emeritus of Law of Personal Status, The
Hebrew University, Jerusalem*

Translated by Ben Zion Bokser

Edited by Marvin S. Wiener

THE BURNING BUSH PRESS

NEW YORK

Original Hebrew Title: *Kakh Darko Shel Talmud (Principia Talmudica)*
Faculty of Law of the Hebrew University, Legal Studies No. 8
Published by *Mif'al Hashichpul*
The Hebrew University Students' Press
Jerusalem

ISBN: 0-8381-3112-3
Library of Congress Catalog Card Number: 73-76348

MANUFACTURED IN THE UNITED STATES OF AMERICA
BY THE BOOK PRESS

Contents

Translator's Introduction

The modern state, like its earlier predecessors, has as its primary objective to save society from lapsing into either of the twin perils—anarchy or tyranny. It does so by trying to reconcile the conflicting claims of man against man and—on occasion—of man against the state. Without the intervention of the state, the conflict between opposing claimants would go unresolved and each would seek to go his own way, without regard to the other. Society would thus become a battleground among claimants, which is anarchy, or the stronger might gain control and impose his will by arbitrary force, which is tyranny.

In fulfilling its mission, the state may have to engage in many involved and far-reaching enterprises, depending on the claims which require reconciliation. Consumers may claim that a company promotes its products through fraudulent advertising. Tenants may claim that a landlord allows health hazards in his rental property. Employers may claim that their employees fail to fulfill equitably contractual obligations for performance in their job assignments. The unemployed may have a claim against society as a whole for maintenance during times of hardship. The aged may have a claim against society for proper care, after they have made their contribution to the public good during their years of productivity. Minorities may have a claim against society that widespread discrimination denies them the opportunity for dignified and honorable livelihood. All the complex involvements in which the modern state engages derive from meeting some claim against particular individuals or groups in society, or society as a whole.

The state resolves the conflict by reference to "rights," on the basis of the merits of one claim over the other. By what criteria are these merits to be determined? This is the contribution made by law which sets forth a body of criteria by which to assess the "rights" of the litigants. The contention of both claimants may have merit. The state must then mediate between these competing rights, assigning the particular scope where each is to prevail. Law emanates from a basic charter of principles setting forth the norms under which a society seeks to conduct itself, from legislative enactments, and from precedents established in the course of time for dealing with such problems. Because law is often unclear in its cogency for a particular conflict, courts are established, and because claimants are not always ready to obey the decisions of the courts, the state has created a variety of sanctions to assure compliance.

A jurist is always concerned with precedent which illumines the present with the experiences of the past. And a wise jurist will extend the concern with precedent to societies other than his own. He will seek the norms by which societies everywhere have established criteria of "right," both through the enactment of law and the interpretation of law. The human spirit in its groping for equity, in whatever time or place it pursued its quest, offers relevant experience that always illumines our own world today.

The study of talmudic law is, of course, of special interest to the Jew. The Talmud is a precious treasure of Jewish wisdom in dealing with life. It mirrors the testing ground of experience where biblical idealism was translated into life and found efficacious—or wanting—in the search for equity. But talmudic law is of unique interest to all concerned with jurisprudence and with the search for equity and justice in our own time. For talmudic law has one aspect which is singularly its own: its major epoch of development occurred at the time when an autonomous Jewish state had ceased to exist and it had to operate without the recourse to force in order to gain conformity to its demands. It based its authority on religious and moral grounds. It had to rely on consent. It takes a people of unusually high ethical sensitivity and a legal system of unusual compassion and wisdom to function on the basis of free acquiescence, without resorting to coercive sanctions.

Justice Silberg's book is a brilliant exposition of talmudic law from this perspective of its inner dimension which enabled it to speak to the human conscience and gain obedience without coercion. It assesses legal norms in the Talmud in terms of their relevance for dealing with the problems of the modern state. It touches on areas where talmudic law needs supplementation in the light of new juridical experience. It assesses especially the relevance of talmudic law to the problems of the State of Israel. For while Israel is *a priori* committed to the utilization of classic Jewish sources in dealing with the manifold and complex problems it faces, Israeli society is religiously heterogeneous and cannot automatically enthrone a legal system based essentially on Jewish religious presuppositions. Some of its citizens, though Jewish, regard themselves as non-religious, while others adhere to various faith communities, as is the case with any other democratic society. Justice Silberg presents intriguing proposals for the proper utilization of talmudic law, within the heterogeneity of Israel's growing population.

Justice Silberg's book originated in a lecture series delivered at the Hebrew University in Jerusalem. The lectures, and the Hebrew volume which resulted from them, were followed with great interest by the Israeli public. We are confident that the English translation of this book will also find a wide and enthusiastic reading public in the English-speaking world.

I acknowledge with thanks the assistance I have received in preparing this translation. Justice Silberg examined the translation and made various suggestions to assure that the English text prove faithful to the Hebrew original. Rabbi Marvin S. Wiener edited the manuscript and also resolved the many technical and stylistic problems entailed in its publication. Mr. A. G. Kraus offered a number of criticisms with a view of simplifying the English version. My wife Kallia offered me her wise counsel and her encouragement, which have aided me in all my literary work. My son, Rabbi Baruch Micah Bokser, assisted me in researching a number of problems in talmudic law. Mrs. Shirley Tendler typed the manuscript in all the stages of its preparation and rendered me many other kindnesses. Miss Dorothy Sachs, of The Burning Bush Press, was most helpful in preparing the manuscript for the printer and in reading the galleys and page proofs. To them all and others unnamed here who assisted me, I am profoundly grateful.

I express, above all, my gratitude to Almighty God who has enabled me to begin and complete this study, which I hope will make for a wider knowledge and appreciation of the rich treasures in the jurisprudence of the Talmud.

BEN ZION BOKSER

Shevat 5733
January 1973
Forest Hills, New York

Author's Preface

The aim of this work may appear overly ambitious: to enable the modern individual to appreciate the modes of thought of the talmudic sages and to open a window into that strange, distant world of talmudic dialectic.

Everyone, nowadays, studies the Bible. Interest in the Aggadah has become intellectually fashionable thanks to Bialik and Ravnitsky's distinguished compilation, *Sefer HaAggadah*. But the Talmud—that monumental work which nurtured generations of Jews—remains in splendid isolation, in an obscure and neglected corner of our culture. It has ceased to function as an effective educational factor shaping the features and character of our people's spiritual life.

The leaders and teachers of our generation are, to a considerable extent, responsible for this state of affairs. I speak of the leaders and teachers from all camps, "religious" and "non-religious" alike, since both parties have not as yet devised an approach that would allow for an objective evaluation of the Talmud. The "religious" camp is uncritical in its praise; the "non-religious" camp, equally uncritical in its hostility. Both camps, then, have contributed to the resulting inaccurate and tendentious picture of this major historic creation.

I do not, of course, wish to belittle the value of the many monographs that have explored various talmudic themes, whether from legal or other perspectives. The worth of these works is unquestioned. But it seems doubtful to me whether these monographs which, after all, are limited in scope even when they exhibit the highest scholarly standards, will succeed in uprooting all the prevailing misconceptions concerning the Talmud. What is required, first and foremost, is an overview of the Talmud as a whole and an understanding of its unique climate and atmosphere through a critico-topical analysis—in modern terminology—of its modes of logic and forms of expression.

The author is well aware that his work is only the beginning of a new approach to the rich and complex world of talmudic thought, an approach that will engage neither in polemics nor in apologetics. May others, more competent and able than he, continue and complete the task. Then will the Talmud regain its rightful place among the spiritual treasures of the Jewish people.

The author's fundamental thesis is that the Talmud is a legal, juridical creation *par excellence.* He endeavors to examine this thesis from various perspectives in the first seven chapters of the work. The eighth and last chapter—"At the Crossroads"—is devoted to an analysis of an actual problem facing the State of Israel: the crisis that has overtaken the decisions in Israeli courts as a result of the absence of an independent Israeli code firmly grounded in the principles of Jewish law.

Eight years have passed since I wrote the above lines. During that time a lively debate has been carried on in the scholarly literature and in the public press between those who affirm and those who negate the revitalization of Jewish law. A complete polarization has taken place, similar to the polarization between religious belief and freedom of thought in society at large. We still await that *magnum opus* dealing with the unique historic challenge presented to the judges of this generation: to delineate the fundamental qualities of Jewish law and to examine the vitality of its institutions in the light of the Israeli reality and its experience.

MOSHE SILBERG

28 Menahem Av, 5730
August 30, 1970
Jerusalem

CHAPTER I

Legal Character

1. The ultimate basis for any appreciation of the unique features of the Talmud is the realization that the Talmud is a collective work of many generations, possessing a clear legal character both in those sections dealing with relationships between man and man and those dealing with relationships between man and God.

Jewish law, unlike practically all other legal systems, does not limit itself to the sphere of "between man and man." It also places the relations between man and God in juridical categories, it speaks of them in juridical terms, and it approaches them with a juridical conception. The Holy One, praised be He, in all His glory, is deemed as a kind of legal person, enjoying rights, being subject to obligations, heeding His own precepts, and entering as a subject of civil jurisdiction, as it were, in the complex of relations between Himself and His creatures.[1]

Many manifestations of this approach can be found throughout the Talmud. We will take the liberty of illustrating our thesis from the aggadic as well as the halakhic material, for the Talmud as a whole is one organic unit.

Consider, for example, one of the legends describing the

Sinaitic event—an event that by definition is pre-Torah-itic, for it was then that the Torah was given, and there can be no law prior to the giving of the Law, a legal norm cannot engender itself. Even so the Rabbis have attached legal concepts retroactively to this constitutive event.

The Talmud states:[2]

> "And they stood under the Mount" (Exodus 19:17)—this teaches that the Holy One, praised be He, suspended the mount upon them like an inverted cask, and said, "If ye accept the Torah, 'tis well; if not, there shall be your burial." Rabbi Aha bar Jacob observed: "This furnished a strong protest against the Torah."[3] Said Rava: "Yet even so they reaccepted it in the days of Ahasuerus, for it is written, 'The Jews confirmed and accepted upon them' (Esther 9:27), *i.e.,* they confirmed what they had accepted long before.

At Mount Sinai God established a covenant between Himself and His people.[4] A covenant is, in essence, a contract, and a contract requires mutual consent. This mutual consent was lacking in this instance for one of the contracting parties coerced the other party through suspending the mountain. If we could picture a tribunal competent to pass on litigations between God and Israel and were God to summon the Jews before this high tribunal, then the Jews would have a cogent protest [*moda'a*] against the Torah.[5] They could validly claim that the whole transaction of the acceptance of the Torah was null and void. They could claim, "We were coerced by the other party who gave the Torah." And the Torah itself states that an act of one who is coerced entails no legal consequences either in terms of punishment or obligation.[6] Then came the miracle of Purim to repair the defect in the Sinaitic covenant. Its binding authority was confirmed retroactively. For at that time, because of their gratitude for the miracle that God had wrought on their behalf, the Jews reaccepted the Torah out of their own free will.[7] From that time on no one would have grounds for bringing a lawsuit disputing the authority of the Torah.

This is a daring *aggadah*. Aside from anything else it depicts the warm intimacy existing between the Jews and their God. The God of this *aggadah* is not the great, awesome, mighty God of the Bible. Rather He is the "folk" God of the Talmud about whom one can ask: "Where are His mighty deeds? Where are His wondrous acts?"[8] Moreover, one may quite "defiantly" lodge before Him the protest, "You coerced us at Mount Sinai." But it is not this very interesting concept which concerns us here. What we wish to emphasize is the unique interplay between Halakhah and Aggadah, how the world of Aggadah can become suffused with normative halakhic concepts.

This interweaving of Halakhah and Aggadah is not in any sense ill-fitting. Rather each stream of thought complements the other. The Halakhah injects a note of reality into the free-floating, imaginative world of the Aggadah; the Aggadah softens the "austere" appearance[9] of the Halakhah, adding to it a touch of grace. Both benefit, then, from this blending together of diverse motifs. There is no perversion therefore in the retroactive projection of halakhic motifs to personalities and events preceding the giving of the Torah, and we are not to view as a "falsification of history" statements such as these:

> Our father Abraham kept the whole Torah . . . even the law concerning the *eruv* of dishes.[10]

> And Rebecca said to Jacob, "Go now to the flock and fetch me from there two choice kids" (Genesis 27:6,9). Did then two kids form a meal for Isaac? But this occurred on Passover: one he offered as his paschal sacrifice, and from the other he prepared the savoury food.[11]

> And Esau was a cunning hunter (Genesis 25:27)—cunning

in ensnaring and deceiving his father with the words of his mouth. He would ask him, "Father, how should salt and straw be tithed? . . ."[12]

Such statements have as their sole purpose the elevation of the authority of the Halakhah by endowing it with this retroactive power which is seen as being in force at the very dawn of our history. These statements were made deliberately; they may be termed, as it were, "transgressions performed for an ideal end" for were it not for these "distortions" there would be nothing left of the ties that link us to our early ancestors.

2. Any talmudic law—be it civil and secular or religious and ritualistic in nature—never stands alone. Rather it always forms part of an organic thought-complex in which all elements are bound up one with the other.[13] Both laws regulating relationships "between man and man" and those regulating relationships "between man and God" became embedded and integrated within a comprehensive legal structure, as we have already mentioned. The specific juridical character of these relationships is expressed by the word "between" which presumes even in the man-God relationship a reciprocity which engenders rights and obligations on the part of both parties. The religious commandment is not to be seen merely as a commandment. It should be viewed as a legal obligation that man owes God—an obligation that, in turn, creates an obligation that God owes man. Just as Jews put on *tefillin* [phylacteries], so does God![14] We might even go so far as to say that the Torah is not just a decree thrown at man from on high. Rather it is a covenant based on the relationship, "Fulfill your obligation and I will fulfill Mine." This view is set forth in a startling statement of the Palestinian Talmud:[15]

Rabbi Lazar said: "The law is not binding on the king."[16] A human king issues a decree. He may choose to obey it; he may choose to have only others obey it. Not so the Holy One, praised be He. When He issues a decree, He is the first to obey it, as it is stated: "And they shall observe My observances, I am the Lord," I am He who was the first to observe the commandments of the Torah.

This outlook in which the concept of the rule of law[17] finds such striking expression must necessarily have broad consequences for all branches of the Halakhah. First and foremost it renders impossible any division of religious and civil law into separate spheres. Both religious and civil law are cast into similar molds since both types of law involve the structuring of legal patterns of relationships, whether between man and man or between man and God. As a result of this obliteration of all boundaries, the entire range of religious practice is embraced within a network of purely juridical concepts.

A striking illustration of this is to be found, in my opinion, in the quality of "thingness"—an old and well-known legal concept—which surrounds in an ascending and descending manner the religious prohibition. The prohibition—even if it is a "personal" prohibition[18]—is not merely a categorical imperative, but something substantive, real, which applies (that is to say, descends or falls) on the forbidden object. Once the prohibition has descended and taken hold of the forbidden object, then— as in the physical world, so to speak—occupies space in it, a subsequent prohibition has no room where to apply. The result is: "One prohibition cannot apply where a previous prohibition is already in existence."

If he committed a transgression which involves two death penalties . . . Rabbi Jose says: "He is dealt with according to the prohibition which came into force first: If he offended with a married woman who was formerly his mother-in-law, he is dealt with according to the offense with a mother-in-law; if he offended with a married woman who subsequently became his mother-in-law, he is dealt with according to an offense with a married woman."[19]

Rabbi Simeon said: "If one eats *nevelah* (food not slaughtered properly) on the Day of Atonement, he is exempt from *karet* (excision from the people, the penalty for eating on the Day of Atonement).[20]

It is a major principle with regard to all prohibitions in the Torah that one prohibition cannot take legal hold where another prohibition already exists, unless both are coincidental or the second prohibition introduces factors additional to the first or is more comprehensive in its application than the first.[21]

We see that the second prohibition cannot take legal hold because the first prohibition has already possessed the forbidden object. That is to say any prohibition—insofar as it relates to a concrete object—is not merely a commandment against performing a certain act; the prohibition flows necessarily from the character or status of the forbidden object. We have here, *mutatis mutandis,* the basic concept of "institutions" and "classes" or *iura in rem,* which pervades the entire field of Jewish legal theory. This principle is similarly at work in all constitutive acts which change the status of a particular object from holy to non holy. I use the term status in its widest sense, including the task of imparting to the object a different character or use. Let us examine an incongruous collection of laws: renunciation of property, *terumah* [priestly perquisite from produce], *get* [bill of divorce], *eruv,* redemption of the tithe and the paschal sacrifice. The concept which underlies and unifies this diverse group is the well-known juridical principle that no act can have the effect of endowing or withdrawing the status of a specific object, unless the object's individual identity has been clearly established at the moment the act is being performed.[22] In the talmudic sources this principle has never been defined in such abstract and precise terms, but it becomes apparent with the fullest certainty in the dispute as to whether or not there is retrospective designation [*bererah*][23]—a dispute which affects, in equal degree, all the diverse laws mentioned above. We mention them in their proper order:

Rabbi Judah says: "In the morning the owner of the field should get up and say, 'Whatever the poor shall glean during the day should be considered ownerless' "; Rabbi Dosa says. . . .[24] "If a person purchases wine from Cutheans he may say: 'Two small bottles (out of a hundred) which I shall separate are to be *terumah;* ten, the first tithe; nine, the second tithe'; and then he may begin to drink." This is the view of Rabbi Meir; Rabbi Judah and Rabbi Jose and Rabbi Simeon forbid it.

If a person purchases wine: This refers to a Friday toward sunset, as it is taught in the Tosefta, and the day became hallowed and he does not have wine to drink on the Sabbath, and he does not have time to separate *terumah* and *ma'aser*[25] [the tithe].

Any writ of divorce written without specification of the woman is invalid. . . . If he said to the scribe, "Write for the one who will first leave my door," what is the status of the document?[26]

A person may attach a condition to his *eruv* and say: . . . "If the sage should come from the east, my *eruv* shall be for the east; if from the west, my *eruv* shall be for the west."[27]

If a person says, "The tithe which I have at home shall be redeemed for the *sela* which I will bring up from my pocket"—Rabbi Jose says that it is redeemed.[28]

If one declares to his sons, "I shall slaughter the paschal

sacrifice for the one of you who will be first to enter Jerusalem," once his head and the greater part of his body were first to enter—he merited his portion. . . .[29]

Because we say there is retrospective designation, and from the time of the paschal sacrifice's slaughter he had become entitled to it, and this paschal sacrifice was offered with the intention of his sharing in it. . . .[30]

In all of these cases the Sages viewed the legal force of the act—that is to say, the declaration which was to effect the renunciation of the property, or the designation of the *terumah,* or the validity of the divorce, etc.—as being dependent upon the question whether or not there is "retrospective designation." And practically all the Sages are of the opinion that there is no retrospective designation, that the future will not, when it actualizes, impart an unequivocal retrospective meaning to the potential, undefined present situation. Consequently we must say that because the object of the legal act was not individuated at the moment of the performance of the act, the act cannot effect the "real" change desired.[31] We see once again, quite clearly, how a juridical approach can embrace all the branches of the law.

In sum, as I have written elsewhere:[32]

The rule of Jewish law is not limited to the sphere of relationship between man and man. The relationship between man and God, which, practically speaking, is the relationship between man and himself, between man and his own deepest moral and religious sentiments, is caught up in the network of juridical relationships, is integrated into the complex of juridical categories that were created by the lawgiver.

3. Indeed, we find God Himself a veritable participant in legal action, as a subject of material rights and obligations —similar to a mortal—with respect to all matters involv-

ing sacred objects. And not alone objects which are intrinsically sacred, but also and perhaps even more so those which are set aside for the maintenance and repair of the Temple buildings, that is to say, objects—whether movable or immovable—which their owners have consecrated, explicitly or implicitly,[33] for the purpose of the administration of the Temple.[34] Scholars have disputed as to who is considered the legal owner of Church property, according to Roman law.[35] With reference to Temple property in Jewish law, the matter is seemingly clear: the realm of the sacred is not in itself to be treated as a legal person, it is rather "heavenly property," property belonging to Heaven. The deity itself—the *Shekhinah*—is, from a strictly juridical point of view, the owner of the property.

> The unconscious, profane use of Temple property is like the conscious use of secular property; in connection with Temple property the category of "unconscious use" does not apply, for there is the awareness of God.[36]
>
> In that case, the reason there is need to exempt Temple property from the law of interest, is that Temple property is like money consecrated to One, that is, to God himself.[37]

It is true that the ownership of God is not like the ownership of man in all respects; it is for this reason that it is stated in the Mishnah,[38] and this is also the view of the sage, disputing Rabbi Simon ben Menasya in the *baraita* quoted there, that:

> If the ox of a lay owner[39] gored an ox belonging to the Temple, and an ox belonging to the Temple gored an ox belonging to a lay owner—there is no liability, as it is written (Exodus 21:35) "an ox of his neighbor," but not an ox belonging to the Temple.

The same applies toward many other subjects, such as interest, deception, and the laws of watchmen.[40] But it is precisely this emphasis, that the lay person is not the neighbor of the divine property owner, or that he is not His brother, which places us before the elements of legal similarity between the two owners.[41]

The legal mentality has truly penetrated the most exclusive spheres of talmudic law.

CHAPTER II

Casuistic Form

1. There is a *mishnah* in the first chapter of the tractate Bava Kamma[1]—a veritable jewel of language—the like of which in abstractness and brevity and conciseness of expression we have not found in all the six mishnaic orders. The splendor of antiquity hovers over it, and it appears that this is one of the "old *halakhot*,"[2] or a relic of an ancient book of laws, "A Book of Enactments."[3] Thus is its golden formulation:

> If I be responsible for the care of anything, I have legally rendered possible the damage it may cause. If I be the partial cause of that injury, I am responsible for damages as one who had caused the entire injury.

The meaning of this, according to simple statement of the text, is that whatever a person is obligated to watch over (lest it cause damage), and he did not watch over it and it caused damage, then he has rendered possible the act of damage and he must make restitution. If two "contributed" to the act of damage, each one is liable to make restitution for the full amount.[4]

But in truth, this is not the law, and the final decision does not agree with this. One cannot equate all monetary damages that may be caused by a person's property, and the failure to fulfill the obligation of watchfulness does not always involve the duty of restitution. In the very *mishnah* which precedes the one quoted, and in many talmudic discussions which precede and follow it, there is a division of damages and the damaging agents into various categories and sub-categories: the ox, the pit, the grazing animal [the Hebrew term is *maveh,* which is also applied to ransacking by an intruder], and the fire;[5] the horn, the tooth, and the foot;[6] *tam* ["innocent" goring] and *mu'ad* [confirmed goring];[7] pebbles[8] and various others. And it goes without saying that the laws governing them are also different: the one pays full indemnification, and the other only half;[9] the one pays from his "choicest," the other from the carcass;[10] the one is not liable for damages caused in the public domain,[11] the other is not liable for damages to concealed property,[12] and yet another is not liable for damages to humans and vessels.[13] And many other distinctions are drawn in the entire realm of damages, and from various points of view.

How can we reconcile all this with the blanket and unqualified statement of our early *mishnah?* The *Tanna* of the *baraita,* it seems, sensed this contradiction and attempted to reconcile these two divergent approaches to the subject of torts, through use of an *ukimta,* a restrictive interpretation. With one stroke he narrowed the formerly wide purview of the principle of our *mishnah* and limited its application only to certain carefully defined, specific situations.

> Our Rabbis taught: "If I be responsible for the care of anything, I have legally rendered possible the damage it may cause." How is that? When an ox or pit which was left with a deaf-mute, an insane person or a minor does damage the owner is liable to indemnify. This, however, is not so with a fire.[14]

This interpretation changes the entire meaning of the statement "If I be responsible for the care of anything." The *mishnah* no longer refers to the passive absence of proper care; rather it only refers to a positive act which negates the possibility of proper care, that is the handing-over of the tort-feasor to one who is not qualified to guard it properly.[15] Only by employing this new concept of an act which negates the possibility of proper care, is the *baraita* able to distinguish between "the ox and the pit" on the one hand and "the fire" on the other, for reasons which the Gemara in its analysis of the *baraita* makes clear. As a result of this two-stage process of interpretation —the *baraita*'s interpretation of the *mishnah,* and the Gemara's interpretation of the *baraita*—the very broad principle of our *mishnah* is transformed into the principle of "vicarious liability"—the responsibility of a principal for his agent's acts, the responsibility of the owner of the tort-feasor for the acts of the deaf-mute, insane person or minor—a principle which allows for the opportunity to distinguish between the various types of damages.[16]

And as for the joint and individualized responsibility of those who have jointly contributed to a particular tort, this principle is altogether interpreted out of existence by another *baraita*'s restrictive interpretation of the second half of our *mishnah.*

> Our Rabbis taught: "If I be the partial cause of the injury, I am responsible for damages as one who had caused the entire injury." How is that? If one had dug a pit nine handbreaths deep and another came along and completed it to a depth of ten handbreaths, the latter person is liable."[17]

Not every partner to a tort, then, can be held liable for full damages but only the partner who completes the tort. Once again we have a restrictive interpretation which fundamentally alters the principles expressed in our *mishnah*.

Elsewhere, and this too in connection with the interpretation of our *mishnah,* we are given an important interpretive principle by the great *Amora* Rabbi Yohanan. It is this:

> No inference may be drawn from generalized statements even where an exception is actually specified.[18]

This is to say that whenever the Mishnah reads "all" it must not be taken at face value, and it is possible to limit the ruling solely to a few particulars. This, in effect, is precisely what the two *baraitot* cited previously accomplished in connection with our *mishnah.* An interesting detail, of great significance, is to be noted: Rabbi Yohanan was of the same generation (approximately) as the early formulators of *baraitot,* and he himself "taught *baraitot*";[19] we have a coincidence which must not be ignored.

The question which confronts us then is: What are the causes for this daring method of interpretation, and whence its legitimacy?

2. The Talmud is not a book of laws. Unlike law books—codexes as they are called—it does not, or it does not solely formulate laws. This is correct not only for the latest part of the Talmud, the Gemara, but also for its earlier part, the Mishnah. Rabbi Judah HaNasi (*Rabbi*)—whether he was the first and only editor of the Mishnah, as some scholars believe,[20] or whether he was the third and last, following Rabbi Akiba and Rabbi Meir, as is the view of others[21]—his goal was not to render decisions, and indeed he did not formulate decisions. This fact has been established with uncontestable evidence by Albeck,[22] and his strongest and most persuasive proof is that in many instances in the Tosefta and *baraita* Rabbi Judah himself

disputes an anonymous view in the Mishnah, which is, according to the opinion of Albeck's opponents, the authoritative law.[23] The view which appears plausible is therefore this:

> The editor (the reference is to Rabbi Judah HaNasi) did not set himself the objective of arranging in his Mishnah the authoritative law . . . but he formulated each *mishnah* in the form in which he received it, and he preserved even the distinctive character of his sources.[24]

But whatever the role of the Mishnah may be with reference to its role in codification, the Gemara—the major portion of the Talmud—is certainly not a code in the accepted sense of the term. Its advantage is also its defect, from the point of view of this designation. Endless numbers of laws were indeed formulated in the Gemara, "established laws,"[25] meant to guide practice, but its major preoccupation and the greater part of its massive material is devoted to the discussion which precedes the formulation of law—to all those amoraic debates, in the academy and outside it, whose objective was to clarify the laws recorded in the Mishnah, or to add laws of their own, either through the use of logic which needs no other support,[26] or through dependence on biblical verses, or—and this is basic—as a result of the careful analysis in the statements of the *Tannaim*.[27] What the *Soferim* and the early *Tannaim* did in their day with the text of the Bible, the *Amoraim* did now with the Mishnah. Both "expounded" the text,[28] the original source, its form of expression; they contemplated and searched into every minute aspect of it, except that the "Midrash on the Mishnah" of the *Amoraim* was much less formal and free, and was not confined by a limited number of interpretive categories. In the meantime the circumstances changed, the vicissitudes of life wrought their catastrophic transformations, for the prevailing institutions through which our people lived its life were destroyed: the Temple was in ruins, the state was dissolved, the Sanhedrin disappeared, and all that remained was the Torah, to be watchman—in this devastated country and outside of it— of the unity of the nation and its very existence.

The task that the *Amoraim* assumed was not an easy one: to fix the law which would guide the people "along the path wherein they should go." True, the Mishnah was already written[29] but, by itself, it did not suffice. For the collection of *halakhot* which Rabbi Judah HaNasi gathered, compiled and edited were, by their very nature, often fragmentary, casual, nondefinitive utterances. The Mishnah represented a compilation of statements made by many different sages, spanning many different generations in greatly different circumstances. Naturally, then, there were many gaps and lacunae present in the Mishnah as a whole. The very first *mishnah* of the Talmud poses the question: From which moment on may one recite the *Shema* in the evening?[30] It replies: From the moment the priests enter to eat their *terumah* (priestly perquisite of produce)—until the end of the first watch. The *mishnah* does not even bother to explain what the recitation of the *Shema* is, in the first place, or when the first watch ends. These lacunae, very often, had to be filled through various other texts, and frequently the solutions had to be arrived at through challenges, comparisons, and contradictions (*remiot*)[31] in discussions of remote themes. And indeed, at times these contradictory texts could not be harmonized except by radically limiting the scope of application of either one or several, or all of the texts in question. While this changed materially the tannaitic Halakhah, it did preserve the continuity of the law by reading its "interpretations" back into the Mishnah's very words. The actions of the fathers provide the model for their descendants.

The *Amoraim*, in the method of exegesis they adopted, were merely following, *mutatis mutandis*, in the footsteps of the *Soferim* and the *Tannaim*. Just as the earlier sages had often "crushed" (*akvu*)[32] the scriptural text, so the later sages "crushed" the text of the Mishnah. Both, of course, were always careful to find a support for their rulings and decisions in a text (*asmakhta*)[33] in order to blunt the originality of the ruling and to remove its sting.

3. We now come to a discussion of the *ukimta*,[34] this revolutionary method of interpretation which we have touched upon in the beginning of this chapter. Its role was to limit the application of the anonymous law in the *mishnah* (or *baraita*) to a particular case—on the face of it, of narrower range of applicability—through such formulae as: "what type of case are we dealing with here?," "the above is meant to apply only to," "the statement is incomplete and it was meant to read thus," and various other such expressions.[35] In considering the matter we shall see that very often the reconciliation is only a shortcut which leads from the unqualified tannaitic law, via the particular case to which it was applied, to a new abstract principle implied in it. It thus turns out that this restriction is for the sake of expansion; for every abstraction is an expansion of boundaries, since it removes the law from the concrete trappings in which it is set in the original text. The following citations will clarify this conception.

Mishnah: If witnesses said, "This is our handwriting but we were forced" . . . they are believed.

Gemara: Rami bar Hama said: "They taught this only when they said, 'We were forced with regard to life,' but if they said, 'We were forced with regard to money,' they are not believed because no man can make himself a wicked man."[36]

Our Rabbis taught: "If a defendant disposed of all his

lands to one person or to three persons at one and the same time, they have all stepped into the place of the original owner". . . . We are dealing here with a case where the property purchased last was of the best quality. . . . But the reason the creditors cannot be paid out of the best is that the vendee may [repudiate their demand and] say, "On what account have the Rabbis enacted that property disposed of by a debtor cannot be attached by his creditor so long as there are available possessions still not disposed of, if not for the sake of protecting my interests. In the present instance I have no interest in availing myself of this enactment." Exactly as Rava stated, for Rava elsewhere said that whoever asserts, "I have no desire to avail myself of a Rabbinic enactment, such as this," is listened to.[37]

In the first case cited the Gemara, through the use of the *ukimta,* derives a very important principle whose range of application goes far beyond the particular mishnaic law. The principle is that no man can incriminate himself if such incriminatory testimony, when accepted by the court, would disqualify him as a competent witness.[38] To accept such testimony would merely create a vicious circle. In the second case cited the Gemara derives, via the *ukimta,* the substantive legal principle that the beneficiary of a particular enactment may retain control over its scope of application. Whenever an enactment was, from the outset, designed to benefit a particular group of individuals— property buyers, married women, etc.—if in a particular case the enactment, through an unintended side effect, will be to the disadvantage of the beneficiary, he can negate the legal force of the enactment as it affects him, stating: "I desire neither its sting nor its honey; I prefer to let the law take its course as it did prior to the issuance of the enactment."[39]

An element of this process is to be found in almost every *ukimta* of the Talmud. The distinctions and qualifications through which are created fresh nuances give rise to new categories and aspects of law. The law is enriched despite or rather because of the limitation imposed on the law as formulated in the earlier text. The interpretations of the *Amoraim*[40] made the law of the Mishnah "poor in one sense, and rich in another." It was not in order to recast the tannaitic law in a new code consisting of abstract and improved principles; the *Amoraim* lacked the authority for this. What they accomplished was not a renewal of the legal system, but innovations of specific individual laws, and the result was a growth of the new abstract conception out of the concrete seed of the particular case under consideration. It is thus that we can understand the relative freedom which the interpreters of the tannaitic law arrogated to themselves, and here, too, is contained the legitimization of the interpretive procedure represented by the *ukimta.*

4. We have spoken of "specific, individual laws," and this is indeed the case and it is this which has determined the casuistic nature of talmudic law. Talmudic law generally takes the form, not of abstract principles, but of brief recitations of incidents which appear to be—because of the constellation of details included—summations of cases, decisions or resolutions which were actually rendered in life situations that had come before the court for adjudication.[41] This casuistic method, which is prominent in the civil law of the Talmud, characterizes especially the law of Gemara. And it is only natural that this should be so. The Mishnah was the center around which moved all the discussions of the Talmud, and since the Mishnah itself, as was indicated,[42] is a collection of individual laws which were formulated in different generations by different sages, it is only natural that the new laws which were adopted in the academy[43] when the Mishnah was expounded,

should be, for the most part, fragmentary, concrete, dogmatic, through which shone the new thought contributed
by the *Amoraim*. They left it to later generations to draw
up the generalizations, which were to be reached by the
inductive method—from the particular to the general.
And while this method led to many disputes—in the epoch
of the *Geonim* and the codifiers and in the literature of
the responsa—it led, on the other hand, to a great flexibility in the law and adaptability to change, and it pre-
vented its hardening within a rigid framework of rigorously formulated principles. Jewish law would not have
developed, as it did develop, in the rich rabbinic literature
of later times, were it not for "the freedom of movement"
given it in other branches of the legal tradition, as a result
of the casuistic style of talmudic law.[44]

5. This leads us to another aspect of the same theme—to
the origin of a phenomenon which has aroused much
bafflement and even mockery among critics of the Talmud.
I have reference to those seemingly grotesque examples,
particularly uncommon in real life, which are sometimes
cited to illustrate the laws of the Gemara. For example:

> In the case of one falling from the top of the roof violat-
> ing a woman.[45]
> If one was told, "You and an ass shall acquire posses-
> sion."[46]
> If one joined two wombs [of two animals] to each other
> and the foetus issued from one womb and entered the
> other.[47]

and many similar cases. Why, the skeptic asks, does the
Gemara find it necessary to render decisions with regard to
these strange, peculiar cases? Should not the Sages have
found more natural illustrations for their legal opinions?
I believe that this question indicates a lack of a basic

understanding of the structure of amoraic law. The reason
for such cases is really quite simple. Precisely because the
Gemara employs the casuistic approach, where the general,
abstract principle has to be derived from the particular
case, through use of the inductive method, the Gemara
had to make sure that the particular case which served to
exemplify the general principle was "monistic" in character, that is to say that the case exemplified one and only
one legal principle to the exclusion of all others. And this
was often only possible through the construction of these
drastic and artificial examples. The advantage of a hypothetical, artificially constructed case over a real-life situation is that in such a case it was possible, in an artificial
manner, to eliminate all accidentals—that is, all the incidental details that usually accompany the real-life situation
—and thus isolate, free from all extraneous considerations
the legal principle that it wished the case to exemplify as
being the sole determining factor in the decision rendered.
It is the casuistic approach, then, which necessitated the
use of such grotesque, unreal examples and, conversely,
the use of such examples clearly demonstrates that a particular law was not always set forth so much for its own
sake, as it was for the sake of exemplifying the general,
abstract principle which could be logically derived from it.

CHAPTER **III**

Evasion of the Law

1. The expression "evasion of the law" [*ha'aramah*], has acquired, in popular parlance, a negative connotation. It signifies an act whereby an individual, through deceit and trickery, escapes from fulfilling his lawful obligations. For example, an individual will keep irregular books in order to falsify the record of his real income. Or he will "import" Swiss watches hidden in meat cans. The first act deliberately undercuts his obligation to pay the proper amount of income tax; the second undercuts his obligation to pay the required custom duties. What is common to both acts is that as a result of secret manipulations unbeknown to the authorities, the citizen avoids fulfilling his legal obligations. It is not the law which is being evaded here but rather its administrators. Such evasion is equivalent to one person defrauding another except that in the above-mentioned situations the citizen defrauds the authorities.

Such, however, is not the proper classical meaning of the expression in the Jewish legal sources. Here, too, there is evading and circumventing the law but such evasion—which is a manifestation of wisdom and not of guile—is

22

directed against the law itself. It plays the law off against itself; one evades the law by means of the law itself.

> Is it permissible to evade the law? But did not Rabbi Tarfon, the father of Israel, evade the law? He married three hundred women in order to feed them *terumah*.[1]

Terumah [the priestly perquisite of produce] may only be eaten by priests, not by the general public.[2] The wife of a priest (with respect to this law) enjoys the same rights as her husband and may also eat from *terumah*.[3] Food of *terumah* is less expensive than ordinary food since, as it is forbidden to non-priests, the demand for it is very limited. This was a time of famine,[4] and Rabbi Tarfon was a priest[5] and a very wealthy man.[6] He married three hundred women from the poorer classes in order to feed them *terumah* or to enable them to buy it for themselves at low cost.[7] The evasion of the law, in this instance, consisted in the fictitious nature of the marriage whose purpose was not the usual one of enabling a couple to live together as man and wife but rather that of enabling these women to be included—in an artificial manner—within the legal category of the wife of a priest.

We find a similar evasion discussed elsewhere, one which demonstrates how, through an artificial, formalistic act, an object can become subsumed under a new legal category. The motivation in this instance does not stem from a sense of generosity and sympathy but rather from the more prosaic desire to save money.

> If one was standing in his granary and he had no money with him, he may say to his fellow, "This produce is given to you as a free gift." Then he can go on to say, "Let this be exchanged for money which is in the house."[8]

The discussion here concerns the second tithe [*ma'aser sheni*]—the tithe that one sets aside in the first, second, fourth, and fifth years of the sabbatical cycle after one has already separated the first tithe.[9] The second tithe must be eaten in Jerusalem, within the city walls.[10] One may, however, redeem the fruits with money and bring the money to Jerusalem to be expended there.[11] If the second tithe that the person is redeeming is his own, he must redeem it with one-fifth more money than its value.[12] If an individual, however, redeems another person's second tithe, he may redeem it at its value and need not add the fifth.[13] The *mishnah* above advises one who is about to redeem his tithe and wishes to avoid the obligation of the additional fifth, to give the fruits to another person as a gift so that he, the redeemer, will no longer be their owner and consequently the law governing one who redeems the tithe of another will apply. This procedure, as the *mishnah* indicates, should only be followed when one has no money at hand. If, however, a person does have money at hand it is preferable that he give the money as a gift to a friend and let the friend redeem the tithe—"since this mode of evasion of the fifth is less blatant."[14] Thus we are told:

> An evasion may be practiced regarding the second tithe. How? A man may say to his adult son or daughter or to his Hebrew bondman or bondwoman, "Here is this money, redeem with it the second tithe."[15]

This procedure, of course, also constitutes an evasion, as it is so characterized, but it is less blatant, and since it suffices, one may not resort to the more glaring procedure.

A very interesting situation involving a *ha'aramah* occurred during World War II. The purpose of the *ha'aramah* was to free a young widow from the bonds of the levirate relation. A childless Jewish couple was living in this country [*Eretz Yisrael*], the husband having an unmarried brother, the wife, an unmarried sister, both living in far-off New Zealand. The husband was stricken with a fatal disease and at the last stage of the illness the pain and suffering caused him to lose his mind. The problem facing the family was that after the husband would die the wife would require the rite of *halitzah* to release her from the biblical ordinance that a childless widow be married to her deceased husband's brother. Considering that it was wartime and the brother lived halfway around the world, this would be very difficult to arrange. Because of the husband's deteriorated mental condition he was unable to divorce his wife.[16] What, then, could be done? The question was put to a halakhic scholar and he devised a very brilliant solution. The family was to instruct the brother in New Zealand that he marry the wife's sister immediately. The woman in *Eretz Yisrael* would then be the sister of her brother-in-law's new wife, which would relieve her of the biblical ordinance that she be married to her brother-in-law or, when this cannot be effectuated, to have him release her through the rite of *halitzah*.

> If the widow of a childless brother be forbidden (to her brother-in-law) because of the prohibited degrees of near-relations[17] she may neither perform *halitzah* nor may she contract the levirate union.[18]

And so it was. The brother in New Zealand married the wife's sister, whereupon he immediately divorced her—since the sister of one's former wife is also a forbidden relation[19]—and when the husband in *Eretz Yisrael* died shortly thereafter, the widow was permitted to remarry without having to undergo either *yibbum* (levirate union) or *halitzah*. This marriage was fictitious in nature; nevertheless, it succeeded in freeing the woman from the bonds of the levirate relation.

In all three cases cited above the purpose of the *ha'aramah* was: to free oneself from the "gravitation" of a particular law—the prohibition of *terumah* to non-priests, the obligation to add the fifth in redeeming the tithe, the requirement of *halitzah*—by bringing another law into play—the marital bond created through betrothal, or the transfer of ownership from the donor of a gift to its recipient, or the forbidden relationship of "a man and his wife's sister" which was created between the *yavam* (brother-in-law) and the *yevamah* (sister-in-law). And these marriages and this transfer of ownership are not in any way disqualified by the fact that they are fictitious in nature, that is to say, that they are not effected for their own sakes but, rather, to bring about certain legal consequences which, as it were, only incidentally and accidentally result from these acts.

The law does not look with disfavor upon such *ha'aramot* which use one law to evade another law, for the law itself is "guilty" inasmuch as it supplies the individual with the apparatus wherewith to perform a *ha'aramah*. We must assume that a legislator is aware of all possible situations that may arise, that he is aware of all the paths that may be taken in order to escape from the obligations that the law imposes. And if the legislator has not closed off these escape routes—has not decreed, for example, that only a "real" wife, that is to say, one who maintains a normal marital relationship with her husband, is permitted to eat *terumah,* or can free her sister from the levirate relation—it is an indication that he is not perturbed by this, and that he is prepared to apply a legal norm even to those who came under it in an irregular manner.

The giver of the Torah did not distinguish between a "real" wife and a "fictitious" wife with reference to the legal consequences of marriage, nor did he distinguish between various types of conveyance of ownership with reference to a redeemer of the second tithe ceasing to be its owner. The three hundred wives of Rabbi Tarfon, the *yevamah* in *Eretz Yisrael,* and the individual who, in accordance with the advice of the two *mishnayot* cited above, sought to evade the obligation of the additional fifth in the cost of redeeming the tithe, were all beneficiaries of this equation—an equation made freely and knowledgeably. We see, then, that the evasion of the law, in these instances, was a legal evasion which utilized one aspect of the law to temper another of its aspects and thus achieve a desired effect.

Rabbi Tarfon's marriages for the purpose of feeding his three hundred newly-acquired "wives" *terumah* bring to mind similar fictitious marriages of our time which have as their purpose the enabling of one of the partners to acquire the status of a citizen. It is a fact that many, if not most, modern legal systems[20] endow even the fictitious wife with the citizenship that her husband possesses. And why is this so? Simply because:

> There is no overseer who can penetrate into these innermost regions, there is no one who can determine the intent and the design with which a couple enters into the marriage relationship. And an understanding legislator will not be eager to disallow an evasion of the law which it is impossible to prevent. To vary an aphorism of our Sages (Yevamot 65b) we may state "as the legislator is commanded to say that which will be heeded so is he commanded to refrain from saying that which will not be heeded." If he will not act in such a fashion he himself, in effect, will be a contributing cause to the transgression of the law.[21]

This same explanation applies with equal force to the recognition of fictitious marriages as they effect permission to eat *terumah,* and the freeing of a *yevamah* from the rite of *halitzah.*

In sum: whenever a juridical norm is set forth in broad, general, all-inclusive terms, then, of necessity, there will be some shelter for those who really are not interested in the law for its own sake but rather have in mind certain inadvertent benefits that result from its consequences. Evasion of the law is the exploitation of the gap between the broad juridical norm and the purpose for which the norm was instituted in order to include within its scope of application acts and events which the law, in terms of fulfilling its purpose, was not really designed to cover. The primary aim of the law in permitting a priest's wife to eat *terumah* is, clearly, that husband and wife should be able to eat together.[22] But the norm itself is broader; it includes any priest's wife. And the beneficiary of this gap is the fictitious wife who does not share a common table with her husband. Such also is the case with the gap between one who, in actuality, is not the owner of the second tithe which he redeems and one who transfers ownership of the second tithe for the specific purpose of not being obliged to add the fifth. The latter exploits the gap between the purely formal-legal transfer of ownership and the standard economic transfer of ownership.

2. We have spoken of "the exploitation of the gap." But such exploitation is ineffective and the *ha'aramah* is of no avail if all it legally effects is to subsume an object under a particular legal category *solely with respect to* the purpose of the *ha'aramah*. That is to say it is of no avail unless all of the other legal consequences that normally flow once an object has been subsumed under that particular legal category are applicable in these circumstances as well. This is a rather subtle point but a very real one and it delimits the borderline at which point a legal *ha'aramah* turns into a forbidden one, or—to be more precise—an ineffective one. The talmudic tale of Beth-Horon will both illustrate and prove my point.

A certain man in Beth-Horon whose father was forbidden by a vow to have any benefit from him was celebrating his son's marriage, and he said to his neighbor, "The courtyard and banquet are given to you as a gift, but they are yours only with respect to[23] my father coming and eating with us at the banquet." His neighbor said to him, "If they are mine then they are dedicated to Heaven." He replied to him, "Did I give you what is mine that you should dedicate it to Heaven?" His neighbor replied in turn, "Did you give me what is yours only so that you and your father might eat and drink and be reconciled and that the sin should rest on my head?!" The Sages said, "Any gift which is given with the stipulation that if one dedicated it, it is not to be considered dedicated, is not a gift."[24]

But cannot a person give a gift on the condition that his neighbor not dedicate it? So is the *mishnah* to be read: "Any gift which is a clear *ha'aramah,* which is not given with the understanding that if the recipient dedicates it, it is to be considered dedicated, is not a gift."[25]

One "who is forbidden by a vow" is a person "whose friend had forbidden him to derive any benefit from him in any manner whatsoever,"[26] that is to say, the individual who made the vow forbade the individual subjected to the vow, using the proper form, to derive any benefit from him. Such a vow is effective[27] since "a person can prohibit others from benefiting from his property."[28]

In this very fascinating tale of the man from Beth-Horon,[29] Reuben vowed that his father, Jacob, should not derive any benefit from him. A while later Reuben was about to celebrate the marriage of his son Enoch[30] and wanted his father, Jacob, who had been subjected to the vow, to partake of the wedding feast. Reuben, thereupon, gave his friend Simon both his courtyard[31] and the feast as a gift, adding the proviso: "they are yours only with respect to my father coming and eating with us at the banquet." Simon, however, immediately dedicated both the courtyard and the feast to Heaven. Reuben berated his friend: "Did I give you this gift that you should dedicate it to Heaven?" Simon, unintimidated, staunchly replied: "Did you give me this gift only so that you and your father might eat and drink and be reconciled, and that the sin should rest on my head?!"[32] When the case came before the Sages they decided: Any gift which is a clear *ha'aramah* —which is not given with the understanding that if the recipient dedicates it, it is to be considered dedicated—is not a gift.

The explanation of this tale, and this is undoubtedly the proper explanation in light of the above-cited comment of the Talmud Yerushalmi[33] is this: Reuben could have given his belongings to Simon as an *unconditional* gift, and then Jacob, who had been interdicted by the vow[34] would have been allowed to partake in the wedding banquet even though the sole purpose of the gift was to enable Jacob to enjoy this benefit. This would have been a permissible evasion of the law, in which the evader invokes as law the advantage accruing to him from another law, negating this one. Reuben could even have stipulated explicitly with Simon that he presents him with this gift on the condition that he does not dedicate it, and yet the grandfather Jacob would have been permitted to eat at the banquet in honor of the wedding of his grandson Enoch; for even in this case the gift is complete, unlimited in content, except that if Simon violated the condition, the gift would have been voided retroactively, reverting to its original owner. But Reuben did not do this! In giving the courtyard and the banquet to Simon, he added:

> They are yours only with respect to my father coming and eating with us at the banquet.

He thus cut at the very roots of the gift by limiting its legal effect. He limited it in advance so that it not be efficacious except with respect to the father's benefit. But a gift which is not effective in all respects is not effective in any respect. For if one wishes to utilize a law as a "palliative" to another law, he must realize that the effect of the law he is utilizing cannot be limited solely to that of a palliative.

We have stated—guided by the Yerushalmi cited above —that Reuben could have given the gift to Simon *on the condition* that he not dedicate it and that had Simon violated this condition, the gift would have become void retroactively. At this point the reader may very well ask: How can this be? After all, if the gift is voided retroactively, then the act of dedication is, *ipso facto,* also voided, in which case the condition was never violated. The answer to this is that this very difficulty was raised and the solution found in connection with a similar condition discussed in the talmudic tractate Gittin. The *baraita* discusses the opinion of Rabbi Eliezer who states that if a man divorces his wife on condition that she may not marry so-and-so, she is permitted to marry anybody except so-and-so. After Rabbi Eliezer's death "four elders," among them Rabbi Akiba, differed from his view. Rabbi Akiba argued thus:

> Supposing this woman went and married some other man and had children with him and then was widowed or divorced from him, and she afterwards went and married this man to whom she had been forbidden, would not [according to Rabbi Eliezer] her original divorce have to be declared void, and [consequently] her children illegitimate?![35]

The Ran, in commenting on the argument of Rabbi Akiba, raises a similar question to the one we have just asked:

> And if you will ask: "How can the divorce be declared void and her children illegitimate? The woman will never be able to violate the condition for if she will marry the

man who was forbidden to her, the divorce becomes void, and her marriage to anyone else can no longer be efficacious. . . ." Nahmanides has already answered this question thus: when the husband stipulated that his about-to-be divorced wife should not marry so-and-so, he did not mean to stipulate that the divorce is to be declared void only if the wife entered into a legally valid marriage with so-and-so since such a marriage could never be realized. Rather, he meant to stipulate that she should not go through the form of getting married to so-and-so. Therefore, even though this ceremonial form is not legally valid, the condition was violated and the divorce must be declared void. And from this we may infer that one who gives a present to his friend, on condition that he not give it to anyone else and the recipient went and gave it to someone else, even though the second recipient did not, in actuality, become the owner of the gift, the presentation is void retroactively, since the first recipient went through the form of giving it to someone else. . . .[36]

The conclusion of the Ran's analysis spoke about the condition "that the recipient not give the gift to anyone else" but the same conception applies to the condition "that the recipient not dedicate it to Heaven" since dedication is also a presentation except that its recipient is the Heavenly realm [the Temple as surrogate for God] and not a human being.[37]

The gift of Beth-Horon was declared ineffective because of the defect that Reuben read into it at the very time it was to go into effect. If Reuben would have omitted those fatal words and given the gift to Simon without any qualifications, so that if Simon would dedicate the gift or give it to someone else his act would be effective, then the transaction between them would have been one based on pure faith alone—with the emphasis on "pure"—for, unlike the Roman *pactum fiduciae*,[38] Reuben could not have sued Simon for any loss that Simon might have caused by choosing to dedicate the gift. Reuben's sole reliance would have been on the good faith and trustworthiness of Simon. This is, it would seem, the reason why Simon—who evidently believed in the efficaciousness of the gift—felt free to dedicate it to Heaven.

A transaction in Jewish law which does resemble, to an extent, the Roman institution mentioned above is the *urkhata*,[39] whereby a plaintiff delegates power of attorney to an individual so that the delegated attorney might be able to sue the defendant in his place. On the one hand, the plaintiff must write in the authorization: "Go, sue, and win and take for yourself."[40] Otherwise the defendant can tell the attorney: "You are not my claimant."[41] On the other hand, the attorney upon obtaining from the defendant the object for which he was suing cannot keep it for himself but must return it to the plaintiff. If he attempts to keep it for himself and refuses to return it, the Court will forcibly seize it from him since "he is only an agent"[42] —the plaintiff had only made him his deputy to receive the object from the defendant. We seem to be confronted by a blatant contradiction: "take for yourself" and "he is only an agent." Why here, unlike the rule in the case of the gift of Beth-Horon, is there no need that the hands of the one who receives the gift be free of all restrictions, and it is permissible to "impose a guardian" to watch over his faithfulness? The difference is clear, and it sheds precious light on the entire subject of the evasion of law: it derives from the variation in the legal objectives of the two gifts. There, in the case of the gift of Beth-Horon, the objective was to "alienate" the one who had made the vow, Reuben, from the courtyard and the banquet, so that the father who had been interdicted by the vow shall be able to benefit from them, and Reuben cannot be deemed a "stranger" in relation to them so long as the recipient of the gift, Simon, cannot dedicate it or give it to another. With respect to the law of the *urkhata,* however, the transaction does not have as its purpose that the plaintiff divest himself of ownership of the object claimed. The purpose of the transaction is rather to enable the attorney to *acquire an interest* in the claim thus preventing the defendant from refusing to recognize him through arguing: "You are not my claimant." And in order to forestall such an argument even this "weak transfer,"[43] this limited ownership with its dual character—ownership with respect to the defendant, agency with respect to the plaintiff—suffices.

> Power of attorney even with respect to recovery of a deposited object is not a full-fledged transfer since we have established that the attorney is only an agent. It is only with respect to the bailee (the defendant) that the attorney acquires possession of the deposited object . . . thus preventing the defendant from refusing to recognize him through arguing: "You are not my claimant."[44]

This very same construction, according to Sohm,[45] characterizes the Roman *pactum fiduciae:*

> The effect of the fiduciary clause was not merely obligatory but also *real, i.e.,* it *altered the character of the right of property* itself; in other words, *fiduciary ownership was different in kind* from ordinary ownership.[46]

The *urkhata* of Jewish law, then, resembles in several respects, the Roman *fiducia.* In contradistinction to this, the gift of Beth-Horon, to fulfill its purpose, must be a transaction based on pure faith alone where the donor has to rely solely on the fairness of the recipient, as—in the opinion of some scholars—was the case with the ancient *fiducia* of earlier Roman law.[47]

3. The *ha'aramah* of the gift of Beth-Horon—upon examination—was not forbidden but merely ineffective. It

was, of course, forbidden to depend on it and to have the person interdicted by the vow partake of the banquet, but the presentation of the gift itself involved invalidity, not a prohibition, since there is nothing to forbid the presentation of a gift which is devoid of efficacy.

We find precisely the reverse situation obtaining by another *ha'aramah* which, according to some codifiers, is effective even though it is prohibited. I refer to a particular form of evasion of the prohibition against taking interest.

> Rav Safra learned in the collection of *baraitot* on interest of Rabbi Hiya: "There are some matters which are in themselves permissible, but they are forbidden as an evasion of the law against interest. How is this? If a man said to another, 'Lend me a *maneh*,' and the other replied, 'I have no *maneh* but I have wheat in the value of a *maneh*[48] which I will give you.' If he gave him the wheat in place of a *maneh*, and then repurchased the wheat for twenty-four *selaim*— this is permissible in itself, but one is, nevertheless, forbidden to do so as an evasion of the law against interest."[49]

Maimonides offers us a version of this law dealing with units of ten, citing it thus:

> There are some matters which, in themselves, are permissible, but it is forbidden to do them as an evasion of the law against interest. How so? If one man said to another, "Lend me a *maneh*," and the other replied, "A *maneh* I do not have, but I have wheat to the value of a *maneh*," and he gave him the wheat as the equivalent of a *maneh*, then proceeded to repurchase it for ninety *zuz*, this is, strictly speaking, permissible, but the Sages forbade it as an evasion of the law against interest, because he gave him only ninety *zuz*, and took for it a *maneh* [one hundred *zuz*]. If a person, however, transgressed the prohibition, and acted thus, he can even claim his hundred in a court of law, for it is not even regarded as quasi-interest.[50]

The legal construction of this *ha'aramah* is clear. Rather than lending the borrower ninety *zuz* and receiving one hundred in return—which is forbidden by the Torah[51]—the lender sold wheat on credit to the borrower for one hundred *zuz* and then bought it back, paying cash, for ninety *zuz*. In terms of the economics of the transaction, this, of course, constitutes a loan on interest since the lender paid out ninety *zuz* and received one hundred *zuz*, with the merchandise ending up right where it started. But if we view the transaction in terms of its legal form, we have before us a double sale, involving an exchange of roles: first, the lender sold the wheat for one hundred *zuz* to the borrower, whereupon the borrower sold it back to the lender for ninety *zuz*. The law is that initially one is forbidden to do this—not because it constitutes quasi-interest,[52] but because it looks like interest. However, if the transaction was completed then it is legally binding, and when payment is due the creditor can recover the one hundred *zuz* from the debtor—not as principal and interest but as payment for the wheat which he sold to him on credit.

In any event we are confronted by a unique *ha'aramah*, legally effective yet forbidden. But how can these two conflicting judgments dwell together in such unity? The answer is: they are not "dwelling together" at all. The evasion is effective—since in casting the transaction in the form of a double sale, the principals have evaded the prohibition against interest and even of quasi-interest;[53] it is forbidden as a result of another norm, which has nothing at all to do with the prohibition of interest, it is the prohibition against any transaction which looks like interest. The prohibition against quasi-interest is a preventive measure to safeguard the laws concerning interest[54] itself, which widens, through a rabbinic ordinance, the prohibition against interest; "something that looks like interest" is like "something that looks like a falsehood,"[55] or "something that looks like pride,"[56] a concern about appearances, which cannot be included precisely in the scope of the prohibition against interest. Therefore—so Maimonides and those who follow him explain the *baraita* of Rav Safra and Rabbi Hiya—we cannot deny to this evasion its efficacy because of an unrelated prohibition, which is outside the law that has been evaded.

Those who differ with Maimonides,[57] on the other hand, are of the opinion that the prohibition of the evasion involved in this double sale is no extraneous prohibition but one that is rooted in the laws against interest as such, that it is a case of quasi-interest, and the creditor, therefore, cannot recover legally from the debtor the interest due him—that is, the last ten *zuz* of the hundred—despite the fact that this interest was included originally in the price of the wheat.[58] The terms "permitted" and "forbidden" which the *baraita* uses, according to this view, mean that while biblical law permits such a transaction, the Sages have prohibited it as constituting quasi-interest, for in order to evade the biblical prohibition, an evasion must change the juridical and formal aspects of the transaction. It might appear paradoxical but it is a fact, and an important fact at that, that biblical laws can be more easily evaded than rabbinic enactments. Since "the reasons for biblical laws were not disclosed,"[59] what fixes those laws is the written text[60] together with the interpretations derived through the application of hermeneutical principles. And it is easier to find a gap in the scriptural verse through which one can slip through than in the abstract and reasoned formulations which are usually the basis of rabbinic enactments.

4. All of these *ha'aramot* and many others like them serve to demonstrate the creative ability and power of the

Sages in forging juridical instruments, tools that slice clean through the definitive law and which, using very fine, subtle reasoning, differentiate among interconnected concepts. It was this ability which enabled the talmudic sages and the sages of later generations to carry the *ha'aramah* from the confines of the private sector to the public domain as well and to utilize the effective and permissible evasion of law as the basis for enacting various legal reforms. We find, upon examination, that several enactments, whose purpose was to lighten the burden of existing prohibitions, display distinct traces of the *ha'aramah*—that is the utilization of an aspect in the old law for the purpose of mitigating the severity of the law as it was being applied.[61] I would like to illustrate this idea with a few examples. Let me begin with a very well-known rabbinic enactment—the *prozbol*. The Mishnah states:

> The sabbatical year cancels any loan whether confirmed by note or not confirmed by note . . . a *prozbol* is not cancelled. This is one of the things which Hillel the Elder instituted; when he saw that the people refrained from giving loans to one another and transgressed what was written in the Torah, "Take heed lest there be a base thought in your heart etc." (Deuteronomy 15:9), Hillel established the *prozbol*. This is the essential formula of the *prozbol:* "I declare before you, judges, that as far as any debt due me is concerned, I shall be able to collect it whenever I shall desire"; and the judges sign below, or the witnesses.[62]

The sabbatical year cancels any debt resulting from a loan or from any transaction where the money due was entered as a loan,[63] somewhat in the manner of the Roman *novatio*.[64] The sabbatical year should not be seen as a "statute of limitations" proscribing any action after a specified period has elapsed from the inception of the debt, since the sabbatical year is a particular year[65] which at its end[66] cancels all debts, even those deriving from loans contracted a day before.

As long as the economy of *Eretz Yisrael* was primarily agricultural in nature there was little need for a developed credit system and, consequently, no pressing need to limit the legal effects of the sabbatical year. But during the Herodian period when a semi-capitalistic system was introduced in the country,[67] the need for such a credit system sprang up, a system whose development, obviously, would be greatly hindered by the sabbatical cancellation of debts. The creditors, in violation of the scriptural injunction, "shut their hands from their destitute brother," and people ceased lending money to one another. In order to remedy this situation Hillel instituted the *prozbol*. Scholars have offered various theories as to the legal basis of the enactment, most of them lacking any foundation. One scholar even went so far as to suggest that the source for the *prozbol* was the Hellenistic institution of a specific declaration in court.[68] I believe that the most acceptable view is the one that the Tosafists have suggested.[69] They are of the opinion that the *prozbol* is merely the conscious utilization of a provision of the early *halakhah*. One of the biblical regulations governing the sabbatical year is that "he who delivers his notes to the Court [that the Court should reclaim the debt], the debts owing to him are not cancelled,"[70] since once a note has been delivered to the Court it is as if the debt were already being collected and it is not the creditor who recovers the debt but the Court.[71] What did Hillel do? He activated this early law and turned it into a vehicle for the institution of the *prozbol*. The judicial construction of the *prozbol* is as follows: the creditor assigns his claim to the Court. It, in turn, endows him with the power to institute the action *in its name* and recover the debt for himself.[72] If you will

—we are dealing with an actual law or, if you will—we are dealing with an evasion of the law, by means of the law itself. However we may look at it, a law which had its own justification was utilized by the creator of the decree and became a beneficial tool that, in a practical and permissible manner, abolished the sabbatical cancellation of debts. And if there were those who took a negative attitude toward this enactment—Samuel, the *Amora,* termed the decree "presumptuous"[73]—and if the Rabbis, in order to justify the enactment, felt the need to call upon their "power to expropriate" (for the benefit of the public),[74] this was not because the legal basis of the enactment was ever questioned, but, rather because (as the Tosafists have already noted),[75] the *prozbol,* in effect, uprooted the whole institution of the cancellation of debts among the Jewish people. In any event the *prozbol* may serve as an example of an "institutional" *ha'aramah* which resorts to the same technical style of operation as does the "private" *ha'aramah.*

Both types of *ha'aramah* involve the transferring of an act from one sector of the *halakhah* to another of its sectors (always keeping within halakhic limits) in order, thus, to effectuate a particular consequence of that act which will have as its result the rendering of the forbidden, permissible, or the broadening of the scope and field of application of an already permissible area of law. At times the enactment was introduced at such an early period in our history that it appears as though the prohibition and the permission, the writ of indebtedness and the receipt of its satisfaction, were presented simultaneously. The Torah stated: "Let everyone remain where he is; let no one leave his place on the seventh day."[76] The prophet warned: "Take heed for the sake of your lives . . . and do not carry a burden out of your houses on the Sabbath."[77] Whereupon the Sages introduced the *"eruv* of the courts"[78] and the "partnership in an alley" together with the "*lehi*" and the "form of the gate" all for the purpose of permitting the transportation of movables from one end of a city to the other even if it be twice the size of London or New York. The Torah stated: "You shall not lend him your money at interest nor give him your food for profit."[79] This is the well-known prohibition of interest whose stifling of transactions on credit, and of commerce generally, became ever more oppressive from generation to generation, with the development of society. As far back as the talmudic era and continuing into the time of the *Geonim* and the codifiers, many Sages attempted to devise new legal arrangements and formulae that would eliminate even the slightest taint or tinge of interest from commercial transactions. Some of these attempts proved to be acceptable; others, unacceptable. Finally the legal formula embodied in the writ known as the *heter iska*[80] was generally accepted as the most satisfactory means of resolving this problem. Similarly, other institutional *ha'aramot* were devised which had as their aim the removal of the sharp, bitter sting that might result from a strict application of some of the injunctions of the early law.

CHAPTER **IV**

Quantification

1. The aim of the law is to order relationships between two litigants, and these relationships are established by drawing boundaries and delimitations. In some instances the outlines of the boundaries are objectively marked; in others they float in the air of indefiniteness and depend on the pronouncement of the judge to concretize them and bring them down to the realm of reality. Modern jurisprudence follows the second method; that of Jewish law follows the first. For in modern jurisprudence the judge is "sovereign" over the law, while in Jewish jurisprudence the judge is the servant of the law.

The above tendency expresses itself in the inclination of Jewish law to definite dimensions and quantity. No system of law can escape this altogether, but here the inclination is primary and "numerical frequency is turned into a quality."[1] It is a fact that Jewish law, both in its civil part as well as in the religious and cultic, does not look favorably on abstract norms which call for discretion, but prefers specific quantities which can be weighed and measured by the objective standards of weight, time and distance. Moreover, and this is most important: the assumption of Jewish law—an assumption come by necessity or conscious deliberation—is that the computations established by the Sages overshadow any rational factor, and are characterized by precision, unlike modern jurisprudence which invokes quantitative measurements only in the absence of alternatives, out of the knowledge of the imprecision and the uncertainty of things.

2. The following illustrations will clarify the concept; they will also underscore the hesitancy of some sages— hesitations that never reached to the establishment of another school of thought[2]—toward the specification of weights and measures in principles of law:

> A bird found within fifty cubits of a nest belongs to the owner of the nest; if outside the fifty cubits, it belongs to the finder. . . . Rabbi Jeremiah raised the question: "What if one of its legs is inside the fifty cubits and the other outside?" For raising such a question Rabbi Jeremiah was asked to leave the academy.[3]

The subject under discussion is a young bird found near a bird's nest. The question posed is whether the finder may keep it as an ownerless object or whether he is obligated to return it to the owner of the nest. An absolute arithmetical quantity was fixed that up to fifty cubits and not a hairbreadth more, we assume that the young bird escaped from the nearby nest and must be returned to the owner; beyond fifty cubits we assume that the bird came from beyond and belongs to the finder. This is certainly not an arbitrary measure; it is based on an empirical consideration that "a hopping bird does not hop more than fifty cubits."[4] But the very exactness of the law is its weakness, for what if one leg is within fifty cubits and the other outside the fifty cubits? For raising this vexing question, Rabbi Jeremiah was disciplined: they removed him from the academy; but the law remained unchanged. Better that one in a thousand birds become property of doubtful ownership, than that the principle of objective delimitation shall be uprooted in Israel!

Here is another illustration:

> As long as she remains in her father's household she can always collect her settlement stipulated in the *ketubah*. . . . The Sages say: "As long as she is in her husband's household, but if she is in her father's household she collects the settlement in the *ketubah* up to twenty-five years. . . ." Said Abaye to Rabbi Joseph: "If she came on the final day before sunset, she collects the settlement; if after sunset, she forfeits it." Within this fleeting moment can we assume that she renounced it? He answered: "Yes; all the measures laid down by the Sages are thus! In a pool of water of forty *se'ah* one may immerse himself; in forty, minus the tiniest measure, he may not."[5]

This law is based on considerations of common sense, and it distinguishes between one kind of widow and another with reference to the obsolescence of her claim to the settlement provided by her departed husband under the *ketubah*. There is no real obsolescence here, where the rule applied is based on grounds of public policy or "the perfection of the world." Here the question is probed on the basis of waiver or renunciation. A widow who remains in her late husband's household with other heirs, can always claim her allowance; her silence—that is, the failure to make a claim—does not prove anything, because "since they treat her deferentially she is too embarrassed to claim the settlement."[6] On the other hand, a widow who has returned to her father's household, and does not receive any benefit from the heirs,[7] has the right to the settlement only for twenty-five years. If this period has passed and she has not made a claim,[8] her prolonged silence is the equivalent of a renunciation, and she has forfeited her settlement. But when is the renunciation of the settlement established, from the point of view of law? At the end of twenty-five years precisely, at sunset of the final day of that period. How is this possible—Abaye asked—how can we assume that in that fleeting moment she was able to make a renunciation of the *ketubah?!* Rabbi Joseph's reply is: Indeed, all measures fixed by the Sages are thus! Consider, for example, the pool of water needed for immersion after ritual impurity. In the Bible it is written: "and he shall immerse his whole body in water,"[9] on which the Talmud adds:[10]

"His whole body in water"—this means that his entire body can be immersed in it;[11] and how much is this? One cubit square, by a height of three cubits, and the Sages computed that the quantity of water needed for ritual immersion is forty *se'ah.*[12]

The reasoning is then clear: his entire body must be immersed, but the Sages did not distinguish between a tall man or a short man, a fat man or a lean man. The Sages established an objective measure—forty *se'ah* and not a *kurtuv*[13] less. Similarly here, the Sages estimated that a silence of twenty-five years—and precisely twenty-five— amounts to renunciation, and therefore the widow may come one second before the last day's sunset and claim her settlement.

All measures of the Sages are thus, they established them as a peg which cannot be moved.[14]

"Which cannot be moved"—the meaning is: such is the law! In this brief sentence did Rashi express for us the entire concept: the measurement is a peg on which the law rests, for otherwise the law would become uncertain. We shall discuss this again later on.

The Talmud returns to this very theme in connection with another subject in the realm of religious law, a question that deals with the fruits grown in the sabbatical year. We encounter the same question and the same answer, but here a new element is added, stressing what we have quoted in the name of Rashi previously: the function of the formal measurement is to safeguard the stability of the law.

In the seventh year, the sabbatical year, work in field and garden must cease, as we are instructed: "The seventh year shall be a year of total rest for the land, your field shall not be sown and your vineyard shall not be pruned."[15] But not only is the work of the sabbatical year itself forbidden, also included is "the plowing just prior to the seventh year carrying over to the seventh year, and the reaping of the seventh year which carries over to the eighth year."[16] For we add from the ordinary to the holy, so that the work of the sixth year shall not be an aid to the growth of the seventh year and the eighth year shall not benefit from work in the seventh. But the sages of the Talmud imposed a limit on the latter prohibition: only if the crop "grew a third prior to the new year are you to treat the growth of the eighth year with the same prohibition which applies to the seventh year."[17] If the crop ripened and was harvested at *Sukkot* time, then "it is certain that a third grew before the new year."[18]

On the above statement there developed the following argument among the talmudic sages:[19]

> Said Rabbi Jeremiah to Rabbi Zera, "Could the Sages distinguish precisely between a third and less than a third?" He replied: "Did I not tell you to cease stepping outside the zone of the law! All computations given by the Sages are thus! In forty *se'ah* of water he may immerse himself for ritual purity; in forty, less a *kurtuv*, he may not. Ritually unclean food the size of an egg will contaminate other foods with impurity, but if less than an egg by the size of a sesame seed it will not contaminate.[20] A seating area of three cubits

square may be contaminated with ritual uncleanliness, but if less by the breath of a piece of string, it is not contaminated.[21]

"Did I not tell you to cease stepping outside the zone of the law"—did I not tell you: do not withdraw from the domain of the law! The measures given are the skeletal fabric of the law, on which grow flesh and skin, and if you do not submit to their discipline, you find yourself beyond the law. This is the peg to which Rashi referred in his wonderful statement quoted above.

3. This exactly is the nature of the measurement, a pillar on which the law rests, which one encounters from one end of the Talmud to the other: laws bearing on monetary matters, on legal capacity, on qualities of body and soul, on relations between husband and wife, on permitted and forbidden foods, on capital cases, on things consecrated to the Temple, ritual purity and many others.[22]

But the question yet remains: What, in the final analysis, justifies the computation: is it its absolute necessity as a "natural law," or a practical necessity as a general procedure in the law? The answer is: both are responsible! For without the joint effect of both reasons, we shall be unable to grasp the value placed in our sources on all the computations of the Sages. One may believe the statement of the Sages and say, that it has indeed been established on the basis of observing the behavior of birds, that a hopping bird does not hop more than fifty cubits. But this cannot be maintained, obviously in connection with other computations. Thus no one will assert—if he should say it he would only invite derision and the dismissal of his statement as absurd—that in a pool of water of forty *se'ah* minus a *kurtuv* "the whole body" cannot be immersed, even in the case of the smallest dwarf, but if one *kurtuv* be added[23] the whole body can be immersed, even if he were the tallest giant! Is the difference in dimensions between a dwarf and a giant no more than a *kurtuv?* We must necessarily conclude that the quantity of water computed by the Sages for a ritual immersion served for them not as an absolute law of nature, but as a statistical average,[24] appropriate for the average person, and for this reason, because it is statistically sound, they converted it into an absolute juridical principle which remains valid for all persons. The same applies to some other statistical computations.

4. Why is Jewish jurisprudence so inclined to give fixed measures and delimitations?

The answer to this was already hinted at in the beginning of this chapter, but now it becomes appropriate to elaborate on it.

Jewish jurisprudence—if we may say so—is a jurisprudence which does not depend on judges. The function of the law is not to prescribe for the judge how to decide; it prescribes for the person how to conduct his life. Even the paying of a debt—the basic foundation of all civil law—is a divine commandment,[25] and the right of the claimant is only a reflection of the religious obligation which rests on the debtor. This is a unique, Jewish outlook, which is diametrically opposed to the cynical, propertied outlook of Roman law, as well as to the more moderate outlook of its modern inheritors. The turning of Jewish jurisprudence directly to the person is based on, or follows as a logical inference from, the commandment to study Torah. It is for this reason that this commandment has been declared as the "equivalent of all others."[26] It is striking—I do not know if anyone has already called attention to it— that the term "decision in law" [*pesak din*] in the sense of a concrete determination is found in the Talmud only once.[27] It is surely noteworthy! In the Bible itself we read:[28]

If there arise a matter too hard for thee in judgment . . .
between plea and plea . . . then thou shalt go to the priests
the Levites and to the judge that shall be in those days, and
thou shalt inquire and they shall instruct thee the judgment and thou shalt do in accordance with what they instruct thee. . . .

The text says "thee" [in the singular], not "you" [in the
plural], which makes it clear that according to the original
Jewish conception, even in a case of pleas by two litigants,
the judge does not decide—determine—between the two,
but he notifies each how he is to act. "And thou shalt instruct them the way they are to go and the work they are
to do."[29] He notifies the defendant who lost how much he
must pay, and he notifies the claimant who won how much
he is permitted to accept. Herein is the total competence
of the judge and herein is his sole authority. For the two
litigants themselves are obligated by the Torah—they are
obligated even prior to the rendering of the judgment not
to transgress the commandments "thou shalt not rob," or
"thou shalt not oppress."[30]

The commandment to pay a debtor or the prohibition
of robbery and oppression is the religious foundation of
civil law; herein is the pinnacle and the peg holding together all the rights and obligations which constitute it.
At times a companion commandment or some other prohibition makes its bid for relevance, then juridical logic
comes to the rescue and attempts to distinguish between
those laws, or to reconcile them; this contributes to the
growth of the body of jurisprudence.

A striking illustration of this is afforded us in the treat-
ment of the subject of interest. This is one of the most
developed themes in all of Jewish jurisprudence. No won-
der, in one instance, did our own Supreme Court, in a
practical case before it, find itself obliged to turn to the
Jewish laws pertaining to the subject of interest—it could

find no clearer precedent.[31] This theme was dealt with by the Sages of the Talmud, and the codifiers after them—commencing with the Mishnah and continuing down to the latest authorities—in a most modern fashion, and with almost scientific analysis, embracing all the issues which probe the nature of money and exchange. For instance: the classic definition which has not become obsolete of what is interest;[32] the criteria for distinguishing between money and merchandise, "coin" and "fruits";[33] which precious metal is to be regarded as current money, and which is not;[34] what are the economic factors that produce a rise or decline in market values, or—in other words, who lowers and who raises prices—is it the one who raises or lowers the cost of commodities or is it the one who lowers or raises the value of money?[35] If the country—in their terminology: "the king"—raises the value of the national coin, is it permissible to accept a return of the nominal amount of the loan?[36] The point of the doubt is (according to some codifiers) the recognition or denial of the "principle of nominal value in currency":[37] the very delicate distinction between lowering the price against pre-payment and raising the price against a delay in payment.[38] Many other such distinctions pervade the entire field of this subject of interest.

Why all this; why were these distinctions in all their minutiae elaborated? It is because on this subject two prohibitions converged—the prohibition of interest and the prohibition of robbery—and one affects the other. Interest, as we know, is prohibited by Jewish law both for the lender and the borrower: it is forbidden to take interest, and it is forbidden to give interest.[39] The borrower is thus caught in a trap: if he gives too much he violates the law against interest, if he gives too little he will violate the law against robbery.

This is indeed how the question was defined before one

of the last codifiers (Rabbi Mordecai Halevi, d.1682): "May the teacher of righteousness instruct us how to arrange payment so as not to involve interest or robbery."[40] This dilemma of conscience was responsible, in my opinion, for all the rules and regulations and distinctions which were developed—and at times became complicated and distorted—in this field of law.

5. We see the deep impression registered by the religious commandment in the field of law. It touches everything, not alone the specific area of religious or ritual law. Even the code of civil law, *Hoshen Mishpat,* is in practice a way of life, *Orah Hayim,* which defines man's behavior. Therefore must the law—the entire body of law, including what we call civil law—be precise, without ambiguity, without allowances for discretionary judgment and interpretations, which are likely to reflect the subjective inclinations of the judge; and no concepts are less subject to this uncertainty and more objective than the concepts of measurement, of weight, time and space.

The secular law can allow itself to invoke abstract criteria, imprecise and obscure, such as "reasonable care,"[41] "reasonable behavior,"[42] "proximate cause,"[43] "reasonable time,"[44] which the judge in a specific litigation will bring down to concreteness and convert into tangible terms. For here generally the non-payment of a debt or the failure to meet an obligation is not a transgression, and the maximum that the guilty party faces is the payment of compensation and the cost of litigation. But this is not so in Jewish law, which, because it is by nature a religious law, does not define norms for deciding the law, but norms of behavior. The one who owes payment, who evaded paying what is due from him without justification, is not forgiven by paying damages which he caused by his action for the claimant. He must know at the outset how to act, and for this kind of precise knowledge there is no other source but a law which is clear and explicit.

6. An interesting parallel to this which rests on a similar—similar but not exactly the same—concept is found in secular law insofar as it deals with the fixing of penalties. *Nulla poena sine lege*—there is no punishment without a law—declares the well-known Latin legal aphorism, and scholars are still divided as to the source of this dictum, whether it is in Roman law, the British Magna Carta of the early thirteenth century,[45] or western liberalism of the eighteenth century.[46] It is conceivable—and here I offer a conjecture for which I have no proof—that the source of this concept is in Jewish law, which already in the time of the Mishnah and the *baraitot* (that is, at the end of the second and the beginning of the third century) declared: "We do not impose penalties on the basis of inference,"[47] which means: We do not impose penalties on the basis of "logical considerations," and even if the most cogent inference supports it. But whatever the historic origin of this maxim, it is a fact that beginning with the eighteenth century, it gradually won its place in various parts of the world and it presently appears in the criminal codes in most enlightened countries.[48] There is no punishment without a law specifying it which preceded the action,[49] and the term "law" here means: a written and explicit law, which does not require amplification or clarification through external considerations. It is, moreover, forbidden to the judge to invoke analogies or identity of terminology in order to create by his own action an offense not specifically included in the law.

> The principle is that one may not impose penalties unless the action under consideration has been defined specifically in the legal code as involving penalty. . . . The judge is denied a creative role here. . . . In other words, it is forbidden

to impose any punishment, basic or supplementary, except in cases defined by the law. The legislator alone may define the category of offense and he alone may define penalties. The additional inference follows that one may not impose penalties on the basis of the common law,[50] or by analogy. . . . One may not regard actions as punishable except those that are covered by the terms defined in the law. In the case of a lacuna, the criminal judge must render a verdict of not guilty, even if the public welfare requires that such an action be punishable.[51]

The reason for all this is that criminal law directs itself primarily to the citizen and prescribes for him his mode of behavior. What it forbids is forbidden, and what it does not forbid is permitted. Therefore must the law be explicit in its own terms, that the citizen reading it shall know decisively the dividing line between the forbidden and the permitted. The principle "No punishment without a law" is—according to the well-known expression of List—the "Magna Carta of the lawbreaker" (to be more exact, of the one accused of violating a law); from the "no" which forbids he infers the "yes" which permits, but he could not depend on this "Magna Carta" if its boundaries were widened, to his bewilderment, by an unanticipated interpretation of the judge.

This thought applies similarly, if not as rigorously, to the civil part of Jewish law. This law, too, turns to the citizen and establishes his behavior in life, and for this reason must the quantification which has been established be definite and explicit, weighed and measured without involving the additional factor of an interpretation by the judge. Hence the well-known talmudic formalism, which so many have disparaged. "The question is: Which is preferable in the law, precision and explicitness, or flexibility and better adaptation to reality? These two objectives cannot always be attained simultaneously, and at times it is necessary to choose between them, to forego one in favor of the other. The question is: Which is more important? If the goal of the legislator, the ideal toward which he aspires, is not the resolution of conflicts between persons *post factum,* but incipiently to set forth to each his ethical behavior, then the first consideration—precision and clarity—prevails and the inevitable result is: legal formalism."[52]

CHAPTER V

The Law and Its Rationale

1. Every law has its rationale, but the rationale is not sovereign over the law, and is not necessarily a condition for its authority. And the rationale itself sometimes seems apparent and sometimes not, or it may not even be discernible at all. Thus it is that in most cases a person must not invoke a rationale to undermine the law, and that the benefit gained by knowing the rationale shall not be paid for by a disparagement of the law.

Why were the reasons for the commandments of the Torah not disclosed? Because in the case of two verses in the Torah the reasons were disclosed, and the greatest person in the world stumbled over them.[1]

"Two verses" is inexact since the number of the commandments whose reasons were disclosed is more than two,[2] but with the others there did not occur any stumbling, at least not to the great of the world.

Nevertheless, and perhaps especially because we face here an element of mystery, the Sages sought to discover the reasons for the commandments.[3] But when they exerted themselves and discovered the reason, they did not make it a *sine qua non* for the applicability of the law, as we stated previously. Only concerning one *Tanna,* Rabbi Simeon ben Yohai, is it stated that "he expounds the reasons of Scripture,"[4] but even he—according to the opinion of some sages—did so only where the reason is indicated in the text, or becomes apparent from the substantive demand of the commandment.[5]

As an inevitable result from the dissociation of the two, there developed a gulf, that is, there continued to develop a wide separation between the law and its rationale. The assumption behind this separation, once it began to proliferate, tended to appear even in the case of enactments or prohibitions adopted by the Sages, in earlier and later times, whose reasons were explicit and significances well known, and the circumstances of their origin clear, and which were adopted *because* of their reasons and their goals. Even in such cases were the laws and the cause behind them no longer a unitary conception; and in the course of the generations the paths of the law became sometimes wider than its rationale, and sometimes narrower, and there now developed an excessive appendage, a kind of no-man's land between the boundaries of these two concentric circles. In this no-man's land there also began to develop the culture of legal evasion and legal fiction which we have dealt with at length previously.

2. This phenomenon, by itself, is an inevitable development; it is almost inherent in every legal system. It is not surprising, for the norm of law itself is plausibly clear to all, open for all to see. It is unobscured by its outer trappings: it generally fits the representative type of situation, but it does not fit with total precision every particular case. The law in relation to its reason is, as usual, a "shoe bigger than the foot," or a garment bigger than the body wearing it, and the result is that the concrete situation under consideration sometimes appears "devoid of rationale." This

occurs because of the accretion of various tendencies which tend to neutralize the original reason.

We cite an illustration: The accepted English law assumes that the place of domicile of a husband is also the place of domicile of the wife. The reason for this is obvious: a married couple under normal circumstances live together, and every division in their place of residence is bound to lead to legal entanglements. But this assumption continues to be maintained—and this is the "excessive appendage" of the law over its rationale—when the couple is separated by mutual consent, or even when the husband deserts his wife and refuses to allow her into his new residence.[6] The domicile of the runaway husband remains technically the shared domicile of the couple, though there is really no "shared living" between them.

3. Despite the similarity between the Law of Nations and Jewish Law with reference to this gulf, there is, nevertheless, a great distinction between them—both in its extent and in its direction. In what sense do they differ in extent? In modern law, the secular legislator is free to act, and he enjoys a flexibility in decision; he can from time to time change the basic legal norm or distinguish it into underlying norms in order to effect a better adjustment of the basics of the law to the specific situations. The gulf thus continues to diminish. But not so Jewish jurisprudence or the Jewish law. Jewish law does not lend itself readily to change because there is no recognized competence to effect it.[7] Its provisions were set down at their inception for a long period of time, and once the gulf appears it remains so until there is a radical change in the conditions which gave birth to the original law.

And how do they differ in direction? In Jewish law the dissociation between the law and the reason behind it is not one-sided, but two-sided. At times the law proliferates beyond the bounds of the reason, and has its sway beyond it and outside it, like that child who leaves his mother's womb and enters a world of his own; this is the nature of the "outer gulf" of the laws of Torahitic or of rabbinic derivation, which may be circumvented by legal fiction or legal evasion, as was explained previously.[8] But at times the opposite occurs, and the gulf is an "inner gulf." In the course of time and due to a change of circumstances the law shrinks and persists within the shell of the reason, but loses touch with it—even though it remains contained within that shell. In this case there occurs the legal paradox, that the law remains dependent on a reason, but is no longer sustained by it in its actual functioning.

The most striking illustration of the above phenomenon may be seen in the case of a wife's *ketubah*. According to the prevalent opinion among the Sages, the *ketubah* is a rabbinic institution: "The Sages ordained for the women in Israel, that the sum to be paid as *ketubah* in the event of divorce or the death of the husband shall be two hundred *zuz* for a virgin and one hundred for a widow."[9]

The reason for this ordinance as explained in many passages in the Talmud is "that it should not be too easy for the husband to divorce her."[10]

This means: the husband will hesitate to divorce her out of the apprehension that he will have to pay the settlement stipulated in the *ketubah!* This reason continues to underlie the law, in a very special way, as it becomes clear in many different provisions of the law.[11]

Consider, however, that in talmudic times two hundred *zuz*[12] was a substantial sum. It marked the dividing line between poor and rich.

> Whoever owns two hundred *zuz* may not accept the beneficence left for the poor in the gleanings after the harvest, forgotten sheaves, or the crop grown on the corner of a field,[13] or the tithe assigned for the poor.[14]

The Sages estimated that this sum is equivalent to the cost of a person's food and clothing for a year.[15]

In the course of time, however, due to changed circumstances, as a result of the rise in the standard of living and an increase in cost levels, the sum stipulated in the traditional *ketubah* became a paltry sum indeed, that could in no sense be said to inhibit the husband from divorcing his wife. Nevertheless, the original law remained unchanged, although here and there local communities adopted enactments to increase the sum stipulated in the *ketubah*, to bring it up to the monetary values of the original, as distinguished from its present purchasing value.[16] The result of all this remained, however, that the *ketubah*, although hovering close to the reason which engendered it, failed to achieve the objective toward which that institution was directed.

The truth must be noted that the Chief Rabbinate of Israel pioneered in the thought that there is need to correct, not the standard of the money, but the condition of the woman, that is to say, not only to equalize the local currency to two hundred *zuz* of talmudic times, but to find a protective measure for the woman that would safeguard her against too easy divorce. Thus in the enactments of 1944, raising the sum of the *ketubah*, it is stated:

Considering the standard of living in our time and economic realities, it became clear to us that the stipulated sum of two hundred *zuz* for a virgin and one hundred for a widow or divorcee or any non-virgin, which is the prevalent standard, no longer fits current conditions, and that this sum cannot function to effect the objective of the Sages when they made their enactment that it should not be too easy for the husband to divorce her. . . . Since it is permissible to increase the sum stipulated in the *ketubah*, we have resolved to add to every *ketubah* not less than fifty

Israeli pounds for a virgin and not less than twenty-five Israeli pounds for a widow....[17]

The objective of those who adopted the above measure was certainly desirable, but their actions were not as "desirable" or efficacious, for this "mighty" sum, even after it was increased fourfold in 1953,[18] still lacks sufficient inhibiting power to hold back the husband from divorcing his wife. But we are not really dealing here with measures to protect the welfare of women. I only sought to illustrate the "inner gulf" between the law and its rationale which I commented on previously.[19]

CHAPTER **VI**

Law and Morality[1]

1. What is the difference between the prescriptions of the law and the commands of morality?

The law directs itself to the citizen, morality turns to the man. The one is created by an outside source, by government authority; the other is created within man himself, in the depths of his own heart. The one comes to establish a social order, the other comes to pacify the mind. The function of the law is to save the aggrieved, the function of morality is to save the aggressor—from himself. The one ordains the repayment of a debt, the other demands the fulfillment of a duty. In short: the law is a social creation, an institution of a social-utilitarian nature, that looks on the individual from the perspective of the community; morality is a personal phenomenon, a sense of individual obligation, which sees the community itself from the perspective of the individual.

Despite these distinctions, however, law and morality are not two separate realms detached from each other. On the contrary, they cleave one to the other as the fire to the glowing coal. Morality is the ideological basis of the law, and the law is the outer garment, the concretization, of a part of the principles of abstract morality. This garment is standardized, given equal scope for the poor as for the rich, for the righteous as for the wicked; for the significance of the law—for the legislator—is the minimal moral performance which is demanded from each citizen.

I said "for the legislator"—but legislators are not all alike, nor are all "minima" alike. What appears to one legislator as a mountain, the other sees as a hairbreadth, as a demand below what should be the minimum, and he will, therefore, raise the standard of his demands, withdrawing them from the free zone of morality, and entering them into the compulsory zone of law. The realms of morality and law are two concentric circles, which coincide only partially—and as the dividing line between them increases, so will the realm and content of moral law increase. The ideal to strive after is that the two circles coincide fully—as the waters cover the sea.

I wrote these sentences as an introduction to an essay which I published some years ago,[2] and I do not modify the position which I developed in them. But in this chapter I want to shift the center of gravity to another aspect of the question, to expand it in one respect and condense it in another, so as to clarify not the subtle and not so subtle distinctions between law on one side and morality on the other, but the relationship between law and morality in the competence of the law itself—the relationship between the pragmatic and the moral considerations in the content of the law, in the content of jurisprudence, not of jurisprudence generally, but of Jewish jurisprudence.

Here we face a great difficulty which impedes the very opening of our investigation. The difficulty is in defining the concept "Jewish law." This concept is not particularly old; it seems to me that it goes back to no more than fifty or sixty years. But the confusion which developed around it is immense, and let it be stated here parenthetically that this is the cause for the confusion of basic principles and concepts which have beset one of the pivotal issues in our time, the revival of Jewish law.

What indeed is the content of Jewish law? I shall not attempt to offer here an all-embracing, exhaustive definition—I shall say only in a negative way, that Jewish law, unlike other juridical systems, does not confine itself to the categories between "man and man" alone, but it also introduces into juridical categories, it designates with a juridical terminology and it conceives in juridical terms, the relationship between man and God. The Holy One, praised be He, Himself, is treated as though He were a juridical person, who enjoys rights, is subject to obligations, heeds His own laws, and enters as a subject of juridical-civil scope into a hierarchy of relationship between Himself and His creatures.

It is taught in the Palestinian Talmud:[3]

> Said Rabbi Elazar: "On the king the law is not binding." Ordinarily when an earthly king issues a decree, if he wishes he can keep it, if he wishes—only others must keep it; but the Holy One, praised be He, is not so. When He issues a decree, He is the first to heed it. Why is this so? It is written: "And they shall keep My charge . . . I am the Lord" (Leviticus 22:9)—I am He who was first to keep the commandments of the Torah.

This thought, that the Torah exercises authority over Him who gave it, found noble expression in a wonderful legend concerning the so-called "Akhnai stove."[4] A dispute arose among the *Tannaim* concerning a rather dry point of law affecting this stove. The issue was this: a stove was cut into tiles with sand between the tiles,[5] and the whole was then plastered over with cement; shall it still be regarded as a vessel of pottery and as such subject to levitical impurity or shall it be regarded as an earthen object which is not subject to ritual impurity?[6] Rabbi Eliezer[7] declared it ritually pure; the view of the Sages was that it was impure. But this did not terminate the dispute. Rabbi Eliezer wanted to convince his colleagues that he was right. And the *baraita* continues to report:[8]

> That day Rabbi Eliezer brought forth a multitude of arguments, but his colleagues did not accept them. Finally he invoked miracles saying to them: "If the law is in accord with my views, let this carob tree offer testimony." The carob tree was uprooted from its place and moved one hundred ells, and others say four hundred ells. They replied to him: "We adduce no evidence from a carob tree." Then he said: "If the law is in accordance with my views, let this water brook testify." The water of the brook flowed in a reverse direction. They said: "We adduce no evidence from a water brook." Then he said: "If the law accords with my views, let the walls of the academy bear witness." The walls of the academy began coming together and were about to fall. Rabbi Joshua[9] rebuked them, saying: "If scholars debate an issue of law, what business is it of yours to intervene?" They did not collapse out of deference for Rabbi Joshua, and they did not resume their straight position out of deference for Rabbi Eliezer, but remained in a bent position. He then said to them: "If the law is in accordance with my views, let them confirm it from heaven." Whereupon a heavenly voice was heard declaring: "What have you against Rabbi Eliezer, since the law is always in accordance with his views!" Then Rabbi Joshua stood on his feet and said: "The Torah is not in heaven, it has already been given us at Sinai! We pay no attention to heavenly voices! For Thou hast already written at Mt. Sinai in the Torah: 'Incline after a majority.' "[10]

The Talmud adds to this:

> Rabbi Nathan[11] met the prophet Elijah and asked him: "What did the Holy One, praised be He, do at that time?" He replied to him: "He laughed exultantly, saying: 'My

children have vanquished Me, My children have vanquished Me!' "

This legend is well known, and scholars and literary people have marvelled at its beauty. But in my view there is more than literary beauty here. Here in this legend, as well as in the statement from the Palestinian Talmud quoted earlier, is disclosed to us the singular characteristic of Jewish jurisprudence. We have here the rule of law in its absolute sense, the rule of law over the one who decrees the law, the introduction of the lawgiver into the hierarchy of relationships, juridical and administrative, which were created by the law which He himself ordained. He heeds "the commandments of the Torah," that is to say, He takes on himself the discipline of the law and He submits to the authentic interpretation of the authorized interpreters. In other words, He accepts the discipline of the judgment pronounced by an authoritative body—the majority—which was empowered by Him for deciding doubtful cases, even though in this instance the doubtful case is for Him not doubtful at all. If the law is to follow a majority, one must act in accordance with this law, even if the one involved in the litigation is the giver of the Torah Himself.

This is a mighty conception, mightier than can be grasped by our simple common sense, but certainly one clear inference may be drawn from it and it is this: that Jewish jurisprudence is not content to limit its sovereignty to the areas affecting man and man. Also matters between man and God, which are in effect matters between man and himself, between himself and his religious and moral feelings, these too are embraced in the scope of juridical relations, they are joined in the hierarchy of juridical categories that were created by the lawgiver. Whoever has studied Talmud has had occasion to note that in the talmudic dialectic there is no distinction—from the standpoint of the delimitation of concepts and their manner of functioning—whether the issue under discussion deals with money matters, or whether it deals with Temple property or levitical purity. There is no halakhic subject so remote from the practical world as the laws of Temple sacrifices—the codifiers who came after Maimonides, as is well known, did not even include them in their codifications. One, nevertheless, finds in the talmudic order of *Holy Things* all the well-established procedural details that one finds in the order of *Damages* and the order of *Women*—the same dialectic, the same approach, the same conception, the same classification, with only one minor difference—which is wholly unimportant from a juridical point of view—the "transactions" here are between the layman and the heavenly realm, and not between Reuben and Simon, or between Jacob and Leah.

2. What conclusion follows from the preceding? The conclusion is that in the wider zones of Jewish jurisprudence, it would be very difficult to draw a distinction between the practical considerations of the lawgiver and his moral considerations—to establish the identity of any "property" being defended by a given decision of the law, even if the utility of this decision is beyond any doubt, even if it is impossible to envision any civilized society without this decision. The need or the utility are not discernible factors in the identity of the interest that has been defended.

One question, on the face of it rather puzzling, suggests itself: Why, for instance, is a person obligated to repay his debt, or to satisfy an obligation he took on himself? What is the *ratio legis* of this basic requirement? The pundits of Roman law, and similarly every modern jurist, would be baffled by such a question. It is clear—they would say— that the obligation to repay a debt is the other side of the rights of ownership, and one cannot exist without the other. It is inconceivable to have an ordered society, and not alone in a capitalist country, without the existence of an obligation, of civic law, to satisfy the obligations which the citizen took on himself. This is for the jurist a decisive answer which calls for no other elaboration. But in Jewish law the question is more problematic, and was so deemed by the sages of the Talmud.

There is a dispute among the sages of the Talmud whether the repayment of a debt is a "commandment" or not. In other words, whether this is a religio-moral obligation which presupposes, like every obligation of this type, a given personal maturity (and thus does not fall on a minor), or whether it is simply a civic obligation—which is to say: the necessary consequence of the right of the claimant—and is unconcerned with the religio-moral capacity of the debtor to assume obligations. The *Amora* Rav Papa declared:

> The repayment of a debt is a commandment, and minor orphans are not subject to the obligation of performing the commandments.[12]
>
> A debtor is commanded to repay his debt: he is commanded to pay his debt and fulfill his commitment, as it is written: "a just *hin* [a liquid measure] shall you have."[13] [The Hebrew term *hin* resembles the term for "yes," *hen,* which leads to the homily,] Let your "yes" be righteous and your "no" be righteous.[14]

We are not concerned here with the practical results of the question, nor with the final decision in law rendered on this question, but it is most instructive to consider one debate, brief and piquant, which developed around this issue:

> Said Rav Kahana to Rav Papa:[15] "According to you who hold that the repayment of a debt is a commandment, what

if a person declares that he is not interested in performing a commandment?" He replied, "We have studied a precedent for this question: 'When do we say (that he be punished with forty lashes)?[16] In the case where he violates a negative commandment but in the case of a positive commandment . . . , we continue to impose penalties until he conforms.' "[17]

The significance of the answer is: Here, too, in the case of a person who refuses to pay his debt, we force him to fulfill the commandment and repay the debt. The court, in other words, is not primarily concerned with the indebtedness to the claimant, but with the obligation of the debtor, with his religio-moral obligation, with the performance of his commandment, and it is only as though in a side effect, as a secondary result of the process, does the claimant receive his money.

This entire problem does not exist in the systems of modern jurisprudence, and it no longer existed for the Roman jurists. One may say, obviously with a grain of salt (*cum grano salis*), that modern jurisprudence is not interested in obligations, it is only interested in rights, and the obligation of the one who is indebted to pay is only the short expression of the claimant's right to coerce payment. One cannot erase from the modern lexicon the term "he is entitled to," but one may get along—though it would not be especially convenient—without the term "he is obligated." You will only have to write in its place: "You can force, through the courts and the offices charged with enforcement of its decisions, to sustain the right of the claimant." For natural law (*obligationes naturales*), too— insofar as residual elements of these archaic conceptions persist in modern juridical systems—the obligations which involve no enforced adjustment fall under the term "obligation" only in a fictional sense, and its significance is limited only to this: that the one who satisfies the obligation, the one who pays, cannot ask for a return of his money.[18] This is again a reflection—a negative one in this instance—of the rights of the claimant, which alone constitute the principal measuring rod for meeting the civic responsibility.

The condition is not the same in Jewish law, as we have seen. It is certainly not the same for the *Amora* whom we quoted, who holds that the payment of a debt fulfills a commandment. The debtor's satisfaction of a debt is a guiding principle for all forms of civic obligation, and if these be only the satisfaction of a commandment—that is to say: a religio-moral obligation resting on the obligated person—then, according to this conception, the obligation is primary, and the "right" secondary, or even less. But even one who does not adhere to this extreme view, cannot ignore the great importance which Jewish law attaches to the satisfaction of legal obligations. If the repayment of a debt is not a commandment solely, it certainly is, to all opinions, a commandment as well, and this projects and influences, directly or indirectly, the activating party—the side which has a right and makes a claim—of the *obligatio* in Jewish law.[19]

The distinction drawn in Jewish law between an obligation resting on the person and the obligation resting on property is well known.[20] Every loan which is confirmed by note creates both obligations, but later on they are likely to become dissociated. The obligation on the person rests on the individual and affects only the relationship between the lender and the borrower, the original parties involved in the transaction. The obligation on property, on the other hand, rests on the realia of the object and is transferred from person to person together with the property (landed property), or it is transferred—to confer the right—from the lender to the one who purchased the debt, with the transfer of the debt as provided for by law.[21] But what is the obligation on the person, this vague something, if not the commandment to pay a debt which is familiar to us, the religio-moral obligation of keeping faith with a promise, that your "yes" be righteous and your "no" be righteous, as Rashi put it in the passage cited previously.

The conclusion which follows from all this is that the *obligatio* of Jewish law is neither exhausted nor limited by the possibilities of effecting civically the demands of the claimant, but it depends not a little on the religious and moral obligation of the owner to repay the debt. Here come into focus the moral foundations of Jewish law, which stamp their characteristics in diverse ways on the uniquely Jewish doctrine of obligation.

3. We now proceed to another point, somewhat paradoxical, to a phenomenon which appears to contradict the basis of the concept I have developed previously. I have in mind the position of Jewish law with reference to one moral issue *par excellence,* and this is its attitude toward the validity of illegal or immoral contracts. On the face of it, it would appear that here is the testing ground for the morality of the legal system, and that to the extent of its stress on the moral norm, will it oppose the recognition of the legal validity of illegal contracts. But this, surprisingly enough, is not the case, as we shall soon see.

The problem in itself is most interesting, and it has continued to occupy most legal systems, new as well as old. Briefly put, the question is this: What is the attitude of the law toward covenants entered into in opposition to the provisions of the law, or to the accepted moral principles of society? The difficulty here is that the answer to this question is not simple and cannot be given succinctly in the form of "yes" or "no." There are various factors at work here: considerations of morality, of utility, of convenience—ethical and esthetic factors—and not the least:

considerations which have to do with impressions and face-saving.

I shall explain my point, and illustrate it with cases taken from English law which in this instance is based on concepts drawn from Roman law. We find here a rich differentiation, very subtle, and together with it—as is customary among the English—not entirely clear or entirely not clear of internal contradictions. The general principle is that the law does not recognize the validity of a forbidden contract or a contract which runs counter to the claims of morality. In other words—and I stress this—it does not see in such a contract a basis for making a civic claim.[22] If Reuben, for example, hired Simon to kill Levi, Simon cannot obviously sue Reuben to collect his stipulated fee.[23]

Thus far the matter is simple enough, and it will not occur to anyone to grant this agent a right of action against his "principal." But the matter becomes less simple as we descend the ladder of gravity in the criminality of the act and find ourselves confronting contracts contrary to law, but whose illegality is not especially grave. Let us imagine, instead of that murderer, a small shopkeeper, the owner of a grocery store, who does not close his store at the hour designated by the municipal ordinance, or on the day so provided, and he sells his merchandise during one of the forbidden hours or days. In the formal terms of the law he made a contract contrary to the provision of the law, he has entered upon a legal covenant which clearly violates the intention of the legislator. Let us further assume that he sells his merchandise not for cash but on credit, and the buyer who has fallen into indebtedness does not pay his debt. Can this "lawbreaker" claim what is due him from the purchaser, or shall here, too, apply the familiar principle: *ex turpi causa non oritur actio?* Or to cite another, less extreme, illustration: what is the legal status of a manufacturer who sells his product before receiving the necessary license required by one of the Emergency Regulations, or what is the legal status of a liquor store owner who neglected to renew his annual permit? Shall we say that in all instances the purchaser shall be the gainer and be relieved of paying for the merchandise he received?

Such questions arose by the hundreds in English law,[24] and the juridical position taken toward them was not uniformly the same. There occurred a strange incident some one hundred and fifty years ago, when on almost the same day there were brought two cases before the same judge, and the defendant claimed in both cases that the agreement on which the claim against him was based, was illegal and the claim was, therefore, to be denied. In the first litigation,[25] the issue involved two Frenchmen who had immigrated to London, and one of them, a priest by profession, had been stricken with syphilis. His colleague cured him through the use of various drugs, and he sued him for twenty pounds as the fee for curing him. The defendant did not deny the facts. He admitted that he had been fully cured, thanks to the attention of the claimant who was an expert. He argued, however, that his colleague was not legally permitted to attend him because, according to the laws of the period, no one was allowed to practice medicine in London and its environs within a seven mile radius unless he were licensed by the medical association. He therefore claimed that his cure of syphilis was a violation of the law, and that one could not claim to be paid for doing something which transgressed the law, that one had to do it without a fee! The Court did not recognize this argument, and ordered the defendant to pay the full amount of the claim. In the second instance,[26] which was tried the same day and by the same judge, the claim was for payment of the cost of a certain fabricated article—bricks. The defendant claimed that the bricks did not conform to the size prescribed by law, and that it was, therefore, forbidden for the seller to sell them, and that he could not, therefore, now claim their price. The Court accepted the argument and dismissed the claim. Over one hundred and fifty years have passed since the two decisions were given and no one is clear as to the difference between them—except for the relative emotional difference between them, between the ingratitude of the person who was cured and a merchant's refusal to pay.

But even in a later period, and in more detailed and more sophisticated decisions, we still find a multitude of contradictions in our quest for stable principles that shall embrace all sides of this question. Two mutually contradictory tendencies played on the loyalties of the judges: the desire to defend the validity of the legal proscription on the one hand, and the desire to grant redress to an aggrieved claimant, in a particular case, on the other. For the two are not always possible, and sometimes we face a rift, an opposition between them. The goal of a decision in criminal law is not only to punish the offender but also —if this be possible, primarily—to spoil the "pleasure" in the offense, to destroy its temptation, to "slay" the evil impulse drawing to it. In practice, all punishments as fixed have as their objective to neutralize the natural temptation. "Let sins cease—and not sinners!" states a talmudic aphorism.[27] The ideal before the legislator is to effect a condition where the transgression does not seem worthwhile and will, therefore, not be done. If the transgression or one of its bases or one of its accompanying phenomena is the conclusion of a certain contract, or entering into a particular civil relationship, then one means of voiding all this—removing the temptation to transgression—is to nullify the legal efficacy of the illegal contract. In other words: to deny the right of the offender to enter a claim, and thus to deny him the legal fruits of the for-

bidden contract, to declare the contract entered upon as
"illegal," *i.e.*, having no legal effect.

On the other hand, we have a different consideration,
which cannot readily be dismissed either. It is the desire
and the duty to render justice to litigants who stand before
the judge, the desire not to permit a defendant to evade
meeting his obligation through the inequitable claim of a
lack of legality. There is, of course, always, in every branch
of law, a certain discrepancy, a certain gulf between the
standard justice of the law, and the individualized justice
that suits all concrete circumstances of the case under litigation. No law in the world is absolutely cogent for all
conditions which fall within its scope. This is a grave problem from which there is no escape, and the reason for it is
that there is no legislator who can anticipate in advance all
configurations of circumstances which may occur in life.
The abstract justice of the law is, therefore, in practice
only a "statistical" justice—an average justice—a formal-
ized necessity which spares all of us certain deficiencies,
but does not really satisfy anyone. . . .

But this is not the defect which I want to cite here, in
discussing the second consideration which plays in the
mind of the judge, when he deals with a claim based on a
contract counter to law. Here the contradiction is not accidental, partial, or hidden; it is an inevitable fact of
existence and it appears in every instance. The evil arises
from the fact that frequently the Court must accept an absolutely "unsympathetic" claim, a claim that by its every
essence reveals a moral defect in the claimant. The manufacturer who sells his product in violation of the standards
and measures set by the legislator is certainly deserving of
punishment (there is no doubt about it): it is possible to
arrest him, to impose a fine on him, to close his factory.
However this still does not justify the purchaser who was
a party to the offending act—a partner in essence, if not in

a legal sense, and perhaps even more than a "partner," since "it is not the rat that has stolen but the crack through which he came"—that he shall emerge with a big profit from this transaction, and retain the merchandise without paying for it.

For what is the legal principle at work in the question we have raised? The principle is, as the old Roman aphorism puts it: *In pari delicto, melior est pars possidentis,* since both offended simultaneously—both the claimant and the defendant—the one who holds possession has the advantage! I emphasize, and I want the reader to note it: The law does not say that every contract contrary to law or morality is null and void, absolutely and totally, and that we must restore the condition which existed before it went into effect. It is careful not to say this, it avoids saying it with deliberate intention. All it says is: the one who holds possession has the advantage, *beati possidentes!* "Whoever holds possession" this is "the measure of the law." It is for this reason that the manufacturer who turned over the product without being paid, cannot claim the payment of his price, nor the return of the product. The purchaser—if he is also subject to the prohibition— cannot claim a return of his money if he paid the price and did not receive the merchandise.[28] All this means: The Court is not required to deal with such a claim, it is "set aside as repulsive," and the Court does not soil its hands with such a case. The result of this moral indignation is that, while penalizing the offending claimant, it also awards a prize to the offending defendant. The only difference is that it does not directly award this prize but leaves it in the hands of the one who took it by himself.

This is the unpleasant feeling which remains in the heart of the judge, once he has accepted the claim of "lack of legality." It is the "ill sound" of the claim, with which Lord Mansfield dealt in one of his famous judgments.[29] It becomes the duty of the judge—so the modern legislator demands of him—to suppress this inner feeling, to deny his "musical sense," for the sake of attaining another legal maxim, the practical, the utilitarian, that "they may hear and be intimidated," and in order to endow the law with greater efficacy, greater force, in its ordered prohibitions. The Court must not aid an offender, it must not help him enjoy the fruits of his offense, even though its passivity toward the one offender begets, incidentally, an inequitable benefit, which is also forbidden by law or morality—in some instances, much more immoral—to the other offender.

4. Such is, in general outline, the state of the law in the modern system of English jurisprudence. We cannot enter here into the ramifications and modifications of this conception, but I shall merely indicate that the general feeling is that this condition is not satisfactory, and it is both desirable and necessary to find a new mode of thought, one of substance that is not merely a compromise or an evasion of this dilemma. An incident occurred some years ago in England,[30] involving a man who was obliged to send his wife and sick child to Italy for a cure, but he did not have at his disposal the required foreign currency. The circumstances were reported to an acquaintance and she proposed to him—in her great magnanimity—to make available to his wife in Italy the necessary amount in Italian liras, on condition that the husband deposit with her as security his shares in a certain company. The husband deposited the shares, the woman left for Italy, but she did not receive the promised funds and she returned with her sick child. On returning to England the "friend" sued the husband for a repayment of the loan. . . . In the course of the litigation the attorneys dropped the case, acknowledging that

their client had not kept her promise and had not given the woman the liras. Now the husband presented a counterclaim, asking for the return of the shares. The response of the woman was that the claim against her was based on a transaction contrary to law, since—according to fiscal rules then prevalent in England—the husband had no right to commit the shares as pledge of repayment, because the objective of this commitment of the shares was to acquire Italian liras without authorization by the authorities in charge of foreign currency. The Court accepted this argument, and dismissed the claim for the return of the shares. It acted on a sacred principle, a principle not to be violated: where both offend, the one who has possession enjoys the advantage.

This decision is not particularly significant from a legal point of view. But it is in order to contemplate the pangs of conscience which the judges must have suffered when they felt obliged to dismiss the claim of the husband. Indeed, from a purely humanitarian point of view, the results were most tragic: those people jeopardized the health of their child, wasted the travel expenses and lost the shares. The other party—their "friend" and counter-litigant, the person of the most reprehensible behavior—emerged with a great treasure: she did not pay what she had promised, she received a substantial number of securities; she failed to receive only one additional item, court expenses, since they did not award expenses to this victorious litigant.[31]

5. And now let us examine the position of Jewish law toward this question. It is obvious that when we seek to compare two legal systems so different from each other, both in spirit and in time, we must make a certain "discount"—a certain allowance for these differences, but the

core of the question remains. We shall find that it is possible to show parallels between them, despite the great
differences which set them apart.

What then is the position of Jewish law on this question? The Talmud itself devotes an entire discussion to
it.[32] The *Amoraim* Abaye and Rava were the discussants.[33]
Abaye declared: "Whatever the Torah forbade doing, if a
person did it, the action is valid"; but Rava declared:
"The action is not valid." A sharp and lively debate then
arose on this question, difficulties were adduced, counter-
precedents cited[34]—some against Rava and some against
Abaye—answers were offered, distinctions were drawn, so
that in the end, whether we hold that in a dispute between
Abaye and Rava the law follows the position of Rava,[35]
or whether we hold that *in this case* the law follows the
position of Abaye,[36] that discussion does not help us materially in our quest for a full solution to this problem. We
still do not know what is the basic law which was adopted
toward the particular sector which interests us here: to
what extent there is legal validity in civil law to a contract
or a transaction which was enacted in opposition to a prohibition of the law.

The Torah, however, while it offers but a paucity of
material on a given subject in one text, offers us a greater
amplitude in another text, and our question is fully answered in other discussions of the Talmud and in the
discussion of commentators and codifiers. Here, for example, is another interesting dispute between the same
two *Amoraim* we quoted earlier:[37]

> Abaye further said: "If a person sues his neighbor for
> four *zuz* which he gave him as interest, but instead of paying
> in currency he had paid him by the gift of a garment, we
> order the return of the four *zuz* but not of the garment."
> Rava said: "We order the return of the garment so that it

shall not be said: 'The garment he robes himself with came to him through interest.' "

Interest is forbidden by the Torah, as is well known. It is forbidden to the lender, as well as to the borrower. It is forbidden to accept interest and it is forbidden to give it.[38] Whoever gives interest also violates an explicit prohibition of the Torah (for it is written *lo tashikh*,[39] which means literally, "thou shalt not cause interest to be taken"). Nevertheless, despite his offense, the borrower who paid interest can claim that it be returned to him, if it was an exact and definite sum, called in the Talmud: *ribit ketzutzah.*

> Said Rabbi Elazar: "Definite interest [*ribit ketzutzah*] is to be ordered returned by the judges, but what is only indirect interest [*avak ribit*] is not ordered returned."[40]

The lender, obviously, cannot claim the payment of interest in Court[41] for the Court cannot award a person what he is forbidden to accept (this has nothing to do with the question whether an illegal contract can have any legal validity), but it is noteworthy that the borrower who paid the interest is empowered to ask for a return of what he paid, and the Court will order the lender to make restitution to the borrower of the "definite interest."[42]

From this very ruling we can see that Jewish law does not follow the "exclusive" view that it is unbecoming for the Court to deal with a claim which derives from an illegal act. The Jewish legislator does not share this feeling, and it appears to him exaggerated and improper. In any case, the Court is accustomed to dealing with cases which are not untarnished!

It is an established law that the return of "definite interest" can be exacted by action of the Court, that is, it is taken back from the lender and returned to the borrower.

But in the instance cited the question arose as to the status of a garment which the borrower gave the lender in place of the interest—whether he can ask for the return of the garment, or only for its value. The point at issue was whether the sale of the garment in lieu of paying the interest is not itself an invalid transaction because it was incidental to a violation of law. Abaye is of the opinion that the money is refunded, but not the garment:

> The transaction is valid but the specified interest is to be refunded.[43]

Rava, on the other hand, is of the opinion that we demand a return of the garment itself, so that people seeing the lender robe himself in it shall not learn to do as he has done; or, according to another interpretation, that he shall not come under suspicion of being benefitted by a garment which he acquired as a payment of interest after he has returned to the borrower the specified sum agreed upon as interest.

In this regard, the Rosh[44] notes in his commentary:

> It is only so that people shall not say that he robed himself in a garment acquired in a payment of interest, that we demand its return. Otherwise, the transaction would be valid, and we would not say, "Since it was done in an act forbidden by law, the transaction itself is devoid of validity."

We are, therefore, justified in inferring that in principle there is no disagreement between Abaye and Rava, that both agree that a purchase which involved a violation of law is not invalid. The Rosh also adds in his comment the following in the name of Rav Hai Gaon:[45]

> Where a sale was made in violation of law, such as increasing the price in consideration for waiting for payment, . . .[46] and the sale was validated through the usual

token of completing a transaction, and the price level did
not increase, the sale is valid, and it cannot be voided
because it occurred with a violation of the law incidental
to it.

"It cannot be voided," whether the transaction was completed—the merchandise was exchanged for the payment
of the price—or whether it was still incompleted. This
means: the purchaser can demand by law the surrender of
the merchandise, the seller can demand by law the payment of the price, but, obviously, up to the level of the
excess, or: the principal but not the interest.

The view of Rav Hai Gaon, in a slightly different version, is quoted by the Ritva[47] in the name of the Ramban:[48]

> We have found in a *responsum* of Rabbenu Hai, that
> one who sells produce to his neighbor for a price in excess
> of its value in consideration of his waiting for later payment,
> and the purchase was consummated in a standard fashion, if
> one should seek to void the transaction, the transaction can-
> not be voided....[49]

Neither of them can back out of the purchase, not even
the purchaser from whom the seller demands the full price
[including the excess]. This is also the decision of Maimonides:[50]

> One who sells or transfers a gift on the Sabbath . . .
> though he is punished with stripes [for violating the Sab-
> bath], the transaction is valid. Similarly, one from whom a
> purchase was made on the Sabbath, the transaction is valid,
> and after the Sabbath the necessary documents are written
> and payment made.

The first clause deals with the substantive violation of
the Sabbath in a sale; the second clause adds to it the obligatory commitment.[51] The original source of this law is

in the Palestinian Talmud, as is cited in the Code of Rabbi Isaac Alfasi:

> Whoever purchased land or movable property on the Sabbath, the purchase remains valid.[52]

Maimonides supplements the above with a reference to the legal validation of the purchase (through the customary token of the buyer pulling at the garment of the seller). The decision in the *Shulhan Arukh, Hoshen Mishpat,* is similar:

> One does not make a purchase on the Sabbath through the token pulling of the garment; but if he did make the purchase—though he violated the law—the transaction stands.[53]

We see clearly that Jewish law does not establish a causal connection between the commission of an offense and the voiding of a civil contract, or any other legal transaction which occurred incidentally to a violation of the law. The violation of the law or of morality is one thing, and the legal validity of the contract is another—to the extent that the fulfilling of the contract itself does not activate the offense (as, for instance, the payment of interest by the borrower to the lender). Precisely because Jewish law does not distinguish between law and morality, and that practically every performance of an obligation is at the same time a fulfillment of a religio-moral commandment—as "the commandment" of repaying a debt of monetary obligation—the non-fulfillment of a contract entered into through a violation of law will only turn out to be an additional offense to supplement the original one committed by the transgressor. This is the core ideological concept for the distinction between the two approaches. In other words, the distinction between the criminal and the legal content of the action is a consequence of the identity in the legal and moral content of the law generally, and it is precisely this decision which appears on the face of it to contradict the concept I developed which serves, in fact, as an important additional confirmation for it.

6. In the first part of this chapter, I stressed the close relation in Jewish law—the "identity" as I called it—between the legal and the moral content of the law. And, indeed, there is no legal system in the world, ancient or modern, in which the principles of morality and law are so intertwined as in our Jewish law.

There are three reasons for this phenomenon (I have already alluded to this in the essay which I mentioned in the beginning of this chapter).

(a) Jewish jurisprudence is a religious jurisprudence, founded on the religious consciousness of the people. Even the offenses between man and man are also religious offenses, and they also affect man's relation to God. "Thou shalt not take the name of the Lord thy God in vain," and "Thou shalt not steal," are both listed in the Ten Commandments, and from a religious point of view there is no distinction between them. The well-known counsel of compromise: "Render unto Caesar what is Caesar's, and unto God what is God's," was a doctrinal innovation introduced by Christianity. Judaism does not acknowledge a domain that belongs to Caesar; everything is part of God's domain—in a metaphoric sense, of course—and the citizen owes nothing to Caesar which as a person he does not owe to God.

(b) Jewish jurisprudence is a national jurisprudence, whose principal development occurred after the loss of national independence. The Talmud, the formulators of legal decisions, the great codifications of the twelfth century (Maimonides), of the fourteenth (the *Tur*), of the sixteenth (*Shulhan Arukh*), and the Responsa of the early and the later authorities (*Rishonim* and *Aharonim*)—all these arose on alien soil, and their primary objective was to preserve the national character of the people, that it be not dissipated or assimilated in the atmosphere of an alien culture. The people in exile voluntarily confined itself in the "four ells" of Halakhah—ritual law, civil law, criminal law—in the knowledge that only thus, with the help of this shield, would it be able to preserve its national uniqueness until the return to its ancestral land, until the coming of the redeemer.

And this major role of the law necessarily set the path for its development. Every decision, every commandment, every law, every emergency enactment was studied firstly from the perspective of its efficacy toward the needs of the national defense—the defense of the people and its culture, in the widest sense of these terms. Only when the issue seemed neutral from the point of view of this overriding objective, was it weighed from the perspective of other considerations. The dress of the Jew, his diet, his place of residence, his manners, his behavior with people, his family relations, his business affairs—all these were cast from the very beginning in a national mold, in a hierarchy of well-defined rules, strict and detailed, which accompanied him from the cradle to the grave.

(c) A historical factor which is well known and which influenced the later development of Jewish law was the absence of coercive measures, on the part of government or quasi-government agencies, to enforce the decisions of the law.

And this is the reason: At the end of the tenth and the beginning of the eleventh centuries, the autonomous Jewish center in Babylonia disintegrated, and the national hegemony moved to the countries of north Africa and western Europe. After a period of one thousand years of national autonomy in the legal and cultural realms in the countries under the sway of pagan Rome, of Christian Byzantium, of Sassanian Persia, and the Arab Caliphate, the national center was shifted into a strange and intolerant setting which did not recognize any legal status for the remnant of the Jewish exiles. From then on there is no longer any Jewish self-governing authority in the Jewish street throughout the Jewish dispersion, except for certain meager concessions, limited and of little significance, granted from time to time by the local ruler.

In this atmosphere, in the dark walls of the ghetto, without governmental enforcing power, without judges and police authority authorized by an agency of government, our national law continues to develop through only one factor: the free consent of the people. Though this consent can also impose certain sanctions, primarily social, the essence of its efficacy is limited, deriving from the free will of the individual, not to isolate himself from the community, not to forsake the shared spiritual ground of the people.

Under these circumstances, and because of these conditions, Jewish law took on its distinctive moral character. A legal system which is religious in essence, national in its goals and free in the means of its actualization can have only one firm basis: the moral conception shared by the constituent individuals of the people. The simple utilitarian interest of preserving the continuity of the group cannot form such a basis because this interest negates the asocial or antisocial interest of the lawbreaker. The community is, of course, interested that every person meet his obligation to the other person, but the obligated individual is not interested, from a materialistic point of view, to meet his obligation. He is forced into it either by the recognition of the moral claim, or by the fear of coercion at the effective arms which enforce the law. Thus we may infer that every effective legal system—if it is at all effective—in a society that lacks the means of coercion and enforcement, has no other basis, but the moral recognition of the community.

The concept is altogether simple and there is no need to elaborate on it. But what is not so simple, and not so well known, is that these causes formed and delimited not only the substance and content of Jewish law, but also its form, its patterns of thought and its manner of legislation; but more of this in the next section.

7. The Talmud—I refer to its sections dealing with law—is still a closed book for the greater part of our intelligentsia. Our intellectuals have not yet become enlightened enough to take a natural position toward it—by "natural" I mean: neither an apologetic one nor disdainful one—and all this not necessarily out of ignorance, but out of a lack of a proper approach, out of a lack of understanding and a failure to reckon with the special conditions which fashioned this monumental creation. We judge it for the most part by improper criteria taken from the outside—from foreign worlds, from other cultures. The result is inevitably distortion and perversion, either toward apologetics or to the opposite side, all depending on the taste and inclination of the critic.

Let us consider, for example, one of the characteristic features of talmudic law—ritual law as well as civil law—its well-known formalism, a characteristic about which most of the perverted critics of the Talmud have repeatedly complained. Endless scorn has been directed at the "little minds," the "pedantry," and the "narrow views" which characterize, as it were, the thought processes of the sages of the Talmud. This is a very cheap criticism, one easy to come to, and most convincing, if one is satisfied to look at the outer impression, the superficial one, without probing into the depth of things.

What is, in essence, legal formalism? It means: the event on which hinges the outcome of the legal consideration is measured and weighed by standards which are exact and precise, and where the slightest deviation will affect the outcome of the legal decision (by legal decision I refer to the general attitude of the entire legal system). Thus, a given quantity of water—forty *se'ah,* and not a drop less— qualifies the pool of water to remove the ritual impurity of one who immerses himself in it;[54] thirty days—and not "a time which seems reasonable," as a modern legislator would provide—is the duration of time given us for paying a debt, if no specific time was stipulated;[55] so many and so many ells, not more nor less, constitute the dividing line between "near" and "far" in connection with a law about found objects.[56] In practice there is no legal system in the world which is altogether free of formulating measurements and delimitations, but there is a great differ- ence in the tendency toward this, whether it is to maximize or to minimize the imposition of such forms and rigidities. In our case quantity becomes a quality.

But whoever can read between the lines will find in the Talmud itself, from the lips of an *Amora,* a veiled criticism against this tendency to formalism. I have reference to the well-known question by Rabbi Jeremiah[57] in the tractate Bava Batra.[58] The subject under discussion is that of a young bird found close to a nest of pigeons, and it is un- known whether it belongs to the owner of the nest, and the finder would, therefore, be obligated to return it, or whether it is ownerless, and the finder may, therefore, keep it for himself. The Mishnah rules:

A young bird found within fifty ells belongs to the owner of the nest, outside the fifty ells it belongs to the finder.

On this ruling Rabbi Jeremiah raised the challenging question:

> What if one leg is within the fifty ells and the other leg outside?

The Gemara adds that for raising this question Rabbi Jeremiah was excluded from the academy. Rashi explains the action by saying:

> He troubled them.[59]

To me it seems that the problem here was not of troubling or annoyance alone, but a very sharp challenge of all legal formalism by carrying it to absurdity. But the challenge was without results, the official academy ignored it and passed over it to the agenda of the day. In the language of metaphor: they removed Rabbi Jeremiah from the academy and continued with their studies.

Let us pause to consider this classic illustration, for it can disclose to us the basic concept, and let us ask ourselves who was right in this case, Rabbi Jeremiah or his colleagues? It will become clear that the question is not so simple, as it appears on first consideration, and that the answer to it is not easy. Rabbi Jeremiah's question is indeed very subtle but it is not particularly convincing. The occasional "fixing of boundaries" is to be found in every legal system, and it cannot be avoided, even if the legislator prefers to employ more abstract categories. For what, in essence, was the position of Rabbi Jeremiah, and what did he seek to establish, if it be true that his question represented constructive criticism, and not an effort at obstruction? Rabbi Jeremiah sought to obliterate the external, formalistic distinction between fifty ells and more than fifty ells, and to substitute for it a measuring rod that was more abstract and flexible, such as "near"-"far," or, in a more general way: the finder must return the young bird and not keep it, if on considering all circumstances, it would appear that the bird belonged to the owner of the nest and was not ownerless property.

But at once we face the question: Who will decide what is "near" and what is "far," what are the factors that are to be reckoned with, and what is the final conclusion which may be inferred from them? It is clear that if the matter should become subject to litigation, and the dispute come before the judge, he, after listening to witness and experts, will be able to clarify all the circumstances in the case, and draw from them the most plausible conclusion. But what is the ordinary citizen who does not have command of this complex apparatus to do—how can he clarify the subject, and what is he to do in order to be able to decide whether he is indeed obligated to return the bird, or not?

It might be suggested: he need not do anything! The finder can sit with folded hands and wait until the owner of the nest will sue him, and then the matter will be clarified in all its details, as I have described above. This is indeed true, he can behave in this manner, but only if the question before him is one of legality, if the only concern which troubles him is whether his neighbor will bring him to court, and he will become obligated to return his find together with the expenses of the litigation. This is precisely the customary question which faces the average citizen in the average country. But if this is not the primary question, if the question in the first place is not one of legality but of conscience, if the finder wants to be at peace with himself and to know whether he is under obligation to fulfill the religious-moral duty of returning a found object—does not this consideration require that the legal norm be perhaps less elegant but more precise, less flexible and more exact, so that the citizen toward whom the instruction of the law is directed shall be able to utilize it, without the constant intervention of the judge?

This, to my mind, is the decisive factor, here is the turning point of the two systems, the flexible and the formalistic, and here we see clearly the advantages and the defects of each. The question is, which is preferable: precision and exactness, or flexibility and greater adaptability to the contingencies of reality? These two do not always go together, and very often it is necessary to choose between them, to compromise on one for the sake of the other.

The question therefore is, which of the two is preferable? If the goal before the legislator, if the ideal toward which he aspires is not to resolve *post factum* conflicts between man and man, but to provide, in the first place, moral guidance for each person, then the first consideration—of precision and clarity—will prevail, and the inevitable result is legal formalism.

A similar phenomenon is to be found among nonformalistic systems with reference to a particular branch of the law, its criminal division. It is well known that the methods of interpreting criminal law differ from the methods of interpreting every other branch of the law. Here prevails the principle of austerity in explanation, of exactness, and there is no extension of the boundaries of the concept beyond the clear and precise meaning of the language in the written word of the law.[60] One is not permitted to invoke the principle of *a fortiori,* or any other of the usual canons of logical deduction, in order to establish as an offense any action which is not explicitly forbidden by the law. The Talmud itself taught long ago: "We do not impose penalties on the basis of inferences drawn by logic,"[61] and if the Torah commanded concerning a witness whose evidence has been refuted [*ayd zomaym*]: "and you shall do to him as he contemplated doing to his brother,"[62] then we only punish the one who "contemplated to do," not the one who actually "did," although all rules of logic would argue precisely the opposite, but the law remains: "if the one against whom they testified has not been executed—fraudulent witnesses are executed, but if he were executed—they are not executed."[63]

And this maxim has been accepted by the most modern legal systems. *Nullum crimen sine lege* or *nulla poena sine lege,* declares the well-known classic maxim, and it has been adopted by all the most enlightened legal systems. There is no punishment without a law, or there is no offense without a law, and the term "law" as used here means a written law, an explicit law, a law that does not depend for its recognition on interpretations and elaborations through considerations and arguments beyond itself. Some ninety or one hundred years ago, in one of the European countries, a person who stole electricity from his neighbor was brought to Court. However, the Court was compelled to free him. The paragraph in the law of that country dealing with theft employed the term "object," and electricity is not an object, but a force. It became necessary, therefore, to pass a new law, which was explicit in imposing penalty for the theft of electricity. It was not deemed proper to utilize the principle of *a fortiori* to learn the theft of a substantial quantity of electricity from the theft of a small nail. There are many such illustrations, and every person familiar with law stumbles over them constantly, in one form or another. And what is the reason for this approach? There are many reasons for it, but the most important is that the criminal code is directed primarily to the citizen, it prescribes for him how he is to behave in life. It is therefore necessary that this citizen, the potential offender, shall be able to learn, to study from it and in it, what he may not and what he may do, and he shall not be dependent on reflections and considerations which were not explicitly set forth in the legal code. It is for this reason that it has been said that the criminal code is the Magna Carta of the offender, because what is written in it—what is explicitly written—offers an absolute distinction between the forbidden and the permitted, and by being shown the one side, he automatically perceives also the other side.

And so it is—with a grain of salt (*cum grano salis*), of course—in the question under discussion here. Jewish law generally, in its criminal as well as its civil aspects, is a system of law which turns primarily to the citizen and not to the judge. The *Hoshen Mishpat* and *Even HaEzer* are, in a certain sense, really *Orah Hayim,* "a way of life," instructing a person concerning his conduct in relations with his neighbor. It is not the "right" of the claimant the law has vindicated when it established the principle of obligation, but the duty of the person who is under obligation: how and in what way he can fulfill his religious or moral obligation toward his fellow-man. The "quantities" bearing on his case must, therefore, be fixed and specific, weighed and measured so that every ordinary person shall be able to apply them, without any dependence on interpretations by the judge.

The sum and substance of all this is: the moral and popular content of Jewish law determined necessarily its outer form as well, and placed upon it the stamp of its uniqueness which distinguishes it from all other legal systems.

CHAPTER VII

Law and Equity

1. The well-known Roman adage says: *Habent sua fata libelli*.[1] It is possible to say with even greater justice: *Habent sua fata nomina*, each term has its own destiny, or its own angel who directs its rise or decline among the terms of the language or the culture.

And such has been the fate of the Hebrew term *yosher* [equity]. It did not remain constant but went through various plastic changes: its form was corroded, its physiognomy was wind-swept, and it presently conveys no more than a small fraction of the original meaning which the term had in antiquity. Long is the road and vast the distance separating the transcendent *yosher* of the books of the Hebrew Bible and the pragmatic *yosher*—the *yosher* of an action which we find in talmudic literature.[2] We are dealing here with the legal categories of the Talmud— with the *yosher* of the action and not with the *yosher* in the heart of the actor. And the task we have taken upon ourselves is to find the line where law and *yosher* meet, the dividing line between "strict law" and "beyond the strict law," as these terms are defined in the principles of Jewish law.[3] When we delineate this obscure line and learn to define the realms which extend on either side, we discover that it is not a straight line, but a zigzag, adapting itself to the twists and turns of the law under consideration.

We shall also find that the factors which led the Jewish sages to create the rules of *yosher* are similar, in essence, to the factors which led the English jurists to lay the foundations of their structure of equity. Certainly, Hebrew *yosher* and English equity are not concentric circles. On the contrary, they are very different in content, as we shall see later on. But both draw their inspiration from the same source, from the need to dull the sharpness of the law and to create by its side a palliative to sweeten or smooth its rough edges. The task placed upon them was to bridge the gap between strict law and *yosher* or equity, to bridge the gap between them but not merge them! The common denominator—perhaps the most important—between Hebrew *yosher* and English equity is that they did not lower the law from its high pedestal and did not reduce it to subservience to pure morality. Hebrew *yosher*, like English equity,[4] walks in the paths of the law; it is its reflecting shadow. Here lies the difference between morality and *yosher* [equity], and we shall have more to say on this in the course of our exposition.

2. There are three principal references cited by the sages of the Talmud to describe an obligatory action, which does not derive from the law altogether, but which stems from the quasi-legal, in a relative degree. It is graded from the grave to the light—that is to say, from the very close to the very distant from the full norm of the law. These are:

(a) And you shall do what is upright and good;

(b) beyond the strict law (or beyond the merit or the measure of the law);

(c) the spirit of the Sages is pleased (or is not pleased) with him, or—an equivalent expression: to act so, is the standard of saintliness.[5]

The meaning of these expressions and the difference in nuance between them will be explained in detail in the following sections.

3. "And you shall do what is upright and good." This expression is a full sentence in the Bible,[6] and its literal translation to the Latin—*aequum et bonum*—is found in many English legal judgments, especially in the second half of the eighteenth century, in those rendered by the renowned judge Lord Mansfield.[7] "The upright and the good" is an obligating category of law, a category made obligatory by the Sages—without any formal *takkanah* [enactment][8]—because it embodies uprightness and goodness. The distinctions between this and a *takkanah* enacted by the Sages is very subtle, and it has not yet been fully explored. It is not identical with the law, but it robes itself in the garment of the law; it effectuates the concept which is its basis, but it removes from it its rough edge, and makes it non-troublesome and non-damaging. Its penetration into the severe realm of the law is in the spirit of "breaking the barrel but keeping the wine." These characterizations will be clarified through the analysis of the laws, on which was first imposed the duty of doing what is upright and good.

(a) "The law is that property appraised and foreclosed and then transferred to the creditor in payment of debt due him must always be returned on the lender repaying the debt, because: 'You shall do what is upright and good.' "[9] This law brings us to the boundary of the law of obligation in Jewish jurisprudence, and it is appropriate to clarify its basic elements. What is important for us here is especially the "general mortgage," as it were,[10] which hovers over all landed property belonging to the borrower

in favor of the creditor, if the loan was effectuated by a
note, and which enables the creditor to seize land from a
purchaser who bought it from the debtor after the execution of the loan. The Gemara states:[11]

> Ula said: "According to the law of the Torah whether a
> loan was executed with a note or orally, it is collectible
> from the debtor's transferred property." What is the reason
> for this? The obligation on the creditor is prescribed in the
> Torah! Why then did the Sages say that an orally executed
> loan is collectible only from free property? In order that the
> purchaser of such property shall not suffer loss by having
> the creditor seize it. If so, should not the same argument
> apply also to the case of a loan excuted in writing? In that
> case the buyers have brought the loss on themselves. But
> Rabbah said: "The law of the Torah is that a loan, whether
> effectuated by note or orally, is collectible only from the
> debtor's free property." What is the reason? The obligation
> on the creditor is not prescribed in the Torah. Why then did
> the Sages say that a creditor can collect from transferred
> property? So as not to shut the door in the face of those who
> need to borrow. In that case, why not extend the creditor's
> right to the case of an oral loan? In that case the loan is with-
> out general knowledge.

The disagreement among the two *Amoraim* whether the
obligation on property is sanctioned by the law of the
Torah or not, has its importance in connection with other
matters,[12] but as to the subject before us they both agree
in deciding the law, that an oral loan is not collectible
from the buyer of the debtor's property, that a loan confirmed by a note is collectible. The reason, in substance,
is the same for both: a loan confirmed by a note has publicity, it becomes widely known,[13] and the purchaser can
exercise caution; an oral loan has no publicity, the would-
be purchaser does not know of it, and we must, therefore,
protect him against loss. The entire distinction between

them is in the legal construction: Ula[14] is of the opinion
that the Sages voided the obligation in the case of an oral
loan to protect the purchaser, and Rabbah is of the
opinion that the Sages *created* the obligation in the case
of a loan with a note in order not to shut the door in the
face of one who needs to borrow.

But when do we say that a loan with a note is collectible
from the buyer of the debtor's property? When the property in question is land, but not if it is movable property.[15]
For only landed property "offers security" in the language
of the Mishnah,[16] and the reason is, according to the well-
know explanation of Rashi:

> "Offers security," that is to say, land which offers security
> to each person, the borrower and the creditor, because it
> is always available, and they depend on it.[17]

It is true that so long as movable property remains in
the possession of the borrower, the creditor can seize it—
the debt is collectible "from him, even through the seizure
of the garment he wears."[18] It is collectible from him (from
the borrower), even through the seizure of the garment he
wears, but this derives not from the obligation which rests
on his property, but from the obligation which rests on his
person; the borrower is obligated to repay his debt, and
with what is he to pay it—with whatever property he has
at his disposal.[19]

And how does the creditor collect his debt? It appears to
me that we shall be unable to formulate a better explanation than the one offered by the commentators of the
Talmud:[20]

> The order is as follows: The creditor comes to Court and
> asks redress from the debtor, to pay his debt. We cite the
> debtor to Court. . . . If he does not appear, we excom-
> municate him, and we issue a writ of seizure [*shetar tirpa*]
> to the creditor that he may go and undertake a search

whether the debtor has any landed property. And wherever he should discover his property, even if in the possession of those who purchased it from him after the loan was made, he is to show the writ to the Court of that city, and they will transfer the property to the creditor, and they are then to write him a writ of assignment [*shetar adrakhta*], that he may control and utilize the property of this person until he collects his debt from it. The writ of seizure is then to be destroyed lest he submit it to another Court and duplicate the seizure. The property is to be assessed according to the usual assessment of the Court . . . and on the basis of the assessment he is to collect his debt. And the Court is to issue him a writ of assessment [*shetar shumat ha-nekhasim*] to disclose at what value he took the property over, because the seized property is always returnable to the debtor when he has the funds to repay his debt . . . and when the Court issues the writ of assessment they are to destroy the writ of assignment, lest he use it again in violation of the law.[21]

This formulation is based on a version of the talmudic text as generally current among us.[22] There is another version which precedes the writ of assignment to the writ of seizure. But the difference between them is only one of terminology.[23] What one version calls the writ of seizure is called in the other version the writ of assignment, and vice versa. Both agree that three basic writs are to be issued. Their chronological order, on the basis of their essence, is as follows:

(1) a writ to search for property;

(2) a writ of attachment which transfers to the creditor the possession of property;

(3) a writ of execution[24] which transfers to the creditor— from the debtor or the one from whom it is seized[25] —ownership of the property. Once the writ of execution is written, the creditor may use the property which has been assigned to him "as one uses his own

property";[26] in other words, it becomes his own in all respects.

Now let us examine from the perspective of "the upright and the good" the laws concerning the return of foreclosed property mentioned earlier. According to the accepted principles of the law, the property which was appraised with the issuance of the writ of execution was transferred to the ownership of the creditor.[27] He can use it as a person uses any of his own property, and included in this is the right to sell it, to mortgage it, to grant it as a gift to anyone he likes, and, obviously, he can refuse it to anyone to whom he prefers not to sell it, even to the original debtor. This is the law, and the Sages did not void this law. What then did they do? They analyzed this law, and divided it into its component elements. What is the reason that after search, seizure and assessment the property is assigned to the creditor? Obviously it is to pay the debt due him from the debtor! This is the only legitimate interest the creditor has in acquiring the property, this and nothing else! He has no right to enrich himself through the loan which he extended to the debtor, and such enrichment is forbidden him even if it does not take the form of interest. It is for this reason that the Sages ruled that the upright and the good—the upright and the good for both sides—demands that if the debtor or the purchaser[28] from whom it was seized finds the means of repaying the creditor the original loan—or that portion of the loan for which the property was assigned to the creditor—in short, if he acquired the means to repay the amount of the assessment, the assessed property reverts—and it reverts forever—and the creditor must return the land to its previous owners against the repayment of the sum due him. The integrity of the law is preserved. The proposal to repay does not void the assessment retroactively; the land which was assigned to the creditor is still his property, except that he is now obligated—for the sake of doing what is upright and good—to transfer it back[29] to the debtor or the purchaser from whom it was seized.

The result of all this is that the principle of *yosher* is advanced and the law is not diminished. It (*yosher*) "vanquishes the law on its own premises," and does not permit it to inflict injury in the realm of its justified authority, out of consideration for the reason which was provided for in the foundation of the law itself. *Yosher* does not affect the rules of acquisition and ownership laid down by the law; the property which was appraised and assigned to the creditor remains his, and, moreover, if he sold it or gave it to another, his sale or gift remains valid, and the debtor or the one from whom it was seized cannot claim it back from the new owners.[30] But as long as the property remains in the possession of the creditor, he must return it through the process described above because this return is within the meaning of the upright and the good for both sides: the one (the creditor) is repaid his loan, and the other (the debtor or the one who purchased it from him and from whom it was seized) reacquires his possession. There is no legitimate interest of the creditor which can be affected adversely through the return of the foreclosed property, and for this reason the Sages declared: "Foreclosed property is always returned." We say to the creditor: "The only claim you had against the debtor is money, and here you are getting it,"[31] take it and return the land to its owner!

(b) "The sages of Nehardea say: Even for the sake of the law of the neighbor, we remove him, because 'you shall do what is upright and good in the eyes of the Lord.' "[32]

This is the second case in which a law was formulated on the basis of the obligation to *yosher* deriving from the verse, "You shall do the upright and the good." The case deals with the law of the neighbor [*dina devar mitzra*], and it means that the person who has land bordering on the land of the seller enjoys a right of preemption with regard to the land that is for sale.[33] And if the seller proceeded to sell it to another, the person whose land borders the land for sale can displace the buyer by paying the same price which he paid to the seller.

This law is, in a greater measure than the previous one,[34] bound together with the concept of the "good" in *yosher,* as we shall soon see; it is as though it were written, "and you shall do the good *yosher.*" It was created as a shield against the one who insists on his legal right, saying: let the law pierce through the mountain!

Who is here really obligated to do the upright and the good—is it the seller or the buyer? The sources indicate that the obligation rests primarily on the buyer and not the seller.

> The verse imposed the law of the neighbor only on the buyer.[35]
>
> The law of the neighbor was not made obligatory by the Sages on the seller.[36]
>
> The Sages did not ordain the law of the neighbor on the seller but on the buyer, that he drop his intended purchase, and automatically the seller will have to sell to the one who has the law of the neighbor.[37]

But if we probe deeply into this law we shall see that from the point of view of pure law this is not the case. The "timing" when the obligation begins, naturally, places its fulfillment on the would-be buyer. For since one obviously cannot force a person to sell land he does not wish to sell, the obligation to give preference to the person with the prior right goes into effect after the seller has made the sale, and then the land is no longer his possession and he cannot transfer it to the person with the prior right. But if the intention of the seller to sell is open and well-known to all, and both the seller and the buyer enter a deal to keep the person with the prior right out of this deal, this person can sue both, and obligate the seller as well to do all that is needed to enable the person "on the boundary" to acquire the land.[38] This view, that the obligation to transfer the land to the person on the boundary falls essentially on both the buyer and the seller, becomes clear when we study the subject critically in the Talmud,[39] as well as the various laws formulated by the codifiers.[40]

The law of the neighbor is "a weak law which hangs on a hair,"[41] because its source is in the injunction to do what is upright and good, and one cannot introduce into it tight delimitations and precautions. The assumption is that the purchaser loses nothing as a result of his displacement by the person with the prior right, since he receives from him a return of whatever money he spent without any loss whatever;[42] and as for the land—he can acquire it elsewhere.[43] The only one who may possibly suffer loss is the seller—for the buyer may withdraw from other intended purchases,[44] or this incident may interfere with a deal he may be eager to consummate with a third party.[45] Since the purpose of the law of the neighbor is to do what is upright and good, the Sages decided that where its application may cause loss to the seller, this law is not to be invoked:

> We have no right to cause loss to the seller in order to do what is upright and good to the person with the prior right, for just as we are obligated to do good to the one, so are we obligated to do good to the other.[46]

Despite all these limitations which were introduced into this law, the law of the neighbor remains a law, and if all the required conditions are shown to prevail, the buyer is asked to transfer the land to the person on the boundary, and we apply this law with all the rigor of any other law.

We may say here, paraphrasing the well-known statement,[47] "In consideration of the mitigation with which we approached this law initially, we proceed rigorously in carrying it out and confirming it." Not only this, but here in this seemingly weak law, the Sages proceeded (as it were) beyond the law, and applied a legal construction which has no precedent in other areas of the law: they made the buyer—against his will—into the agent of the person with the right of preemption, so that his act of closing the deal with the buyer automatically transferred the property to the person with the right of preemption:

> For we have already shown that the acquisition by the buyer has also acquired the land for the person with the right of preemption, and no other formal act of acquisition is necessary. . . . Though the seller did not intend to transfer it to anyone other than the buyer and he protests that he did not transfer it to the person with the right of preemption, but only to the buyer, and the buyer protests similarly that the acquisition was meant only for himself, we say—for the sake of doing what is upright and good—that the acquisition which occurred effected an acquisition for the neighbor, unless. . . .[48]

This unusual legal construction finds its source in the Talmud itself,[49] and it was adopted by all the codifiers.[50] The law concerning the neighbor, if we may say so, owes its conception to considerations of *yosher,* and its birth to the ways of the law. For in the final analysis, the neighbor claims the property, not as something which he obtains, but as his own, his own by law, as a result of this "synthetic" agency. This is the reinforcement that the law accords to *yosher,* in order to endow it with full efficacy. This aid which a "rabbinic" ordinance receives from a law prescribed in the Torah is not an unusual phenomenon in Jewish law; we encounter it in the case of many ordinances established by the Sages[51] and in all kinds of legal constructions. This only shows that the two zones, the rabbinic ordinance and the Torahitic law, nourish one another. This is a theme deserving of further contemplation.

These two laws—the return of assessed and seized property and the law of the neighbor—are alike in their origin, but they are unlike in their final development. Both find their support in the commandment to do what is upright and good, but while the law of returning seized property continues to operate to its final climax under the aegis of *yosher*, the law concerning the neighbor robes itself in the end with the covering of legality itself. Both have this in common, that they are laws which command obligation, that is to say: the obligation to perform, which will be enforced by the Court. The debtor sues the creditor in Court, and the Court will obligate the creditor to effect legal transfer to the debtor of the field which had been seized for non-payment of the debt; the neighbor sues the buyer in Court, and the Court will order the buyer to transfer to the neighbor the field which he, the neighbor, had purchased. The explanation for the difference in their development is to be found, in my opinion, in this, that there is no readily available legal formula which will help transfer the property to the debtor who has acquired the means and now comes and offers the creditor the sum of his debt. "Agency" was obviously not considered, and other suggestions would have endangered the hierarchy of principles which govern the acquisition of property.

4. Different from the first type is the category of *yosher* described by the term: beyond the strict law. Its content and nature will be clarified on examining the cases in the Talmud to which it was applied. We shall cite them not according to the order of tractates of the Talmud, but according to a conceptual order, from the simple to the more complex.

(a) The first case has to do with the laws of unloading and loading:[52]

> Rabbi Ishmael ben Yose was walking on his way. He was met by a man who was carrying a bundle of wood. He put it down on the ground and stopped to rest. He said to him: "How much is it worth?" He replied: "Half a *zuz*." He gave him the half *zuz*, and he renounced ownership of the wood. The man thereupon reacquired possession of it (as ownerless property). Rabbi Ishmael again gave him a half *zuz* and renounced ownership of it. He saw that the man was again about to reacquire it. He said to him: "I have renounced ownership of it as far as the rest of the world is concerned, but not for you." . . . But Rabbi Ishmael was a sage and it was not in keeping with his dignity to reload the wood! Rabbi Ishmael acted beyond the strict law. . . .[53]

Here the principle of acting "beyond the strict law" came to expression in the fact that Rabbi Ishmael relinquished the privilege granted him as a "sage"[54] and submitted himself to the obligation of the Torah[55] to help a person with a load, as though he were an ordinary individual. We shall have occasion further to deal with this theme.

(b) The second case deals with a law in the field of damages—the obligation to pay compensation for erroneous information given unintentionally.[56]

> It was said: If a person showed a *dinar* to a moneychanger and he recommended it as good, but it was later found to be bad—one *baraita* states that if he were an expert he is not liable, but if he were an amateur he is liable, while another *baraita* states that whether expert or amateur he is liable. Said Rav Papa: "When we declare that an expert is not liable, we mean one like Danko or Isur,[57] who need no instruction at all.". . . A certain woman showed a *dinar* to Rabbi Hiya and he said to her that it was good. The next

day she came and complained to him: "I have shown it and have been told that it is bad, and I cannot spend it." He said to Rav: "Go change it for her, and write in my ledger that this was a bad transaction." Now what was there about Danko and Isur, who were not liable—that they did not need to be instructed, but neither did Rabbi Hiya require instruction! Rabbi Hiya acted beyond the strict law. . . .[58]

In the first case, Rabbi Ishmael relinquished the privilege he enjoyed as "sage"; in the second case, Rabbi Hiya relinquished the immunity which he enjoyed as an expert on coins, that is, one in the same class as Danko and Isur, who "did not require to be instructed."[59]

(c) The third case deals with the law concerning the return of a found object. It is the law, as is well-known, that if one finds an object after its original owners had despaired of its return, he is not obligated to return it.[60] But, lo and behold:

> The father of Samuel found donkeys in the desert and he returned them to their owners after twelve months, beyond the strict law.[61]

The meaning of the case is as follows: Samuel's father[62] found donkeys in the desert over twelve months after they had been lost[63] and returned them to their owners, though, according to the law, he was not required to do so, for after an object has been lost twelve months the presumption is that the owner has despaired and no longer expects its return.[64]

"Despair" is an event—an event in the mind, of course. "Presumption" is a factual determination *ex lege,* which the legislator permits us to depend on, though this has not been demonstrated by tangible and clear evidence.[65]

The inference to be drawn, therefore, when we examine the case carefully, is that the "beyond the strict law" in the incident with Samuel's father consisted in that he did not depend on the presumption that his find "was transferred to him in heaven." Being severe with himself, he was concerned lest the owners had not yet despaired of the return of those donkeys, in which case he was obligated by law to return them.

(d) More complicated is the fourth case, which deals with one of the laws of sale. We are dealing here with the action of a certain *Amora* which, as a matter of fact and as the case was finally decided, is not to be included in the category of "beyond the strict law," but is actually within it. It is only in the intermediate state of the discussion in the Talmud, which was in doubt at first about the mandate of the law, that one can draw certain conclusions about the nature of the "beyond the strict law," and while such evidence is usually weak, its value must not be disdained altogether. I shall explain myself. "The words kept in one's heart are not efficacious words," the Talmud declares in many instances.[66] If a person sold his property because he wanted to settle in *Eretz Yisrael,* but said nothing at the time of the sale, and then he was forced by circumstances not to go to *Eretz Yisrael,* the sale is valid,[67] "since he did not express" the contingency.[68]

The reason for this principle is doubtless to ensure the ways of buying and selling. For there is no guardian for words which have remained in the heart, and if we were to say that every unspecified condition hidden in one's bosom can void a sale, then you would have no son of Abraham[69] who would take the risk of engaging in business.

From this there developed two qualifications, one definite and the other with some doubt (which was resolved later on). If there exists a "clear presumption"—a conjecture logical to the mind, clear to everybody—that the only reason which moved this person to sell his field, for example, was his decision to conclude his affairs to go to *Eretz Yisrael,* or that he sought to purchase in its place another property more advantageous than this one, and it is clear to all that without this expectation he would not have sold, then if his expectation was disappointed—"he was forced by circumstances not to go to *Eretz Yisrael*"—or if the owner of the second property refuses to sell it—then his sale is voided and rescinded; in other words, the field which had been sold returns to its original owner.[70] For so clear a presumption is like an explicit condition, and if the buyer of the field objected to involving himself in such an uncertain purchase, he should have been cautious not to buy.[71] In this instance there was no "deception" on the part of the "silent" seller,[72] for what is well known does not have to be publicized.

But what shall be the law in a case similar to the previous but yet not so similar, close to it but yet not identical with it. It is the following: there was no conclusive presumption as to the objective of the sale, nor was there anything like a condition to affect the validity of the sale, but at the time of the sale, the seller disclosed a particular purpose why he was selling the land. Shall the frustration of the purpose in a case such as this invalidate the sale, or not? This question was discussed in the academy:

> The question was raised by them: "If he sold and then did not need the money, is the transaction cancelled or is it not cancelled?"[73]

The meaning of the inquiry is this: Reuben sold a field to Simon without any conditioning stipulation, but at the time of the sale he disclosed that he was selling it in order to buy another property from Levi. Subsequently Levi changed his mind, and because of this Reuben no longer needed the money. Shall we say that under the circumstances the sale becomes void and the field reverts to Reuben, or not?[74] The final decision was that the sale is voided.

> And the law is that if he sold and then did not need the money, the sale is voided.[75]

But prior to the final decision, and in the course of the discussion, one of the students sought to bring as evidence the action of the *Amora* Rav Papa.

> Come, listen: There was once a man who sold land to Rav Papa in order to buy oxen, but subsequently he did not need the money, and Rav Papa returned him the land.[76]

We thus have a case here that the purpose disclosed to the buyer, not as a condition of the sale, can invalidate the sale. The objection raised against using this case as evidence was: we cannot bring evidence from the action of Rav Papa! It is conceivable that the disclosure of the purpose is not enough, and the buyer need not return the land, but that he, "Rav Papa, acted beyond the strict law!"[77]

We thus see that this objection was raised in order to reject the evidence cited on the basis of that incident, but it is clear that if this sheds any light on our question, it can do so only if we assume—an incorrect assumption—the law to be that if he sold and then did not need the money, the sale is not voided.

We shall now examine the possible reasoning behind this law, for only then will we be able to appreciate the "beyond the strict law" in the action of Rav Papa. We shall see that this hypothetical law could have had only one basis: to preserve—through clear and formal limits— the stability of business transactions. Though the person disclosed the reason and purpose of his selling, inasmuch as he did not bother to stipulate it by word of mouth as a real condition for the sale, we may assume that the seller did not really intend to have its validity hinge on it. This is what the public good demands—in the traditional Hebrew idiom, "the perfection of the world" (*tikkun ha-olam*)—that the validity of the sale he made to depend only on the explicitly stipulated. This, and only this, is the possible reason to justify the law: "If he sold and did not need the money—the sale is not voided."

And on this legal assumption—an assumption that may very well not agree with the concrete facts involved in the incident reported in "There was once a man"—the *Amora* Rav Papa voluntarily returned the land to the seller, acting presumably beyond the strict law.

(e) The fifth example—not an actual occurrence, but an abstract expression of opinion—also touches on the laws of returning a lost object.

> Rav Judah followed after Mar Samuel[78] in the grit market where they sell "ground wheat for cereal, and many people frequent it" (Rashi). He said to him: "If one found a purse here, what is the law?" He said: "It belongs to him" (because presumably the owners despaired of getting it back; see the talmudic commentators). Then he asked: "What if a person came and identified it?" He said to him: "Then he must return it." "Both?!" (In other words: your answers are self-contradictory!) He said to him: "Beyond the strict law, as was done by the father of Samuel who found donkeys in the desert" (and here is quoted the case cited as (c) above).[79]

This law of *yosher* adds nothing to what we have learned previously, and what we are yet to learn from the four previous cases, especially from the third case on which the last instance depends. We may, therefore, ignore it altogether when we come to sum up and define the character of "beyond the strict law."

5. Different from the two previous categories, and more remote than they from the norm of law, is the third and last which is compounded of obligations to *yosher* whose performance or non-performance is not a "commandment" or "transgression" but a "pleasure" or "displeasure" to the spirit of the Sages, or whose obligation of performance is no more than the "standard of saintliness."

(a) One who assigns his property to others and omits his sons, what he has done is done, but the spirit of the Sages is not pleased with him.[80]

Not only are the Sages not pleased with his action but he causes them irritation, for they are angry with him because he has uprooted a principle of inheritance which is prescribed in the Torah.[81]

When a person dies, his property is transferred to his heirs according to the law. When he is in a state of critical illness,[82] however, he can "pass on his inheritance to anyone he pleases,"[83] but the meaning of this sweeping declaration is that he can augment the share of a particular heir, provided the diminution of the other heir's share occurs indirectly as a result of the augmenting of the share of the first heir, not by a direct reduction of any one heir's portion.[84] Such was the concern of the Sages that the institution of inheritance be maintained.

The Sages, however, added that if the will were written in the form of a gift rather than of inheritance, then the person can distribute his property to anyone he likes, even to transfer it entirely to one who is not his heir.[85] The Sages ordained, moreover, that if the person making the bequest is critically ill [*shekhiv mera*],[86] he does not have to employ "a formal token of transfer" [*kinyan*], and the property will be transferred on his verbal instruction, immediately after his death, to the one to whom he has assigned it.[87]

Thus far the substance of the law and of the rabbinic ordinance. But the spirit of the Sages is not pleased with such gifts, and they do not look with favor on the transfer of property from an heir to a non-heir.[88] They did not void the law concerning the right to make gifts by a healthy person, nor the special ordinance concerning the gift of a critically ill person, but they said: "What is done —is done, but the Sages are not pleased with it." This is the only "sanction" they invoked against disinheriting an heir, and the one who does so has not violated an explicit prescription of the Sages,[89] inasmuch as their position was not expressed in the form of a commandment.

(b) We do not accept from robbers and those who lend money on interest and then make restitution; whoever accepts from them, the spirit of the Sages is not pleased with him.[90]

It is forbidden to take interest and to give interest.[91] But once interest was given, the lender is obligated to return it, while the borrower is not obligated to take it back. He can forego it and forgive it, and with the forgiveness, the obligation of the lender to return it will have become voided. The same applies with the forgiveness of robbed property.

It happened that a certain person (a robber) wanted to repent. His wife said to him: "Fool! If you repent, even the belt will not remain yours." He desisted and did not repent. The Sages then said: "We do not accept from robbers and those who lend money on interest and then make restitution; whoever accepts from them, the spirit of the Sages is not pleased with him."[92]

Here, too, the law obligating the return was not voided. It was impossible to void it, for the Sages would thereby have encouraged those who lend on interest. But in consideration of an actual occurrence and "in order to make more accessible the right path for the penitents,"[93] the Sages said that a robber or a lender on interest who repents and "voluntarily returns" the robbery or the interest,[94] one is not to accept it, but it is necessary to "help him and forgive him."[95] If the one robbed or the borrower on interest should not act thus, the spirit of the Sages will not be pleased with him.

(c) At times the position of the Sages is demonstrated, not by expressing a negative attitude toward the action with which the spirit of the Sages is not pleased, but—on the contrary—through the expression of a positive attitude toward the action with which the spirit of the Sages is pleased. "One who returns a debt in the sabbatical year,[96] the spirit of the Sages is pleased with him."[97]

The sabbatical year cancels the debt, and when the end of the year arrives[98] the lender is relieved of repaying his debt.[99] But if he, despite this relief, comes and repays the lender the money he borrowed, the spirit of the Sages is pleased with him. On the other hand, in the case of a borrower who returns a debt in the sabbatical year, "he (the lender) must tell him: 'I cancel it!' But if he (the borrower) said to him: 'Nevertheless'—he may accept it."[100] We have before us a kind of "manual of *yosher*" on two levels, which surround the law of the sabbatical year on every side.

> All movable property is acquired through pulling,[101] but one who keeps his word—the spirit of the Sages is pleased with him.[102]

Jewish law, as is well known, does not recognize the legal validity of a transaction—whether it is a transaction involving a transfer of real objects, or whether it involves solely an assumption of obligations—unless it was accompanied by an appropriate token of acquisition.[103] Each item has its own form or forms of efficacious acquisition, as was established for different categories in Jewish law.[104]

In the *mishnah* before us let us take, for example, the form of acquisition which is efficacious for the transfer of movable property. These are usually acquired by pulling—a symbolic act which betokens the entry of the object into the domain of the buyer. A vague agreement unaccompanied by any token of acquisition—neither a token efficacious for establishing a firm personal obligation,[105] nor one efficacious to transfer ownership—is devoid of significance from a legal point of view, and the seller can change his mind and refuse to sell or surrender the object, the subject of the agreement. But—said the Sages—though the spoken word alone does not obligate, from a legal point of view, the spirit of the Sages is pleased with the person who keeps his word and does not go back on it. Nothing was done here to affect the sanctity of the ordered hierarchy of acquisitional forms, nor did they add a new form of acquisition. Only the being pleased or not being pleased of the Sages spurs on the fulfillment of the vague promise.

(d) There is another expression, of equal weight, to indicate this third type of *yosher;* it is the expression "the standard of saintliness." The equivalence of the two expressions becomes clear from the statement in the Talmud Yerushalmi.

> Rav said: When I say to the members of my family to give a gift to somebody, I do not reverse myself.[106]

The Yerushalmi challenges this on the basis of another decision by Rav—it challenges and replies:

> There he decided according to the law, his action was based on the standard of saintliness.[107]

But "the standard of saintliness" invoked here is no other but the category "the spirit of the Sages is pleased with him" which was mentioned in the *mishnah* in Sheviit concerning the person who keeps his word, as we have seen above.[108]

The phrase "the standard of saintliness"—not as a general characterization of the standard but as an individualized description of a particular law—is found in the Babylonian Talmud three times.[109] The three deal not with matters which pertain to the relation between man and God but between man and man, with obligations of a person to his fellow man, and it is possible to designate them on a relative scale as obligations of the rules of *yosher*. We cite them here:

(1) Mishnah: How much may be missing from a *sela* without its passage being regarded as deceptive? Rabbi Meir said: Four *isars,* an *isar* to the *dinar*[110]. . . . How long does the one who received it have for returning it? In cities— until he has had the opportunity to show it to a money- changer; in villages—till the eve of the Sabbath. If the one who passed it recognizes it, he should accept it even after twelve months, and he can have against the person returning it only resentment.[111]

Gemara: And if he recognizes it—is he to accept even after twelve months? Where did this transaction occur? If in a city, you ruled that the time is until he has an opportu- nity to show it to a moneychanger; and if in a village, you said—until the eve of the Sabbath! Rav Hisda replied: "So to act, is a standard of saintliness."[112]

The coins of those days would be worn thin through use, and their weight continued to diminish until they would no longer be acceptable as currency, at least not in their nominal value. The question raised in our *mishnah* is, what is the minimum weight of a *sela,* below which the passing of it would be considered a deception which obli-

gates the one who gave it to accept the return.[113] The Sages
disagreed on this minimum weight. And how long—in-
quires the Mishnah—does the one who received the *sela*
have for returning it to the one who passed it to him?
Until the end of such time which would have enabled him
to ascertain whether it was still acceptable in the market
or not. Therefore in cities—where moneychangers are to
be found—until he had the opportunity to show it to the
moneychanger; in villages—until the eve of the Sabbath,
because people were accustomed to spend their money on
the eve of the Sabbath for the purchases of needed foods
for the Sabbath. And the Mishnah adds: "If he recognized
it—if the one who gave the *sela* recognizes that this is the
very *sela* which he gave to the one who received it from
him—he is to accept it even after twelve months."

It is the last decision on which the Gemara paused to
raise a challenge: Why is there an obligation on the one
who gave it to accept its return even after twelve months,
when the Mishnah itself laid down specified times for this:
until he had the opportunity to show it, or until the eve of
the Sabbath? Are not these two provisions contradictory?!
The answer offered to this is: It is the standard of saintliness that is referred to here! That is to say, this is not an
obligation on the basis of law, but an obligation of *yosher*
imposed by the standard of saintliness—it is an obligation
that will be met by one who attained the standard of
saintliness.

(2) Mishnah: One may save (from a fire on the Sabbath)
a basketful of loaves of bread, even though there are in it
enough for a hundred meals. . . . And he may tell others:
"Come and rescue for yourselves!" But if they are wise, they
make an accounting with him after the Sabbath.[114]

Gemara: What place is there for an accounting—they
benefited from ownerless property?! Said Rav Hisda: "The
standard of saintliness is referred to here!"[115]

The case dealt with here is that of a person whose house caught fire during the Sabbath. He himself may save edibles and clothes, and in order to increase the items saved he may tell others: "Come and rescue for yourselves." In other words he tells them that whatever they will save from the fire will belong to them. Nevertheless, though he promised them no reward, if they are wise and realize that actually he intended to rescue for himself,[116] they make an accounting with him after the Sabbath and accept compensation for their efforts at rescue while they return the objects which they saved.[117]

The Gemara asks in wonderment: What point is there for an accounting here; did they not acquire from the ownerless domain whatever possessions they rescued, since the owner allowed everyone to take for himself? The first reply offered by Rav Hisda was: The standard of saintliness is described here. In other words, if the one who rescued is a *hasid,* of saintly disposition, and does not wish to take what belongs to others, he returns the possessions and accepts compensation.[118]

The standard of saintliness is involved here in that although according to the law the one who rescued took from the ownerless domain and it now belongs to him,[119] if he is to act not according to law but according to *yosher,* he returns the possessions to their original owner and he claims from him—if he wishes—compensation for his work of rescue.[120]

(3) Come and hear: A houseowner who travelled from place to place and found himself in need of accepting gleanings, forgotten sheaves, the crop grown on the corner of a field, or the poor man's tithe, may accept them, and on returning home he will make restitution, so says Rabbi Eliezer. Said Rav Hisda: "The standard of saintliness is referred to here!"[121]

Only the poor may take gleanings, forgotten sheaves etc.[122] A houseowner—who is "wealthy"—is not permitted to take them. If he travelled from place to place "and found himself in need of food, he takes gleanings, as other poor, inasmuch as he is now poor,"[123] but after returning home he is to make restitution to the poor for whatever he took.

According to the law he has no obligation to make restitution, because the produce he took is "money that has no claimants." It is for this reason that Rav Hisda himself ruled: "One who damages priestly perquisites, or ate them, is free of any obligation to repay."[124] The reason is that the collectivity of priests and the collectivity of the poor do not constitute a juridic person, in whose name a claim can be made, and the individual priest or the individual poor person does not have—in the modern idiom—any "active legitimation," for the houseowner can say to him: "I will give them to another priest or another poor man, and not to you!"[125] But the standard of saintliness demands that he not aggrieve the poor but make restitution to them for what he took.

In the discussion before us we have support for the proposition that when the restitution falls into the standard of saintliness, it is not merely that we do not coerce him to pay,[126] but he is not even obligated to do so "in order to satisfy a duty to God."[127] We infer from this that the standard of saintliness is higher than the usual moral obligation which rests on each person.

6. It remains for us to examine one subject which we have omitted till now, because it does not belong to any of the three categories of *yosher* mentioned above. I refer to the subject known as "those porters."

This subject is treated in two versions, one in the Babylonian Talmud and the other in the Jerusalem Talmud.

Because of the variants in detail between them, we shall cite them here in full.

(a) The Babylonian Talmud:

Rabbah bar Bar Hanah (according to the version of the Rif and the Rosh,[128] Rabbah bar Rav Huna) had porters who broke a barrel of wine. He took from them their garments. They went and complained to Rav. He said to him: "Give them back their garments." He said to him: "Is this the law?" He replied: "Yes! 'So that you may walk in the way of good men'" (Proverbs 2:20). He returned their garments. They said to him [the porters to Rav]: "We are poor, we worked all day, and we are hungry and have nothing." He said to him: "Go and pay them their wages." He said to him: "Is this the law?" He replied to him: "Yes! 'And you shall keep the paths of the righteous'" (Proverbs 2:20).[129]

(b) The Jerusalem Talmud:

Rabbi Nehemiah taught: A potter handed over his pots to a certain person. They were broken.[130] He removed his garment.[131] The worker came to Rabbi Yose bar Haninah. He said to him: "Go tell (that person): 'So that you may walk in the way of good men.'" He went and told him, and the latter then returned his garment. Then he said to him: "Did he pay your wages?" He said to him: "No!" He said to him: "Go tell him: 'And you shall keep the paths of the righteous.'" He went and told him, and the latter paid him his wages.[132]

In considering these two sources, of the Babylonian and the Jerusalem Talmud, we find a surprising parallel between them: in the substance of the incident—the breaking of vessels and the withholding of garments—in the dialogue between the sage and the involved parties, as well as in the verses cited from the Bible. The occurrence of such coincidence is inconceivable! I, therefore, think that these two incidents are really one, and certain errors occurred in the course of transmission from here to there and from there to here. And when the choice is between an error in the text of the Babylonian Talmud and an error in the text of the Jerusalem Talmud, it is plausible to decide that the fault is with the Jerusalem Talmud, and to assume that the error occurred "there" and not "here," that is to say, in *Eretz Yisrael* and not in Babylonia. For, as it is well known, the text of the Babylonian Talmud is much more exact and reliable than the text of the Jerusalem Talmud. It is reasonable to assume, therefore, that the incident which really occurred was the one involving the porters and the wine, but this well-known event was distorted and changed to an incident with a potter and pots, and the litigation concerning the garments and the wages which took place according to the Babylonian Talmud before Rav, was ascribed in the Jerusalem Talmud to an *Eretz Yisrael Amora*, Rabbi Yose bar Haninah.[133]

Consequently, we need to examine only the discussion about "those porters," to discern the nuance it has added— or it has not added—to the concept of the duties of *yosher* in the three categories mentioned above.

Let us probe, therefore, the fundamental elements in the theme of "those porters." They broke the barrel not through negligence, but deliberately,[134] or—according to some commentators—it was for them to prove, and they failed to prove, that they had not been willful in breaking the barrel.[135]

On reading the decision given by Rav in the litigation between the employer and the porters, it appears as though Rav ruled that the employer is legally obligated to return the garments which had been seized, and to pay their wages. Such an impression is false. This was a decision given by Rav to his disciple on grounds of morality only.

I noted previously, as though incidentally, that the version followed by the Rif and the Rosh refers not to Rabbah bar Bar Hanah, but to Rabbah bar Rav Huna. This was not merely a pedantic observation—the matter is of great importance as we shall soon see—and I therefore propose that we accept the version of the Rif and the Rosh as accurate.

Rabbah bar Rav Huna was the son of Rav Huna who was the close disciple of Rav[136] and he himself, in his youth, managed to be a student of Rav.[137] The full relationship of a rabbi and his disciple is not the relationship of teacher and student solely, nor of educator and educated, in the ordinary sense of the term. It is something unique, for which it is impossible to find a parallel or adequate expression in any other language or culture. The rabbi—according to the conception of the Talmud—is the sole authority over the entire personality of the disciple, broader in scope than the authority of the father, for he is progenitor and teacher at the same time,[138] he shapes the spiritual identity of the disciple, and it is to him that the disciple owes absolute obedience.

> Whoever teaches his companion's son Torah, is deemed by Scripture as though he gave him birth.[139]
>
> The lost object of his father and that of his rabbi—the return of that belonging to his rabbi enjoys priority, for his father brought him into this world, while his rabbi who taught him wisdom brings him to the life of the world to come.[140]
>
> And my disciple—for I decree upon you a decree and you heed it like a disciple.[141]
>
> Heed what your rabbi tells you![142]
>
> Whoever engages in a quarrel with his rabbi, it is as though he has engaged in a quarrel with the *Shekhinah*.[143]

It would not be surprising therefore that Rav, knowing the influence he had on his disciple, drew on this influence and instructed him to fulfill the moral obligation of "so that you may walk in the way of good men and keep the paths of the righteous." It is, of course, true that Rabbah bar Rav Huna asked him: "Is this the law?" And Rav replied: "Yes!" But it is clear that Rav did not refer to a *legal* obligation which can be carried out by coercion! The law is clear and explicit in the talmudic discussion and it shows that, under the circumstances, Rabbah bar Rav Huna was relieved of paying the porters their wages. If Rav had ordered Rabbah bar Rav Huna to pay, he himself might perhaps have been obligated to compensate Rabbah bar Rav Huna for the damages he caused him. For "If he pronounced a decision in law and acquitted the guilty or found guilty the innocent, what was done was done, but he must make restitution from his own funds."[144] We must necessarily say that the questions and answers between Rav and his disciple dealt with the *moral* obligation and the word "yes" is to be interpreted thus: If you wish to know what is the "way of good men" and what are the "paths of the righteous," my answer is that these require the return of the garments and the payment of the wages. The verses quoted are not efficacious to create law, for their source is in one of the books of the Hagiographa, and "Law is not derived from Prophets and Hagiographa."[145] But they are efficacious to establish a high moral norm, and on the basis of this norm—the "law" in quotation marks—Rav decided for his young disciple, as mentioned earlier.

It must be explained and emphasized: in the case of "those porters" great significance is attributed to the fact that the porters worked all day, were hungry and had nothing. It would appear that had they been wealthy, Rav would not have ordered Rabbah bar Rav Huna to pay them their wages.[146] This itself indicates that we are dealing with a purely moral obligation, and not a legal obligation or a quasi-legal obligation on the basis of *yosher*. For the laws of *yosher*, like purely legal obligations, apply equally to all people, and do not distinguish between rich and poor, or between the hungry and the sated.[147]

7. And now, after this general survey, let us sum up and define the three types of *yosher* mentioned above. The three are not merely moral obligations, but quasi-legal, whose distance from the legal varies from close to remote, according to the order in which they were recounted in section two above.

The first type—"and you shall do what is upright and good"—is limited in the Talmud to only two cases: the return of foreclosed property and the law of prior right enjoyed by a person to purchase land bordering on his property. But in the instances where it applies it has the efficacy of real law, because it is possible to force the creditor and the purchaser to conform to it, and its characteristic as "*yosher*" expresses itself in this, that its *source* is in consideration of *yosher*, which silences, in the applicable realm—in the sense that "*yosher* overrides the law"—the claims of the general law.

Next to it, and weaker than it, is the category of *yosher* of "beyond the strict law."[148] There is no coercion to fulfill this,[149] and its distinguishing mark is that the one who volunteers to heed it "cuts down the plants," that is to say, he foregoes the qualification which relieves him and returns to the essence which obligates him, or leaves the peripheral thought and penetrates to the central issue. Rabbi Ishmael ben Yose renounced the privilege applying to him as a "sage and it is not in keeping with his dignity" to help load a bundle of wood; Rabbi Hiya renounced the exemption granted him, in a personal way, because he was an expert "who did not need to be instructed" on the status of a coin; the father of Samuel renounced the presumption of a formal despair by a loser to find his lost object after twelve months; and Rav Papa—according to the original interpretation of the Talmud—relinquished the definite assumption of the law which was established for the public welfare, and he agreed to consider reality as it is, which, in the concrete instance cited, invalidated the conclusion of that assumption.

The common denominator in all these cases is: the voluntary consideration not of the surface scene but of the substantive essence, a "bending in" of the strict law and turning it toward its central core.

The third category, the weakest of all—the category which comes closest to the moral norm but does not altogether coincide with it—is the one known under the designation: "the spirit of the Sages is not pleased with him," "the spirit of the Sages is pleased with him," or "the standard of saintliness." These embrace actions whose performance is not a "commandment" and whose violation is not a "transgression"; they are left to man's heart, or to the heart of the saintly man, and the slight fragment of law which clings to them is this, that they represent a principle, a norm, and not merely a spontaneous moral deed which is given to fluctuation and change deriving from all the concrete circumstances surrounding the action.

Thus one who leaves his property to others and passes over his children, the spirit of the Sages is not pleased with him, even if "his children do not behave properly"[150] and moral considerations demand that the property be given to a person who will dedicate them to worthy purposes—something which will not be attained if the estate pass to his "bad" children. Similarly the repayment of a debt in the sabbatical year. The one who repays it—the spirit of the Sages is pleased with him; the one who does not repay it—the spirit of the Sages is not pleased with him, even if the debtor is a poor man begging from door to door and the creditor is a rich man "like Rabbi Elazar ben Azariah."[151] Once the Sages said that their spirit is pleased with one who repays a debt in the sabbatical year, then in relation to this moral obligation, a debt which remains in effect during the sabbatical year has the same status as a debt not in effect during the sabbatical year, and there is no longer any room to differentiate between rich and poor. And the same applies to all those actions whose performance is described as "the standard of saintliness," as the acceptance in return of the *sela* which became depreciated, or the return of "the brand rescued from the fire" in the case of the fire which occurred on the Sabbath, and all similar cases.

8. Finally, we offer some observations, briefly and in condensed form, on the similarity and the dissimilarity between English equity and Jewish *yosher*.

There is no doubt that they were both hewn from the same source and that one progenitor gave them birth: the need to soften the law, and to find a palliative for the hard bind of the legal generalization. The Romans said: *summum ius, summum iniuria;* already the early prophets indulged in a play on the words *mishpat,* "law," and *mispah,* "scab." Every legal norm, even the most just, is likely to bring about a perversion of justice in a particular case. For law is applied equally to all, a garment prepared in advance, standardized, which fits approximately the dimensions of the average person, but it does not fit with precise exactness the body of the particular individual. Hence the eternal cry for the redress of *yosher*, for this flexible palliative which is meant to remove and to straighten out the sharp edges imposed by life's realities, under the reign of the law.

But here the matter ends, and here concludes the similarity between equity and Jewish *yosher*. The content of equity exceeds many times that of Hebrew *yosher*, for the simple reason that—in contrast to the latter—it was operative in a vacuum, and filled lacunae for which no law existed. At the time of the Norman conquest—declares Snell[152]—there was no common law in England, only a tiny modicum of decisions by the king. When the courts of common law arose[153] and began to create institutions of justice—procedural and substantive—they sank, for various historical reasons, into an exaggerated and hard formalism, both with reference to the content of the claim and with reference to its form. Thus there was created a *numerus clausus* of writs, whose forms were examined from the first for most exacting detail so that only the most artificial contrivances succeeded, at times, to overcome the rigors of this defective and complicated legal system; and these matters are part of the story of antiquity.

But here there appeared the Chancellor, "the natural head of Government of the king,"[154] the "defender" of every embittered and oppressed soul. At first the involvement of the Chancellor was occasional and sporadic. He interfered only in solitary cases which were especially difficult, when it was necessary to rescue the oppressed from the might of their oppressors—lawless defendants with a big fist, or perverted legal decisions by the regular courts, to which they were pushed by the hardened formalism. But in the beginning of the fifteenth century,[155] or perhaps earlier, during the reign of King Edward II,[156] this interference was turned into a system, and the Chancellor took upon himself independent authority as head of the special Chancery Court, which was established on the foundations of the King's Council.[157]

From then on, in the course of a span of four hundred years—until the full merger of the courts of law with the courts of equity in 1873—there was developed in the Chancery Court a full array of new juridical institutions, some procedural and some substantive, which were intended to compensate for the defect—to be more exact, the many defects—of the common law courts. Already in the beginning of the seventeenth century the power of the Chancery Court grew to a point where it began, in specific cases, to forbid litigants to bring their claims before the court of common law, or to modify a decision rendered by it,[158] and this to avoid the perpetration of inequity in judgment by the regular courts. From now on there developed two types of courts—of the common law and of chancery—one beside the other as two separate sovereignties: the first stuck firmly and exactly to the provisions of the law, and the second acted "outside the law" and effectuated the principles of *yosher,* which had no foothold in the regular law courts.

I shall not enumerate here—for the lack of space or of need—all the innovations which were introduced in the Chancery Courts. I shall indicate only the most important among them:[159]

(a) The creation of the institution of the "trust," whose general meaning is that if Reuben transfers property to Simon on the condition that he employ it for the benefit of Levi, Simon is indeed, as far as this property is concerned, the legal owner of the property but Levi becomes by this action the equitable owner of the property.[160] This improved considerably the status of the married woman, for while previously all the rights and deprivations of the married woman were tied up in the paradoxical maxim: "Husband and wife are, from the legal point of view, one person, and this 'one' is the husband,"[161] through the force of the jurisdiction of equity of the Chancery Court, the husband was now considered as the trustee of the woman, even if he were not specifically appointed as the trustee of her property.[162]

(b) Supervision of the management of the estate left by a deceased person.

(c) The wide development of Remedies in Equity such

as: the specific performance of a contract, a restraining
order and the like. According to the common law a person
could sue one who breaks a contract for damages, but not
for the specific performance of the contract. An order to
restrain a future violation could not be issued, because
the courts of common law acted only after a wrong had
been committed.[163] A future wrong was a "wrong which
could not be corrected." The jurisdiction of the Chancery
Court came and preceded the affliction with the therapy,
by granting orders to forbid or to restrain actions such as
these.

(d) The development of principles of equity for the
redemption of mortgages.

(e) Guardianship over minors and imbeciles to effectuate
what was said: *Rex est procurator fatuorum.*

These legal institutions with all their derivative partic-
ularities are, according to all scholars of equity, the most
important that were created through the Chancery Court
(and courts similar to it), and one may say that this is the
principal bequest of equity, in which all English jurists
take pride.

In comparing all these with the parallel institutions in
Jewish law, we shall see, to our great surprise, that most
of these institutions of equity have been incorporated in
Jewish law itself for thousands of years, that is to say, in its
juridical division, rather than in its divison of *yoshor.*
There was no need, therefore, for our Sages to mobilize
considerations of *yosher,* to have them serve as support for
these institutions.

Consider, for example, the important institution of
trust. Holdsworth declares[164] that the ownership on the
basis of *yosher* which English equity bequeathed to the beneficiary has no parallel in any other system of law. But this
is not so! We find this type of ownership in Jewish law in
the legal transaction known as *urkhata* or the power of

attorney.[165] The person making the appointment assigns to the appointee the subject of the claim, so that he may enter proceedings in his place with the person against whom he has the claim, and the latter cannot say to him: "I have nothing to do with you!" But this transfer is a "defective transfer";[166] it confers a limited ownership, valid externally in relation to others but not valid internally in relation to the one conferring it. In their internal relations, the owner is the one conferring the appointment, not the appointee. We have here in a nutshell the concept of trusteeship. For the "defective transfer" of Jewish law leaves room for "full ownership" which remains with the one making the appointment, who is the true beneficiary of the power of attorney, similar to the legal ownership, which *belongs*, under equity, *to* the beneficiary of the trust. There is thus nothing new under the sun, and this institution already existed long ago in the sources of Jewish jurisprudence.

As to the married woman, she is well protected, without the trust, according to Jewish law. The verse, "and they shall be one flesh" is indeed found in the Torah of Moses (Genesis 2:24), but the married woman was never robbed of the right of independent ownership. As is well known, the husband was granted the right to enjoy the fruit of his wife's property, but the principal belonged to her, though she is "subservient" to her husband under the force of certain ordinances.[167] If the wife's father, or anyone else, confers a gift upon the wife and stipulates in the terms of the gift that it is being conferred "on the condition that your husband shall have no right to it, but that you do whatever you wish with it," then the husband does not have the right even of usufruct.[168] It turns out then that according to Jewish law it is possible to protect the separate estate of the wife, without the trusteeship under the principle of equity as mentioned earlier.

The same applies to almost all the institutions of *yosher* cited earlier. The remedy of specific performance, which is truly one of the most important of the innovations of equity, exists in Jewish law under the force of law. Most of the acquisitions in Jewish law are acquisitions of objects, that is to say, acquisitions which transfer to the buyer ownership in the substance of the acquired object (or some other right in the object). However, there is one form of acquisition—through the pulling of a scarf [*kinyan sudar*][169]—which is also valid to create an obligation and once the acquisition occurred, the other party can force the one who assumed the obligation to perform his specific obligation, and to transfer to him the property he obligated himself to transfer to him.[170] The claimant is not obligated to content himself with receiving compensation for the damages inflicted on him through the violation of the agreement in force.

The English king is, as we have noted, *procurator fatuorum;* in Jewish law it was said: "Rabban Gamaliel and his Court are the fathers of orphans,"[171] and from this derived the overriding guardianship of the Court over orphans and their property.[172] Through this, Jewish law spread its protective wings over the major situations recounted under items (b) and (e) above.

In conclusion: the content of English equity is much more extensive than the content of the rules of *yosher* according to Jewish law. But this is not because English law includes more *yosher,* but because Jewish jurisprudence includes more "law" which itself meets the demands of *yosher* under English equity. Jewish *yosher,* therefore, turned to other channels for which there was need, and it found expression in the three types of *yosher* which we have explained earlier.

CHAPTER **VIII**

At the Crossroads

1. I have in mind that fateful parting of the ways at which Israeli law now finds itself.

There was a time, not yet far behind us, when we took upon ourselves the accepted pattern of law—common law, as it was called—unreservedly, without any hesitation or doubt whatever. We were forced by the order of Article 46 of the Palestine Order in Council:

> The jurisdiction of the civil courts shall be exercised in conformity with the Ottoman [Turkish] law in force in Palestine on 1st November, 1914, . . . and such Orders in Council, Ordinances and Regulations . . .; and subject hereto . . . shall be exercised in conformity with the substance of the common law and the doctrines of equity in force in England.

This is the channel through which have streamed and through which were introduced to Palestine—in ever-increasing measure since the middle of the thirties—the foundations of the common law and the principles of equity, till they filled all the open areas and all the lacunae found, for the most part, in the old legal system in Palestine. Thus we were privileged with the acceptance of well-known institutions of English law, such as specific performance,[1] the distinction between a "fine" and "compensation" in instances of breach of contract,[2] equitable ownership,[3] and also many important principles in the law of evidence,[4] in addition to the indirect application of common law, as a result of the interpretation "according to the law prevailing in England," about which we were instructed by various Mandatory orders.[5]

It is true that in the end of Article 46 it is stated that:

> . . . the said common law and doctrines of equity shall be in force in Palestine so far only as the circumstances of Palestine and its inhabitants permit it and subject to such qualification as local circumstances render necessary.

But this qualification remained in the category of a law which is actually not being applied. Throughout the period of the Mandate—as far as it is known to me—there occurred only one instance in which the Supreme Court refused to apply the common law in accordance with the said limitation.[6] And even this refusal itself was reversed in another decision given several years thereafter.[7]

Then there arose the State of Israel, which was neither the heir of the Mandatory government nor its "successor."[8] We were concerned about the vacuum that would be created between one system of law and another, and we bridged the intervening period through paragraph 11 of the Ordinance for the Administration of Government and Law, 5708-1948, which stated:

> The system of law which prevailed in Palestine on the 5th of Iyar 5708 (14th of May 1948) shall remain in force to the extent that it does not contradict this Order or other decrees to be issued by the Provisional Council of the State or through it, and the changes deriving from the establishment of the State and its authoritative institutions.

"System of law" means, of course, the common law and the doctrines of equity which were introduced into the land by Article 46 of the above-mentioned Order.

2. Now a number of years have passed, the storm of the war [of Independence] has subsided, the immediate aftermath of the war is gone, and our mind has been freed to take stock of the future of the legal system in Israel. The twilight of the common law has begun: its lustre has dimmed, its exaggerated splendor has passed, and we have begun to probe into its real contents.

In my decision in the Jakobovitz case in 1952[9] I wrote the following:

I am very doubtful that Israeli courts are obligated to follow the innovations in law which were adopted in English courts after the establishment of the State [of Israel]. For if you so decide, you will have made Israeli jurisprudence subservient to the new winds blowing from day to day in the courts of England. In my opinion, it is not this that the Israeli lawgiver intended when he wrote paragraph 11 in the Ordinance for the Administration of Government and Law—not a permanent dependence on the decisions of foreign tribunals. For the one is not the same as the other: the one-time admission of some foreign legal material, fixed and limited, which became "congealed" and was adopted at a certain, specified time, so as to develop it and refine it, through local courts within the boundaries of the State, is not like the acceptance of a body of alien law, unfixed and unspecified, that continues to be created and to be changed through the activity of foreign courts, outside the boundaries of the State. I am afraid that a broad acceptance of the latter situation would not be suitable to meet the particular needs of the inhabitants of the State, and is likely to become a dangerous restraint to the development of an independent original legal creativity.[10]

The posing of the question, and in this form, bore within it half the answer, and after two years passed, the Attorney General (now a justice of the Supreme Court) Mr. Hayim Cohn also identified himself with this position, in one of the criminal appeals.[11] I quote from the decision of Justice Cheshin in that case:

> The Attorney General responds to these arguments and states that what was said in the Newland[12] case can be of no support to the appellant, for the simple reason that it does not bind the Court. And why not? Those statements were made after the establishment of the State, that is to say, after the *Yishuv* proclaimed its political independence and severed its ties of dependence to England. This severance from British rule—the Attorney General claims— brought in its wake the severance of our dependence upon the principles of English law, to the extent that those principles had not yet become incorporated in the legal system of this country. Every innovation effected since the establishment of the State or that may yet be effected, in British jurisprudence—and this includes new interpretations of old principles of the common law—all these no longer have any obligating authority in the legal system of this country.[13]

After Justice Cheshin explained this claim with obvious sympathy, and noted its various implications, he concluded:

> There is no doubt about it, that this question will continue to knock at the portals of the courts, and sooner or later will demand its full and final solution.

However, since the law as decided in the Newland[14] case would bear no influence on the results of the litigation before him, he saw no necessity "to solve it precisely now." The celebrated Justice "concealed a handbreadth and revealed two handbreadths" of what he thought to himself. For at the first opportunity which came to him thereafter in connection with another case,[15] he expressed himself decidedly in favor of the above conception. For he stated thus:

> Even if we say that throughout the Mandatory period, when we were subservient to the political and juridical authority of the Mandatory power, English court decisions flowed constantly into the legal system of this country through the channel laid down in Article 46, this political and juridical dependence has ended entirely with the proclamation of our country as a free and independent state, and automatically there also has stopped the flow of English legal decisions to the extent that it is continually renewed in England day by day. "I am very doubtful," declares Justice Silberg in the Jakobovitz case (Criminal Appeal 125/50, *Piskay Din*, vol. 6, pp. 514, 564), "that Israeli courts are obligated to follow the innovations in law which were adopted in English courts after the establishment of the State [of Israel]." The learned justice also repeated this statement in his decision in Criminal Appeal 53/54. . . .[16]

We too repeat with him and say: It does not make sense that a sovereign state, which possesses a body of law and a system of jurisprudence of its own, shall continue to remain bound to the authority of a body of law in an alien country and to innovations in law due to be adopted in its courts, only because in the past—when there was a connecting tie between the two countries—the one drew upon the legal realm of the other. This was not intended by the legislation of paragraph 11 of the Ordinance for the Administration of Government and Law, 5708–1948. What was, was; and what it received, it received. The principles of the prevalent body of law which were transferred to the legal system of this country and became integrated with it before the establishment of the State, became part of its accepted system of law by force of paragraph 11, and this law—within the limitations mentioned in paragraph 11—continues, and will continue, to develop with the development of the State and

its adjustment to the special conditions of its population
and legal institutions. English legal decisions which came
later are certainly deserving of attention by the courts of
this country, but they have no obligating authority such as
those preceding 1948. . . . And where the courts are not persuaded of their rightness, they are not obligated to follow,
even where they have not come to overturn altogether an
ancient principle of English law, adopted and hallowed
earlier in the English courts.[17]

The sources of power of the old order are no more, and
the dynamic influence of the common law has become only
static.

But this is not the only breach which has appeared in
the "exalted fortress." We shall soon see—in analyzing the
Kokhavi case mentioned above[18]—that between the lines
of the statement of the judges, those cited above and those
to be cited below, is hidden an "explosive substance"
which is due to jolt the common law altogether from the
paths set for it in the Mandatory period, and to fit it a
new face of which its progenitors never dreamt.

3. Let us therefore examine more closely the decision
rendered in the Kokhavi case, and we shall see the new
direction projected, and what condition, necessitated by
circumstances, we are due to reach in the course of time.

The incident which occurred was as follows: A dangerous liquid, methyl alcohol, passed through various
hands via the merchant-seller until it reached the one who
needed it, a government official, fifty-eight years of age,
who drank it and became almost totally blind. The injured
party sued the merchant who sold him the alcohol, and the
merchant before him, and the merchant before the latter
merchant, and the District Court was persuaded by him
and obligated the defendants to pay damages. The calcula-
tion of the damages was made on the basis of the gross

monthly salary that the injured person would have received from the government—had he not lost his eyesight—and this salary was multiplied by the number of months that remained for him to reach the age of sixty-five.[19] From this, twenty percent was deducted as capitalization for the payment in one lump sum and in advance, which the defendants who inflicted the injury were required to make.

In the course of the litigation there arose the interesting question, whether the District Court was not supposed to deduct from the monthly salary the amount that the employer of the injured person—the government office—would have deducted from him as income tax. For if the accident had not occurred, and if the plaintiff were of normal sight and not blind and had continued his work, he would have sustained the loss each month of a sum equal to the amount of the tax, so that it was not those who caused the injury who brought about this loss.

But this very question came up and was dealt with in another case, the case of Grossman,[20] and the Israeli Supreme Court, speaking through Justice Cheshin, decided against deducting the amount of the income tax from the amount of compensation. This is the language of the learned Justice:

> This question is not new. It has come up a number of times in the past, and it was given a clear answer in English jurisprudence. It will suffice for us to cite two cases in this connection:
>
> (1) *Jordan v. The Limmer and Trinidad Lake Asphalt Co. Ltd.* (1946), 1 K.B. 356;
>
> (2) *Billingham v. Hughes and Another* (1949), 1 All E.R. 684.
>
> In the first case—that of Jordan—Judge Atkinson of the Court of the King's Bench said that in computing the amount of the damage one is to take into consideration only the rights of the injured person according to the con-

tract between him and his employer. The fact that a portion of his salary would have been paid to the government treasury is of no concern to the one who inflicted the injury. It is conceivable that an official of the treasury, on noting that the amount to be paid to the plaintiff also includes compensation for loss of wages, will also appraise this amount of compensation for purposes of income tax—but of what concern is all this to the one who inflicted the injury?

An expression more to the point of this principle was given in the second case—of Billingham—which reached as far as the Court of Appeal. In that case—in which a physician claimed damages for the loss of his ability to work in his specialty—Judge Tucker said:

In estimating the amount of damages . . . the sole question is: what is the sum that may bring about, to the degree possible, *restitutio in integrum* from a financial point of view? Therefore, where the basis of the claim for damages is salary or profits, all those considerations apply whether the injury derived from a violation of contract or whether it is a result of civil injuries. . . . The principle of *restitutio in integrum* demands that the claimant be put in a position where he could have found himself in relation to his income, that is, to receive his full earnings. . . . The questions concerning his later obligations to the authorities in charge of taxes have no bearing on the defendants.[21]

Justice Cheshin, in basing himself on these English legal decisions and in reinforcing them with considerations of his own, decided that there is to be no deduction of the anticipated income tax from the amount of the compensation.

We have thus reached a clear resolution of this interesting question by the Supreme Court, but lo and behold, it was posed anew in the Kokhavi case, as we saw above. Why was this question repeated twice, and why was it still in the nature of a "question" after the first decision? Were we not then in the beginning of 1957, about a half-year before the adoption of the new Law of the Courts which provides that the Supreme Court shall not be bound by its previous decisions,[22] and it still guided itself according to the decision of the Supreme Court in the case of Romm[23] which constrained it to follow precedent?

The answer is: because in the meantime—that is, between the Grossman Appeal and the Kokhavi Appeal—something occurred in England. The House of Lords, in the case of *British Transport Comm. v. Gourley,* annulled the Billingham ruling and decided that one is indeed to deduct the income tax from the estimate of compensation payable to the injured party.[24]

The change of the order there, in faraway England, left its mark here [in Israel], and the delicate question facing the Court was: Which is preferable—the earlier decision of the Israeli Supreme Court, or the new, "revolutionary" decision of the English House of Lords? The element of doubt was whether this new decision, since it was a decision by the highest authority in England, did or did not cancel out retroactively the English foundation on which was based the precedent in the Grossman case.

This was an ordinary problem of compensation and income tax, but bound up with it was the troublesome question: On whom do we depend finally in this country—on our own judges, on the judges of England, or perhaps, as a joint arrangement, on our own judges as the "spokesmen" of the English judges? The Kokhavi case, with its unusual coincidence, served as an appropriate "demonstration lesson" for the examination of this basic issue, and the three judges who sat in judgment in the Appeal expressed, each in his own way, their opinions on this matter.

The Deputy President, Justice Cheshin (in the quotation cited above): The later English decision . . . has no obligating authority as does a decision before 1948 (a decision rendered, it is understood, within the limitations of Article 46 of the Order in Council, 1922, and of paragraph 11 of the Ordinance for the Adminstration of Government and Law, 5708–1948), and where the courts are not persuaded of their rightness, they do not have to follow it. . . .[25]

Justice Vitcon: My opinion is that there is nothing in these English precedents to obligate us any more, even if they were issued before the establishment of the State. These precedents may serve to guide and persuade us, but they have no power to obligate our courts. Indeed we are free to depart from them, whether by the explicit provisions of paragraph 11 of the Ordinance for the Administration of Government and Law, 5708–1948, or by the very fact that our courts are today operating in a sovereign state which is no longer dependent on the legal decisions of another state.[26]

Justice Landau: As to the additional question . . . concerning a decision rendered in England before the rise of the State, with reference to issues that have not yet been decided on in Israel—I can see no great difference between the view of the Deputy President that such decisions obligate us, *within* the limitations of Article 46 of the Order in Council and paragraph 11 of the Ordinance for the Administration of Government and Law, 5708–1948, and the view of the honorable Justice Vitcon that they are not obligatory *because* of what is stated in paragraph 11 of the Ordinance for the Administration of Government and Law, or because of the very fact that with the establishment of the State the system of courts was also established anew as one of the authoritative institutions of a sovereign state.[27]

To me it appears, with all due respect, that there is a vast difference between the two views cited above. "Within the limitations" is not entirely identical with "because of the limitations," for these limitations—so it is possible to argue—did not instruct us merely concerning their own substantive essence, but on the entire subject. Especially should one note the words of Justice Vitcon, that we (the Israeli courts) are free to depart from them, from the precedents rendered before the establishment of the State "by the very fact that our courts are today operating in a sovereign state which is no longer dependent on the legal decisions of another state."

But as to the subject before us—the question of the future form of Israel law—we may overlook the variation of views expressed there. The minimum on which all three judges[28] agreed is that English precedents created after the establishment of the State do not obligate our courts, and this itself, in the course of time, is due to change fundamentally the content and the form of those principles of common law which managed to "find a home" here [in Israel] before the establishment of the State.

4. This future result is imperative—almost unavoidable, as will be explained later on.

The legal system—whether its source is in a statutory law or in the decision of the courts—is not a congealed material fixed forever, which will not be affected by the ravages of time. On the contrary: the very opposite is the great advantage of the English common law. For the *lex non scripta* [the unwritten law] of the common law is a *process,* or a free-flowing activity which, in its unfolding, *creates the precedent which preceded it, as it were.* From a logical point of view, this is self-contradictory, but pure logic does not reign in the heights of the world of law, and at times it is precisely fiction which represents the reality within it.

A profound disagreement abounds among scholars of the common law, as to whether the judge creates the legal norm, or whether he only interprets it.[29] The truth is, I would say, that *the judge interprets the law, which he has previously created under the guise of interpretation.* In justice to the judge, the "chief magician," it should be said that he does not act in a vacuum and does not create something out of nothing, for the direction of his creation is rooted or guided through the decisions rendered by early deciders of the law. The question is an old one.

The norm being created in the common law faces the past and the future at the same time—it depends on a fictional past and directs itself toward a changing future. As the decision will be transmuted from present to past, there will not be left in it much more than the interpretive fiction; it is in the category of the maxim in the Ethics of the Fathers: "Because you drowned others, they drowned you; and those who drowned you, are destined to be drowned."[30] As is well known, the Greek philosopher Heraclitus said: "A person does not bathe in the same river twice,"[31] for, by the time of the second bathing, the river has already changed its waters. This is also true of the stream of legal decisions, which sheds form and takes on form in the course of its movement, and maintains its continuity only in the essence of its streaming. The spinal cord holding together the common law is, of course, the precedent, and yet—except for a few instances, which fit together in all their details, as it were—precedent does not act except "with a grain of salt" (*cum grano salis*) in adapting itself, more or less, to the changes deriving from the distinctive circumstances of the new case. The statement "every event is to be judged in the context of its circumstances"—in traditional Hebrew: "you can only consider it in its place and time"—is a statement repeated as an accompanying refrain in almost every English legal decision, and the result is that the "grandchildren" of the precedent are decidedly different from their "grandfather," and all they have in common is the family name. Such a fate befell the concept *assumpsit* ("he took it on himself"),[32] which after some time transgressed the boundaries of contractual undertaking; agency by necessity;[33]

the many-faceted—and in part, zigzagging—metamorphosis which overtook the concepts of "cause" and "negligence,"[34] and many others.

In one of the decisions mentioned above,[35] Judge McCardie declared:

> The object of the common law is to solve difficulties and adjust relations in social and commercial life. It must meet, so far as it can, sets of fact abnormal as well as usual. It must grow with the development of the nation. It must face and deal with changing or novel circumstances. Unless it can do that, it fails in its function and declines in its dignity and its value. An expanding society demands an expanding common law.[36]

These words put together in a nutshell all that was said and written on the function of the common law in the course of hundreds of years. This is indeed the function of every decision, and if it is here attributed, with explication and emphasis, to the common law, it is thanks to the fact that its decisions constitute the major part of English law.

And now let us sum up! Let us see what is likely to be the fate of the common law among us, after its applicability has been limited, as was stated, to decisions prior to the establishment of the State.

The vision which beckons—I see it and not from far away—is that the stream of English legal decisions will no longer obligate us; we shall not suffer from it nor shall we be benefitted by it. The creation deposited with us—that is, the common law which was "congealed" when the State was established—we shall have to develop by ourselves, to transform it into a part of our own evolving legal tradition. There, in England, they will continue to deduct the income tax from compensation for damages, but among us—not![37] The courts of England will proceed according to the law as decided in the Newland case,[38] which established a *numerus clausus* for the offense of "public mischief";[39] our courts will loosen the confinement and leave room for the recognition of new violations of this type. As is well known, the law is not a series of hermetically sealed chambers, but each chapter is tied and entangled with every other chapter in it, influencing and being influenced at the same time. It is clear then, that in the course of time and as we move farther away from the common origin, the division will continue to grow in all the wide areas of the law and the two arms will move farther apart from each other. The legal system to be created through Israeli legal decisions will be neither an English law nor an Israeli law, but a law that is a composite, half English and half Israeli—two parts, differing in form and content, that will never be merged to form one whole entity. The State of Israel will be the only country in the world where two sovereigns will wear one crown, not one after the other or one beside the other but in a state of confusion—a kind of legal "unicum," which will serve as an attraction to nations because of its strangeness and peculiarity.

5. On the other side of this perspective, as we stand facing the sure and grievous conclusion that the legal system to be created in the country through the process of legal decision will be in the nature of "half-slave and half-free," there stirs within us the troubling question: Is this the only choice open to us in this historic epoch? Perhaps we shall dare dream of and aspire to full legal freedom; perhaps we shall erect the new Israeli structure on the foundation stone which we inherited from our ancestors? In other words, briefer and clearer: Has not the time come to create a legal system of our own, to prepare an Israeli code of laws drawing on the basic principles of Jewish law?

We have revived the Hebrew language—surely not that we might have a "secret code" in which we shall be able to converse with ourselves, without fear of an "evil eye" or "evil ear." The aspiration for Hebrew was an aspiration to return to ourselves, to our spiritual autonomy—in the nature of the slogan "The Hope of Israel: Hebrew"—through which we become cleansed and through which we reestablish our soul's severed link with the world of thought and feeling of authentic Judaism.[40] And if we did not go to borrow a language, let us not go to borrow a legal system. For law is the language of the state—the language of the state in which she speaks to her citizens, in which she fashions the forms of their lives.[41]

6. The question of arranging a Jewish code was dealt with —in a practical way—in an essay which I published about a half-year before the establishment of the State, in which I wrote:[42]

The question is twofold:

(a) Is there a need to prepare a new lawbook, in the spirit of the comprehensive codifications of Maimonides, the *Tur* and the *Shulhan Arukh?*

(b) Is there a possibility, in our time and with our limited means, to prepare such a code?

As to the question of need, there is no doubt about the matter—and whoever does not admit it deceives himself— for the existing lawbooks, precisely because of their vastness and gigantic scope and because of their exaggerated and detailed casuistry, are not the kind of lawbooks than can be helpful to clarify the simple law and its ready and immediate adaptation to the needs of life. The law is—or certainly should be—something readily accessible to everybody, judges included. If the judge, in coming to decide a case according to the law, is obliged to plunge into deep waters in order to find the needed support for the concrete case with which he deals; if every judge is obliged to be a great scholar, to whom the pathways of the law are as familiar as the pathways of his own town, the cause of the law will be found to suffer.

But the question is not only technical. From a thematic or content point of view also, the existing codifications cannot serve as a guide for arriving at the law in the practical cases of all branches of life—even if we include the rich rabbinic literature which accumulated in the last four hundred years. There is no need to elaborate here on the basic cause for the development of the law. It is clear and obvious to all that this development, especially in the civil realm, never stopped, from the time of the closing of the Mishnah to the present. Life always won, or nearly always, over the dead letter. But this victory was achieved at great cost: on its altar was sacrificed the simplicity of legal reasoning. For since the overall traditional framework of the law was generally fixed and static, and it was impossible to breach it in any way, the solution in the concrete case had to be found in byways of the law, through the means of an instrument of thought—formidable in power but also pregnant with peril—the dialectic of *pilpul*. The result was that the law, for the most part, ceased to be general and became individualized, and thus was robbed of its positive and vital foundation of firmness which alone endows a legal system with its revered position as a regulator in the life of society. The function of the law is not merely to resolve disputes which broke out in the past; its principal function is to lead the individual in the appropriate way, and to ward off, as a prophylactic, the eruption of future disputes. And the law cannot perform this function successfully, when its principles are an improvised creation—unanticipated in advance—of expert scholars, and when, for the most part, they are also subjects of dispute among the judges-legislators.

This and one thing more. The development of Jewish law did not always proceed hand-in-hand with the unending development of life's demands. This observation is especially pertinent with reference to the last hundred or hundred and fifty years, the period after the Emancipation. If the economic structure and the social relations of life in the ghetto were adapted, more or less, to the established forms of traditional law, the exit from the ghetto brought with it—even internally among Jews themselves—values of life and new social relations that could not easily be bent to those forms. The sale of an object which is transferred from hand to hand within the walls of the ghetto is quite unlike the telegraphic order of merchandise which is made by a Jewish merchant in Hamburg from his fellow-merchant in Venice. Here was created a wide gap between law and life, a vacuum that could not be bridged except through a conscious turning to a foreign legal system, by means of the legal formula of "the law of the land is law," not at all an ideal way out for a national legal system like ours, which seeks to spread its authority over all aspects of life.

This question—the question of the renewal of the Jewish legal system—appears before us in its proper light when we view it from the new perspective of our generation, namely: the vision of the impending establishment of the Jewish state. It is strange to me that this question has not yet drawn the proper attention in the circles of the *Yishuv,* even though the national worth of Jewish law is surely not lower than the national worth of the Hebrew language. For the institutions of law are the letters of the language in which a state speaks to its citizens, the sole means of expression in which it presents its demands with reference to the normative and minimal moral behavior of the average citizen. And the Jewish state, when it is established, will have something to say to the citizen, and it will have to convey its message in its own language, in the spirit of the rich legal tradition of the Jewish people. It is inconceivable and even absurd that when we come to renew the life of the nation on its ancestral homeland, we skip over particularly that spiritual factor which stood at the center of the nation's thought and interest for two thousand years.

We shall have no alternative but to return to Jewish law. For in practice there is no legal system in this country—there are laws, and in this respect, plurality is always less than singularity. We are dependent here, in this small country, on the authority of Turkish, French, English, and communal laws that are piled in layers one upon the other, with no connection or fusion between them. If, for example, cases of damages are tried according to English law, and compensation for the violation of a contract according to French law, and matters of surety and sales according to Turkish law, then the law is not a legal system but a mosaic, destined perhaps to excite the eye of an archeologist, but not able to serve as a firm basis for healthy and normal legal relations. It is clear, therefore, that the present condition cannot long continue to exist, and that the Jewish state will necessarily have to work toward the creation or the acceptance of a unitary legal system, and under these circumstances is there anything more plausible than the return to the sources of Jewish law?!

And now we reach the second half of the question: Is there a real possibility for us to prepare a new Jewish code, adapted to the modern needs of the Jew of this generation? The answer to this, in my judgment, is: There certainly is! We must make one assumption at the outset, in order to see the subject in the proper perspective: this code will not be in the nature of a "condensed *Shulhan Arukh*," and it will not claim for itself the traditional authority—religious and sacred—of the existing codes. This will be a civil-secular creation which will accept, wherever possible, the basic principles of Jewish law, with the explicit exception of the archaic conclusions which are superimposed on them. The objective will be: to winnow and sift, to bring closer and to reestablish what still cleaves to life, and to keep away and reject the dry growth which became shriveled and impoverished in the course of the centuries. In other words somewhat more graphic: to pour out the wine that has become sour, and to keep the barrel so as to fill it with new wine which will become permeated with the aroma that has seeped into it, and that its aroma and its taste may be like the aroma and the taste of the old wine. This is undoubtedly a question of taste, of an historic sense and a sense of reality all at the same time, an attachment to tradition and an attachment to life, the kind of synthesis which we face, and solve, each day in all branches of culture in our renewed existence.

Inasmuch as the work of preparing the new code will be, in large measure, one of choosing and selecting, in undertaking it a great advantage will accrue to us from the very condition which now serves as a major drawback, as was indicated above. I am referring to the many controversies— the controversies among the formulators of law—which are to be found in connection with almost every decision in our legal literature. Our body of legal material is so rich and so controversial that in practice one can find support for any desired view. This does not simplify for the judge the determination of law in the concrete case being tried before him, but it surely simplifies for the legislator-codifier the choosing of the abstract principle. For the task of the codifier is not the same as the task of the judge deciding specific cases. The latter (the judge) must find the acceptable view, while the former (the codifier) may choose the desired view.

But there is also a danger accompanying this advantage: the danger of confusing boundaries and distorting principles. For—from the point of view of principle—what is desirable in one instance does not always go together with what is desirable in another instance. Frequently the opposite occurs: what is desirable in one legal situation actually causes, in a logical sense, an undesirable conclusion in a second situation.

We have already encountered a phenomenon such as this —not exactly like it but similar to it—in the principles of legal decision and determination of Rabbi Joseph Karo, author of the *Shulhan Arukh*.[43] He too proceeded in a schematic fashion: he adopted a general rule to decide according to the majority view among the opinions of "the three pillars of legal decision"—the Rif, Maimonides, and the Rosh[44]—a procedure which involved necessarily, in many cases, a breaking of the underlying unity in the legal institution under consideration. Our new lawgiver, in standing before the overwhelming choice, will have to guard zealously the preservation of the ideological line in its wholeness, and not stray or get lost in utilitarian considerations solely. And this will be the criterion by which he will be tested, for censure or for praise. For the basic and overall purpose is not a new legal system but a new code whose roots will be deep in Jewish law. . . .

Many years have passed since the writing of that essay. The State came into being, it celebrated its *Bar Mitzvah,* but this task to which we are called has remained unattended to and no beginning has yet been made to deal with it— neither by those who vote in the Knesset, nor by those who draft legislation in the Ministry of Justice. Some minor effort in this regard has been made by the Supreme Court. I have reference to the legal decisions rendered by the Court —not in the area of personal status—in which it occasionally probes the case under consideration from the point of view of the principles of Jewish law.[45] But this, obviously, is not enough. This effort is indeed important and very much worthwhile. The decisions of the courts represent an unsurpassed testing-ground for examining the viability of a principle under examination. But by this method we shall not attain a *system;* we may perhaps attain it after hundreds of years. The great advantage of the legal decision— its grappling constantly with cases which have occurred in real life—is here turned to its disadvantage: it grapples *only* with cases which have occurred and does not formulate in advance principles relevant for various future cases which have not yet occurred. For a judge can deal only with what his eyes behold. The judge is a seer, while the lawgiver is a visionary—and vision is what is needed from those who formulate laws.

7. How shall this work be done; what path shall we choose for ourselves in coming to fulfill this great assignment? I base myself on these three norms:[46]

(a) The approach to the material needs to be dogmatic. This means that we must see the Jewish legal system as it is, as one complete entity, without pausing to deal—except incidentally—with the stages in the development of each institution. The knowledge of the paths of development is most important to us, but only from a pedagogic point of view. We must not forget even for a moment that our primary objective, within the confines of our assignment, is not a scientific, historical inquiry into the stages of development in Jewish law, but a pragmatic, contentful retrieving of the *results* of its development.

(b) The choosing of the material. Rabbinic literature, from the eleventh century on, fructified in continually increasing measure the system of Jewish law and turned it into a fertile field for the absorption of new legal ideas. As in the case of the English "common law"—whose first steps also were taken not far away from this period—the Jewish judges, "the formulators of law," began to spin out of old materials of law and custom a new body of principles, limitations and qualifications whose common purpose was to find a solution for the new problems which arose with the unfolding of life. In only one important respect did they remain different one from the other. English common law was created and developed within one cultural center and is all of one piece—one huge pyramid whose lower tiers, the ornament of the tradition, bear upon them in an organic manner all the weight of the upper, perfected tiers. By contrast, our "common law" was created in different cultural centers and in different climates and constitutes a combination of separate pyramids, among which there is frequently no connection or contact. Despite the well-known statement, "No Court can annul the decisions of another Court unless it exceeds it in wisdom and numbers,"[47] the principle of "the obligating precedent" was never firmly established in the wide reaches of Jewish jurisprudence, and this factor caused a profound differentiation—temporal and geographic—in the way it developed. This bears further reflection.

But with all the paradoxical elements in this situation, from this "sharpness" there will derive for us "sweetness" in connection with the task before us. This differentiation is likely to broaden—if we may say so—the "area of conceptual maneuver," and the disputes among these formulators of law will simplify for us the choice of desirable principles for meeting the modern needs of the citizen of the State. For it is clear—as every intelligent person will acknowledge—that only through a strict selection of the material, through the sifting of concepts which have not yet become obsolete, shall we be able to create a modern Israeli code that will satisfy the vital needs of this generation.

(c) The new Israeli code which will arise on the foundations of the Jewish legal system, as mentioned above, will be "a book of civil law" in the accepted sense of the term. It will grapple not with the *surroundings* but with the *core,* that is to say, not with the distinctive branches and growths of the law, but with those basic concepts or primary institutions without which there cannot be any legal system, and thanks to which it is to be designated as a "civil code." These concepts and institutions—such as: obligation, acquisition, ownership, sale, gift, exchange, leasing, deposit, loan, surety, mortgage, partnership, neighborliness and the like— were created at the dawn of human culture and to this day they constitute the "meat" of the law, or—if we prefer it— the skeleton on which all legal institutions grow skin and flesh. Here, in these fundamental areas, there is revealed to us the distinctive characteristic of the national law that from afar sheds its splendor on all subsequent legal growth.

This, therefore, is the "geometrical" area on which we must concentrate all our attention when we come—through the creation of an Israeli code—to renew our national system of jurisprudence.

This difficult task is in our charge. The day is short, the task is great, and the guiding destiny of the nation presses us forward. Given a few more years, we shall manage to "become rooted in sin"—to be satisfied with the offspring of strangers and to be content with the continued existence of the alien systems of law bequeathed to us by the Ottoman empire and the Mandatory government. If I shall not act for myself—who will; and if not now—when?

Abbreviations

C.A.	Civil Appeal
Cr.A.	Criminal Appeal
F.H.	Further Hearing
H.C.	High Court
L.A.	Land Appeal
Mot.	Motion
P.D.	*Piskay Din*
P.C.A.	Privy Council Appeal
P.L.R.	Palestinian Land Reports
Pes.	*Pesakim*

Notes

CHAPTER I: LEGAL CHARACTER

1. M. Silberg, *Hok U-Musar BaMishpat HaIvri* (Jerusalem, 5712), pp. 5–6.

2. Shabbat 88a.

3. "So that if the Holy One, praised be He, should summon them to trial, complaining: 'Why did you not keep what you took on yourselves?' they can reply that they accepted it under duress" (Rashi, *ad loc., s.v. moda'a.*

4. Exodus 34:27; Deuteronomy 5:2, 28:69; Jeremiah 34:13.

5. *Moda'a* is a technical term for the voiding of a specific legal action because of duress. For the most part this term is invoked when the one who makes this claim announces it in advance, before witnesses, prior to performing the act, and hence the term *moda'a* [announcement]. See Bava Batra 40a-b; Rashbam, Bava Batra 40a, *s.v. ve-khen moda'a;* Maimonides, *Mishneh Torah, Hilkhot Mekhirah* 10:1; Ketubot 19b; Arakhin 21b; *Shulhan Arukh, Even HaEzer*, sec. 134, para. 1; and many other places.

6. Except for certain situations where there is some consideration which mitigates the severity of the coercion. See Bava Batra 47b–48b; Maimonides, *Mishneh Torah, Hilkhot Mekhirah* 10:1; *Hilkhot Ishut* 4:1; *Shulhan Arukh, Hoshen Mishpat*, sec. 205, para. 1; *Shulhan Arukh, Even HaEzer*, sec. 42, para. 1; cf. also Maimonides, *Mishneh Torah, Hilkhot Gerushin* 2:20.

7. Rashi, Shabbat, *loc. cit.*

8. Yoma 69b.

155

9. The allusion is to the expression of Bialik in his celebrated essay "Halakhah and Aggadah."

10. Yoma 28b. The *eruv* of dishes is arranged to permit baking and cooking and the preparation of other needs for the Sabbath on the day of a festival which occurs on Friday [by having a token of this preparation on the weekday preceding the festival] (see Bezah 15b–17b; Maimonides, *Mishneh Torah, Hilkhot Yom Tov* 6:1–11; *Shulhan Arukh, Orah Hayim,* sec. 527). The remarkable point in ascribing "even the *eruv* of dishes" to Abraham is that this entire practice rests on a rabbinic enactment to circumvent a prohibition only instituted by the Rabbis (see Maimonides, *op. cit.,* law 1)—yet even this is alleged to have been kept by Abraham.

11. Rashi, *ad loc.,* and the original source of this in *Pirkay De-Rabbi Eliezer.* The version in the original source, Ch. 32 (ed. Warsaw, 1874, p. 61), is "one corresponding to the paschal sacrifice," but there is not much difference in this from the point of view of the anachronism represented here.

12. Rashi, *ad loc.,* and its source in *Midrash Tanhuma, Toledot* 8, and Genesis Rabbah 63:15. Salt and straw do not call for a tithe, but Esau who sought to "trap" the heart of Isaac, sought to show himself to him as a person punctilious in keeping the commandments and, posing as innocent, asked him these questions. On deriving laws from the behavior ascribed to the Patriarchs, which occurred before the giving of the Torah, see a negative view in Yerushalmi, Moed Katan, Ch. 3 (ed. Venice, 1522), p. 4b: "and do we derive any legal position from what occurred before the giving of the Torah?" See Maimonides, *Mishneh Torah, Hilkhot Avel* 1:1.

13. This also led to the tendency to classify laws into categories of "principal" and "derivative," which pervades all realms of the Halakhah, from "principal" categories of damages in monetary matters, through "principal" categories of work in the Sabbath laws, to "principal" categories of uncleanliness in the laws of purity and impurity (Bava Kamma 2a–3b, 4b–5a; Shabbat 73a; Kelim, Ch. 1).

14. Berakhot 6a. Their content is also parallel: in our *tefillin* is written "Hear, O Israel, the Lord is our God, the Lord is One," and in the *tefillin* of the Holy One, praised be He, is written: "and who is like Thy people Israel, a unique nation on the earth?" (*ibid.*).

15. Yerushalmi, Rosh Hashanah, Ch. 1 (ed. Venice), 3a.

16. "For the king—the law is not written." This corresponds to the Latin maxim: *Princeps legibus solutus est.* A relic of this norm is also found in our modern Israeli law, in section 42 of the Interpreta-

tion Ordinance, which states: "No act of legislation shall diminish the rights of the State, or impose upon it any obligation, unless explicitly stated." On the attitude of Israeli jurisprudence to this, see the judgment of Justice Landau, *Van Mirup v. Director of the Shikun Department, Ministry of Labor,* H.C. 194/56, 11 *P.D.* 659. Cf. also the judgment of Justice Landau in *Developmental Authority v. Attorney General,* Cr. A. 134/58, 13 *P.D.* 722.

17. See Silberg, *op. cit.,* p. 7; see also Dicey, *Law of the Constitution,* 9th ed., Ch. 4 ("The Rule of Law"), pp. 183–205.

18. I trust that I will not be misinterpreted. I do not refer to the distinction between a "real" prohibition and a "personal" prohibition which differentiate between a vow and an oath (Nedarim 2b). I refer to this basic "thingness" or "quasi-thingness," which is also found in prohibitions which are "personal" (except in the case of oaths) such as the prohibition of cohabitation with near relations, eating on the Day of Atonement, or forbidden foods. As to the classification of forbidden foods as "personal" prohibitions, see the Ritva on Nedarim, beginning of Ch. *Ve-Aylu Mutarin* (Livorno, 5555-1795), p. 17a: "If a person declare: 'Your food which I might eat shall be to me as the meat of a pig, or of an idol . . .' which means, whatever I might eat of yours shall be forbidden to me as one of those which are forbidden things, his words are without efficacy . . . because he made the prohibition to depend on an object whose prohibition is a 'personal' one. . . ."

19. Yevamot 32a.

20. Kiddushin 77b: "He is relieved of excision [*karet*], because the prohibition of eating on the Day of Atonement cannot fall on the prohibition of *nevelah* which preceded" (Rashi, *ad loc.*).

21. Maimonides, *Mishneh Torah, Hilkhot Isuray Biah* 17:8.

22. See Magella [Ottoman code], paras. 200, 201; the sale in the Magella was a real contract (para. 369). See sec. 16 of the Sale of Goods Act, 1893; cf. *Austin v. Craven* (1812), 128 E.R. 483; *Gabarron v. Kreeft* (1875), 33 L.T. 365; cf. also Komm. d. RGR to sec. 930 of the B.G.B., note 3.

23. The question is quasi-philosophical and indirectly it also bears on the whole question of determinism and indeterminism. "Retrospective designation" implies that the actual present clarifies retrospectively the potential past; and automatically also the future, when it will arrive, will clarify retrospectively the present. It thus turns out that the individuation by means of a future event is as clear as the individuation by means of an unknown event which has already

taken place. The partisans of the view which negates "retrospective designation" deny the necessary identification of the "potential" and the "actual," or of the "anticipated" with the "existing." There may be, in their view, a discrepancy between them; therefore there is no equivalence, and therefore there cannot be a precise individuation by means of tokens which are based on a future event. See Silberg, *HaMa'amad HaIshi Be-Yisrael* (Jerusalem, 5718-1957), pp. 271–278.

24. Bava Kamma 69a. The owner who is especially scrupulous and God-fearing is concerned lest the poor will glean in his field beyond their right under the law, and they will thus violate the law against robbery; therefore, according to Rabbi Judah, he renounces in advance all the sheaves they will glean later on (Rashi, *ad loc., s.v. Rabbi Dosa;* see also Tosafot, *ibid., s.v. kol sheloktu*).

25. Gemara and Rashi, Bava Kamma 69b; Gittin 25a. By "designating the name"—that is, by the declaration about making twenty-one small bottles *terumah* and *ma'aser,* he excludes the wine from the category of *tevel* or the untithed (Rashi, Gittin 25b, *s.v. ve-shoteh*) and he makes of part *terumah* and *ma'aser,* leaving the greater amount fit for lay use. But so that "the name" shall apply and release the rest, it must necessarily apply not to a proportionate amount of the wine at hand, but to an actual, specific quantity, and this individuated designation is accomplished through the formula: "that I *will* separate" (tomorrow, after the Sabbath).

26. Mishnah, Gittin 24a, and Gemara, *ibid.,* 25a. The case deals with a person who "had two wives with the same name," such as Sarah, and, recalling the incident with Jephthah (Judges 11:31), he instructs the scribe to write the divorce for "the Sarah" who will be first to leave his door. The question then is whether this is a writ of divorce written specifically "for her," or not.

27. Mishnah, Eruvin 36b. The distance one is permitted to walk on the Sabbath [*tehum Shabbat*] is two thousand cubits in each direction from the point where he fixed his residence on the Sabbath (where he made his abode on Friday toward sunset); and if he made his residence in the city, the distance of the city (including seventy cubits square outside the city) is not counted, for all of it is deemed his place of residence, and the two thousand cubits are computed from the end of the city limits. When a person makes an *eruv tehumin* on Friday it means: he deposits food for two meals at a specific point outside the city, within the two thousand cubits; we then consider that point as his place of residence and he can then walk two thousand cubits in each direction from that point. It thus

turns out that the person "gains what he loses," for he extends the distance of his permissible walking in one direction, while reducing it in the opposite direction.

The person dealt with in the Mishnah is desirous of listening to a lecture by a scholar who will arrive from his own place to a place away from the city by more than two thousand cubits, but he does not know "in which direction he will come," whether to the east or to the west of the city. Therefore, he deposits two *eruvin*—one in the east and one in the west—and he stipulates that the *eruv* on whichever side the scholar will come from shall become efficacious and establish for him his point of residence. He thus hinges the efficacy of the *eruv* on Friday toward sunset on an event due to occur later (see Gemara, Eruvin, *ibid.*, and Rashi *s.v. mizrah u-ma'arav;* for other aspects of this law see Mishnah, Eruvin 27b, and Rashi, *s.v. bakol me'arvin;* Mishnah and Gemara, *ibid.*, 87b; Mishnah, *ibid.*, 45a; Mishnah and Gemara, *ibid.*, 57a–b; Mishnah, *ibid.*, 60a, and Rashi, *s.v. lo asah ve-lo kelum;* Maimonides, *Mishneh Torah, Hilkhot Eruvin* 6:1–4, 7, 9; *Hilkhot Shabbat*, Ch. 28 and *Magid Mishneh, ad loc.*, law 1; *Shulhan Arukh, Orah Hayim*, sec. 397, para. 1; sec. 398; sec. 408, para. 1).

28. Eruvin 37b. The reference is to the second tithe [*ma'aser sheni*], which one is obligated to take to Jerusalem and eat within the city walls on the basis of the provision in Deuteronomy 14:23: "and you shall eat them before the Lord your God in the place He will choose to dwell there"; but immediately in the two verses which follow it is stated: "Should the distance be too great for you, should you be unable to transport them, because the place . . . is far from you, you may convert them into money. Wrap up the money and take it with you to the place the Lord your God has chosen. . . ." Hence the alternative: to redeem the second tithe, or to "secularize" it through money, and through this "secularization" "the fruits become ordinary, while the money is to be taken to Jerusalem and to be spent there" (Maimonides, *Mishneh Torah, Hilkhot Ma'aser Sheni Ve-Neta Revay* 4:1; cf. Zevahim 112b; Makkot 19a–b; Ma'aser Sheni, Ch. 4). In the case cited here, the person redeems the second tithe with money, but the individuation of the coins by which the *ma'aser sheni* is *now* being redeemed is accomplished by reference to an event which will occur later on: "the *sela* which I will bring up from my pocket" (see Rashi, Eruvin, *loc. cit., s.v. Rabbi Jose*).

29. Gittin 25a; Mishnah, Pesahim 89a.

30. Rashi, Gittin, *loc. cit., s.v. zakhah be-helko;* it is obvious and in

no need of special explanation, except that the paschal sacrifice is slaughtered only to include those who made previous arrangements to be part of the feast, and only they may eat of it (Pesahim 61a; Maimonides, *Mishneh Torah, Hilkhot Korban Pesah* 2:1).

31. See Rashi, Eruvin 37b, *s.v. Rabbi Jose;* Tosafot, *loc. cit., s.v. ela.*

32. M. Silberg, *Hok U-Musar BaMishpat HaIvri* (Jerusalem, 5712), p. 7.

33. Unspecified consecrations were used for the repairs of the Temple (Arakhin 24a; Maimonides, *Mishneh Torah, Hilkhot Arakhin Va-Haramin* 1:10).

34. Or other such uses; see Shekalim, Ch. 4.

35. Cf. R. Sohm, *Institutes of Roman Law,* 3rd ed., pp. 197–198; T. Mommsen, *Roemisches Staatsrecht* (Basel, 1952), Vol. II, Pt. I, pp. 59 ff.; Duff, *Personality in Roman Private Law,* pp. 174 ff.

36. Bava Kamma 20b–21a, and Rashi, *ibid.,* 20b *s.v. zot omeret.* This view was expressed in connection with the dispute whether "a person who lives in his neighbor's court without the latter knowing it, needs to pay rent, or not." And the interpretation of the present statement is that one who lives in a courtyard which is Temple property—it is always deemed to be with the awareness of the owner, for the *Shekhinah* knows of it. It is thus considered that the *Shekhinah* is, plain and simple, the owner of the court. But cf. Tosafot, *ibid.,* 21a, *s.v. ke-hedyot,* and *Shitah Mekubetzet,* Bava Kamma, *ibid.,* in the name of Rabbi Yeshaya and the Rashba; see and reflect on the matter.

37. *The Responsa of the Rashba,* ascribed to the Ramban (ed. Warsaw, 1883), sec. 222, p. 49a. This is also the view of A. Gulak, *Yesoday HaMishpat HaIvri* (Warsaw, 1913), Gate I, Ch. 2, para. 13; cf. Tosafot, Bava Kamma 76a, *s.v. hashta;* Rashi, *ibid., s.v. mukro le-hedyot,* and *Shitah Mekubetzet, ad loc.,* in the name of a pupil of Rabbi Peretz.

38. Bava Kamma 37b.

39. See the comments of the Bah to the Mishnah, *ibid.;* this is also the version of the *baraita, ibid.,* as quoted in our texts.

40. See Bava Metzia 56a–58b.

41. See *Tosefta,* ed. Zuckermandel, 2nd ed., with *Tosefta Supplement* by Prof. Saul Lieberman, Bava Kamma, 4:4 (Jerusalem, 5698), pp. 351–352. There a list is made of the elements in which the lay authority is greater than the "divine" authority and one in which

the "divine" authority is greater than the lay authority; the scales are almost balanced.

CHAPTER II: CASUISTIC FORM

1. Mishnah, Bava Kamma 9b.

2. Zechariah Frankel, *Darkhay HaMishnah* (ed. Sinai, 5719), p. 12; cf. H. Albeck, *Mavo LaMishnah*, Ch. 4.

3. Y. N. Epstein, *Mevo'ot LaSifrut HaTannaim* (Judah L. Magnes Press, Hebrew University, Jerusalem, 1957), p. 155. Cf. I. H. Weiss, *Dor Dor Ve-Dorshav* (Jerusalem, 5684), Pt. I, p. 69.

4. This is similar to the conception of solidarity in obligation by "joint wrongdoers" of Anglo-Eretz Yisraeli law. See section 10 of the Civil Wrongs Ordinance 1944.

5. Mishnah, Bava Kamma 2a.

6. Gemara, *op. cit.*, 2b–3a.

7. Mishnah and Gemara, Bava Kamma 23b–24b; Maimonides, *Mishneh Torah, Hilkhot Nizkay Mammon*, Ch. 6; cf. also *Shulhan Arukh, Hoshen Mishpat*, sec. 389.

8. Mishnah and Gemara, *op. cit.*, 17a–19a.

9. Mishnah, *ibid.*, 16b; in the case of "pebbles" he also pays half-damages. See Mishnah, *ibid.*, 17a.

10. Mishnah, *ibid.*, 16b; the "choicest" means the choicest property; "from the carcass" means from the carcass of the young animal and if its worth be less than the damages—the injured person sustains the loss.

11. For "tooth" and "foot" see Mishnah, *ibid.*, 19b; Gemara, *ibid.*, 3b and 5b; Maimonides, *Mishneh Torah, op. cit.*, 1:8; *Shulhan Arukh, Hoshen Mishpat*, sec. 389, para. 15.

12. For "fire" see Mishnah, *op. cit.*, 61b; Gemara, *ibid.*, 5b; Maimonides, *Mishneh Torah, op. cit.*, 14:8, 9, 11; *Shulhan Arukh, Hoshen Mishpat*, sec. 418, paras. 13, 14, 15.

13. For "pit" see Mishnah, *op. cit.*, 52a; Gemara, *ibid.*, 5b and 53b; Maimonides, *Mishneh Torah, op. cit.*, 13:1; *Shulhan Arukh, Hoshen Mishpat*, sec. 410, para. 21; cf. also Maimonides, *op. cit.*, laws 2, 3.

14. Bava Kamma 9b. In Yerushalmi, Bava Kamma 1:2, this *baraita* is taught in the name of Rabbi Hiya, and in the following version: "If I am responsible for the care of anything . . . Rabbi Hiya taught: 'This applies in the case of the ox and the pit; and fire he does not include?' Said Rabbi Jeremiah: 'In the case of fire he has legally prepared the damage caused. . . .'"

15. See *Shitah Mekubetzet*, Bava Kamma 9b, in the name of the Ri Katz, and infer.

16. "In the case of an ox that is tied down and a pit that is covered and similarly in the case of a live coal . . . the ox tends to loosen himself, the pit will tend to be uncovered, but a live coal grows dimmer; . . . in the case of an untied ox and an uncovered pit . . . we say that the watch of the deaf-mute was responsible, but in the latter case, we do not blame the watch of the deaf-mute" (*ibid.*). On careful examination we shall see that much of the substantive issue in these cases is the question of vicarious liability, though the feeling here is—in contradistinction to the position taken in the Anglo-*Eretz Yisraeli* law (secs. 11–13 of the Civil Wrongs Ordinance)—that the primary cause of negligence is in handing over the wrongdoer to an incompetent watchman.

17. Bava Kamma 10a. Note also the legal conclusions inferred in the Talmud from the consideration that the *baraita* could not exemplify the law except in the case of one who digs a pit.

18. Eruvin 27a, and Rashi, *ad loc.*: "We do not draw inferences from the use of a general term; where the Mishnah uses 'all' we do not assume exactness of terminology, because a general term is often used imprecisely, and there may be cases not meant to be included in this 'all' . . . and even where the text excludes a particular case from this generalization, allowing us to argue that since the text excluded this particular case, it was undoubtedly precise in its generalization— we nevertheless draw no inferences from it, for the author may have omitted, failing to exclude all he really wanted to exclude."

19. Y. N. Epstein, *Mavo LeNusah HaMishnah*, p. 239.

20. H. Albeck, *op. cit.*, Chs. 4, 6.

21. Zechariah Frankel, *Darkhay HaMishnah*, pp. 123, 221–224; Zevi Graetz, *Divray Yemay Yisrael*, 3rd ed. (Hebrew), Vol. III, pp. 76, 85; cf. also Jacob Bruell, *Mevo HuMishnah* (Frankfurt, 5645), Pt. II, p. 13.

22. H. Albeck, *op. cit.*, p. 106, and Appendix 6, pp. 270–283.

23. For example: "It was taught: This (the anonymous *mishnah*) is the *mishnah* of Rabbi Nathan; Rabbi Meir says, 'I do not follow the view of Rabbi Nathan, but they divide equally'" (Ketubot 93a).

24. Albeck, *op. cit.*, pp. 105–106. Actually this is also the view of Weiss, *Dor Dor Ve-Dorshav*, Pt. II, p. 209, who declares: "The primary rule to be adopted concerning the Mishnah is that Rabbi Judah HaNasi did not compose a code to teach the prevailing law, but a collection of laws which embrace the whole oral Torah," and,

as Albeck noted (*op. cit.*, p. 270), Weiss here contradicts what he wrote elsewhere on this subject.

25. See Rashbam, Bava Batra 65a, *s.v. kevuot*. Another more limited interpretation was given to this concept by Nahman Krochmal, *Moreh Nevukhay HaZeman* (ed. Berlin, 5683), Gate 13, p. 201. The conclusion of this statement in Bava Batra, "be careful with these, for these are 'established laws' [*halakhot kevuot*]," does not support Krochmal's interpretation.

26. For instance, Bava Kamma 46b: "How do we learn that the burden of proof is on the claimant? Because it is written (Exodus 24:14), 'Whoever has a claim, let him come to them,' which means, Let him bring the evidence to them. . . . But why do we need a text to prove this—it is common sense: Whoever feels the pain goes to the physician! But the verse is needed to support the statement of Rav Nahman in the name of Rabbah bar Avuha, for Rav Nahman said in the name of Rabbah bar Avuha: 'How do we know that the claim of the plaintiff is to be examined first, for it is written, "Whoever has a claim let him come to them." ' " Or Ketubot 22a: "How do we know that the lips which have created the prohibition may be trusted to create the permission, on the basis of a precedent in the Torah? Because it is written (Deuteronomy 22:16), 'My daughter have I betrothed to this man' (literally, 'to man this'); when he said to 'man' he made her forbidden to all men, but when he added 'to *this*,' he released her from the general prohibition and 'permitted' her to this man. But why do we need a text to prove this—it is common sense. . . . But the verse is needed to support the statement of Rav Huna in the name of Rav. . . ."

27. A classic illustration of this: Mishnah and Gemara, Bava Metzia 2a. Cf. also the exacting linguistic analysis, with the legal and other inferences drawn therefrom, in the first discussion in Kiddushin 2a–3a. It is noteworthy that such minutae of analysis are to be found for the most part in the beginning of a talmudic tractate, as in the two tractates mentioned above, and similarly in the beginning of Yevamot, Nedarim, Nazir, Zevahim, Menahot, and Hullin. I am not aware that anyone has called attention to this.

28. It may now be said that an affirmative answer has finally been given to the question whether the Mishnah was written down in the time of Rabbi Judah HaNasi or not. See Albeck, *op. cit.*, pp. 111–115; Zechariah Frankel, *op. cit.*, pp. 228–230; cf. Y. N. Epstein, *Mavo LeNusah HaMishnah*, pp. 692–702. An illustration of the analysis of individual words in the Mishnah is to be found in Hagigah 2a ("*all*

—what does this mean to include?"); Yevamot 20a ("the *rule* is— what does this mean to include?"); *ibid.,* 22a and 22b ("*nevertheless* —what does this mean to include?"); Ketubot 110b ("and not *all* may divorce—what does this mean to include?").

29. See note 28, *supra.*

30. Berakhot 2a.

31. *Remiah* [contradiction]—related to such terms as *u-reminhu, rami, rami ley merma* (Yevamot 13a; Bava Metzia 25b; Hullin 40a; Hagigah 7a; Pesahim 88a; Ketubot 27a; Bava Kamma 16a; Bava Batra 19a)—means literally "a throwing" or a confrontation of two texts which really or apparently negate each other. This term was coined by Rabbi Samuel HaNagid in his *Mevo HaTalmud* or by Rabbi Samuel ben Hofni, if he is the one, as some believe, who really wrote the *Mevo HaTalmud,* usually ascribed to Rabbi Samuel *HaNagid.*

32. The term *akvu* here used with the general meaning of "crushed" follows the usage in the statement of Rabbi Johanan in the name of Rabbi Ishmael (Sotah 16a), "the law crushes (*okevet*) a biblical verse." It is stated in *Tosefot Shantz, ad loc.:* "*okevet*—this means it removes its footstep and the place where it stood, and it uproots it." I use the term here to signify any "camouflaged" uprooting of the old law. Cf. Nahman Krochmal, *op. cit.,* Gate 13, p. 165.

33. *Asmakhta*—an apparent, or artificial source in which the law is grounded. In many instances, where the Sages supported their decisions by citing a biblical verse, it is stated, "This law is only of rabbinic origin, the verse is only an *asmakhta*" (Yoma 74a; Moed Katan 3a; Yevamot 21a, 24a, 52b, 72a; Bava Metzia 88b). The *asmakhta* of the verse lends greater authority and firmness to the law, and even in the case of later ordinances whose origin is well-known the Sages were particular—for this very reason—to parallel the form of their ordinance to a biblical institution: "Whatever the Sages ordained— they structured it like something paralleled in the Torah" (Pesahim 30b; Yoma 31a; Yevamot 11a; Gittin 65a). In explaining the Mishnah in their own way, the *Amoraim* used it as an *asmakhta* for their legal innovations.

34. *Ukimta*—literally "a placement": "we have placed it in consonance with Rabbi Judah" (Pesahim 11a); "in what situation did you place this statement of Samuel?" (Ketubot 64a); "let him place this statement in connection with the case of a robber" (Bava Batra 44a); "according to Rabbi Sheshet who placed this statement in a situation dealing with one who purchased from a robber" (Rashbam,

ad loc., s.v. u-makshinan; "he places this as dealing with charity and acts of lovingkindness" (Moed Katan 16b).

35. Ketubot 26a, 95a; Bava Kamma 8a–b, 114b; Ketubot 18b, 26b; Gittin 16a, 35a; Kiddushin 26a; Eruvin 97b; Ketubot 89a; Nedarim 37a; Gittin 46a. It is appropriate to note that at times the text of a *mishnah* is indeed defective, through an obvious omission, and "the statement is incomplete and was meant to read thus," restores the omitted part in the most logical way, as in Gittin 66a, Bava Metzia 86a, and elsewhere.

36. Ketubot 18b. The case dealt with here is that of the confirmation of documents—the confirmation of the witnesses' signatures—through the testimony of the witnesses themselves. Their testimony in this case is "broken": they testify that they signed the document, but they add that they acted under duress. The law according to the explanation of Rami bar Hama is thus: If they said that the duress affected their lives, they are believed in both elements of their testimony, and the document is rendered void (Maimonides, *Mishneh Torah, Hilkhot Edut* 3:6), but if they said that their duress affected money matters—"we took a bribe in connection with this testimony" —they are not believed, and the document is valid, "for a person may not render himself to be a wicked man, until witnesses testify that he is a wicked man" (Maimonides, *ibid.*, law 7).

37. Bava Kamma 8a–b. In the case cited, the owner had three fields —of choice, average and inferior quality, and he sold them all to another person, while he, at the same time, owed money to three claimants: a plaintiff in a tort action, a creditor, and his wife's *ketubah;* the choice field was purchased last. The law is that "compensation for damages is paid from the choice field, the creditor from the average, and the *ketubah* from the inferior" (Gittin 48b). But there is a rabbinic ordinance that "payment is not made from encumbered property (property sold to another) when there is unencumbered property" (property still in possession of the defendant). It thus turns out that after the average and the inferior had been sold and the choice still belonged to the original owner—being in the category of "unencumbered property"—it was on this, the choice field, that all claims were concentrated, and all the three claimants can demand that the purchaser make good their claim from the choice field. The counter-argument of the purchaser is: The ordinance was originally established for my benefit, allow me to tell the claimant: "I left you a place from which to satisfy your claim; now that all the fields are in my possession, and it turns out that the

ordinance is to my detriment, I say: 'I do not want this ordinance, and it is for you to collect according to the provisions of the original law, that is to say, the plaintiff from the choice, the creditor from the average, and the *ketubah* from the inferior.' "

Another, more practical example in which this concept is invoked is the allowance for the support of a wife: "A wife may say, 'I do not wish your support and I refuse to work' " (the source is in Ketubot 58b), "for the primary purpose of requiring a husband to support his wife is for her benefit, because at times her own earnings are insufficient for her maintenance. The Sages first established their basic ordinance that a husband support his wife, and later they ordained that her earnings should belong to him so as to avoid enmity; and since the primary purpose of the ordinance was for her benefit, when she claims that she does not wish this benefit, we heed her claim" (Rashi, *ad loc.*).

38. This concept is the basis for the law enunciated by Rami bar Hama and Rabbi Joseph, in Sanhedrin 9b, which involves a claim by a person: "So and so committed sodomy with me with my consent." Rava, who disagreed with Rabbi Joseph, also invokes the principle that a person may not render himself a wicked man, in prefacing this with the statement: "A person has the status of a near relative in relation to himself and he thus cannot testify against himself." But he arrives at the opposite conclusion, because of his view that we "divide his testimony," and we differentiate between the non-incriminating part of the testimony which is accepted, and the incriminating part which is not accepted. But why did Rava, who was a discussant in our case cited from the tractate Ketubot, fail to invoke there also the principle of "dividing his testimony"? Concerning this, see Tosafot, Sanhedrin, *loc. cit., s.v. ve-en adam; Kesef Mishneh* on Maimonides, *Mishneh Torah, Hilkhot Edut* 12:2.

39. Cf. the decision of Justice Silberg, *Dvik v. Lalo,* C.A. 99/49, 5 P.D. 625.

40. And similarly the interpretation by those who arranged the *baraitot* of the text of the Mishnah as in the example cited in the beginning of this chapter.

41. We shall cite a few examples from two tractates only, Ketubot and Bava Metzia which, as is well known, are the most important tractates dealing with civil law: Ketubot 26a–b ("we treat here with a case where the father of this person was presumed to be a priest, but a rumor arose . . . and one witness came . . . and then two witnesses came . . . and then one witness came . . ."); 32a ("this deals

with the one who was retarded and who was seduced"); 65b ("the *Tanna* was dealing with a mountainous region"); 72a ("the case dealt with a woman who claimed to her husband that a particular scholar had examined her blood flow and ruled her menstrually clean, and the husband checked and found that her statement had been false"); 109b ("this was a case where fields of other people surrounded his on all four sides"); Bava Metzia 2b ("the case refers to one who took money from two purchasers, from one willingly and from the other under duress"); 18a ("this refers to a case where caravans pass frequently . . . where two persons known to be called Joseph ben Simeon are known to reside in the same city"); 23b ("it makes a difference for returning it to a learned man on the basis of his recognizing it by sight"); 43a ("this refers to a case where the money was bound up and sealed . . . with an unusual knot"); 71a ("this case deals with scholars"); 76a ("this needs to be said in the case where he stipulated that their wages were to be paid by the owner . . . where some hire themselves out for four *zuzim* and some for three . . ."); 83a ("this needs to be said in a case where he added to their compensation"); 97b ("this deals with a case where the adjudication between them involves taking an oath"); 12b; these are all instances in which the Gemara adds some novel example to the circumstances cited in the law as formulated in the Mishnah.

42. See above, section 2 of this chapter.

43. "It is impossible for a meeting of the academy to be held without bringing forth some new insight" (Hagigah 3a).

44. In truth it must be indicated here that at times the commentators and the formulators of law prevailed also over principles which were cited in general abstract form and limited them through the addition of qualifications. Consider, for example, the general principle of Rava, "any act which the Torah declares must not be done, if he did it, it is devoid of legal efficacy" (Temurah 4b), and cf. Tosafot, *op. cit.*, 6a, *s.v. ve-hashta; Sema, Hoshen Mishpat*, sec. 208, para. 1, small para. 3; *Shakh, Hoshen Mishpat, loc. cit.; Taz, Hoshen Mishpat, loc. cit.; Responsa of Maharam Alshikh*, sec. 75; *Responsa Panim Me'irot*, Pt. I, sec. 34; *Responsa of Rabbi Akiba Eger*, sec. 129. See decision of Justice Silberg, *Jacobs v. Cartuz*, C.A. 110/53, 9 *P.D.* 1401. Or the principle, "there is no deputy to perform an illegal act" (Kiddushin 42b) and cf. the qualifications applied to this principle on the basis of the talmudic statement in Bava Metzia 10b, among others, by Tosafot Bava Metzia, *ad loc., s.v. de-amar; Shitah*

Mekubetzet, ad loc.; Ketzot HaHoshen, Hoshen Mishpat, sec. 105, end of small para. 1; *ibid.,* sec. 182, para. 1, small para. 2.

45. Bava Kamma 27a.

46. Bava Batra 143a.

47. Hullin 70a.

CHAPTER III: EVASION OF THE LAW

1. Yerushalmi, Yevamot 4:12.

2. Leviticus 22:10; Sanhedrin 83a; Ketubot 30b; Maimonides, *Mishneh Torah, Hilkhot Terumot* 6:5.

3. Mishnah, Eduyot 7:9; Niddah 44b; Gittin 28a; Maimonides, *op. cit.,* law 3. A priest's wife has the status of one "acquired by him through purchase" in the sense of Leviticus 22:11 (Ketubot 57b).

4. See the version of the story in Tosefta, Ketubot 5:5.

5. Kiddushin 71a; Bekhorot 51b.

6. Nedarim 62a.

7. "According to biblical law, the daughter of an Israelite who has been betrothed to a priest may eat *terumah,* for it is written (Leviticus 22:11), 'and if a priest should acquire a person by purchase,' and the betrothed also has the status of one who has been acquired by purchase. Why then did the Sages say that she may not eat (that is, that she does not eat *terumah* until after the consummation of the marriage)? It is a precaution lest they give her a cup of *terumah* wine to drink in her father's house, and she give it to her brother or sister" (Ketubot 57b). Rabbi Tarfon had only betrothed those women, but he nevertheless gave them *terumah* to eat, "because it was a time of famine" (*Tosefta,* Ketubot, *loc. cit.,* ed. Zuckermandel, 2nd ed., with *Tosefta Supplement* by Prof. Saul Lieberman, Jerusalem, 5690).

8. Mishnah, Ma'aser Sheni 4:5; Bava Metzia 45b–46a.

9. Maimonides, *Mishneh Torah, Hilkhot Matnot Aniyim* 6:4; *Hilkhot Ma'aser Sheni Ve-Neta Revay* 1:1.

10. "You shall tithe a tenth part of all the field of your sowing . . . and you shall eat it before the Lord your God in the place He will choose to establish His name" (Deuteronomy 14:22, 23); Zevahim 112b; Temurah 21a–b; Mishnah, Bikkurim 2:2; Maimonides, *Mishneh Torah, Hilkhot Ma'aser Sheni Ve-Neta Revay* 2:1.

11. "Should the distance be too great for you, should you be unable to transport them . . . you shall convert them into money, and

wrap up the money and take it with you to the place the Lord your God has chosen" (Deuteronomy 14:24, 25); Maimonides, *ibid.*, 4:1.

12. "If a person wishes to redeem any of his tithes, he must add one-fifth to them" (Leviticus 27:31); Mishnah, Ma'aser Sheni 4:3; Maimonides, *ibid.*, 5:1.

13. "If the person redeeming the tithe does not own the tithe and the redemption money, he does not add the fifth" (Yerushalmi, Ma'aser Sheni 4:4; Kiddushin 24a and Rashi, *ad loc., s.v. ishah podah;* Maimonides, *ibid.*, laws 7–11.

14. Rashi, Bava Metzia 46a, *s.v. dehakhi adif;* also Gemara, *loc. cit.*

15. Mishnah, Ma'aser Sheni 4:4.

16. Mishnah, Yevamot 112b; Maimonides, *Mishneh Torah, Hilkhot Gerushin* 2:17; *Shulhan Arukh, Even HaEzer,* sec. 121.

17. "A prohibited degree of near relations" is any woman that a person will bring on himself the penalty of *karet* [excision] by cohabiting with her, and his wife's sister is in this category (Mishnah, Keritot 1:1). Cf. Maimonides, *Mishneh Torah, Hilkhot Isuray Biah* 1:1.

18. Mishnah, Yevamot 20a, and see Rashi, *ad loc., s.v. lo holetzet;* Maimonides, *Mishneh Torah, Hilkhot Yibum Va-Halitzah* 6:9; *Shulhan Arukh, Even HaEzer,* sec. 173, para. 1.

19. "Do not marry a woman as a rival to her sister and uncover her nakedness in the other's lifetime" (Leviticus 18:18); Yevamot 8b; *Shulhan Arukh, Even HaEzer,* sec. 15, para. 26.

20. Cf. *H. v. H.* (1953), 2 All E.R. 1233–1234; *Martens v. Martens* (1952), 3 South African L.R. 771; *aliter: United States v. Rubinstein* (1945), 151 Fed. R., 2nd Series, 915.

21. The decision of Justice Silberg, C.A. 238/53, *Kohen-Buslik v. Attorney General,* 8 *P.D.* 4, p. 34.

22. On the connection between the obligation to provide sustenance and the eating of *terumah,* cf. Mishnah, Ketubot 57a, and the discussion of the Gemara, *ad loc.* There is no contradiction between this conception and the derivation of the law from the verse "acquired through purchase" (Leviticus 22:11), *op. cit.,* 57b.

23. See the *Hagahot HaBah* [critical notes] on Nedarim 48a, *hagahah* 2.

24. Mishnah, Nedarim 48a.

25. Yerushalmi, Nedarim, end of Ch. *HaShutfin,* and, according to the version of the Ran, Nedarim 48a.

26. Rashi, Nedarim 32b, *s.v. eyn beyn ha-mudar*. Cf. the juxtaposition of *mudar* and *nadur*, Nedarim 46a.

27. Mishnah, Nedarim 47b; Maimonides, *Mishneh Torah, Hilkhot Nedarim* 5:1; *Shulhan Arukh, Yoreh De'ah*, sec. 224, para. 1.

28. The Radbaz on Maimonides, *loc. cit.*; cf. the discussion of the Talmud, Nedarim 47a–b.

29. Beth-Horon, a city in the portion allotted to the tribe of Ephraim, about 20 kilometers northwest of Jerusalem, which is mentioned many times in the Bible and the Talmud. See Joshua 10:10 (*ma'alay* Beth-Horon); 16:3, 5; 21:22; I Samuel 13:18; I Chronicles 6:53; 7:24; II Chronicles 8:5; Sanhedrin 32b (*be-ma'alot* Beth-Horon); Berakhot 54a (*be-morad* Beth-Horon); and elsewhere. According to the view of S. Klein (*Sefer HaYishuv*, Vol. I, p. 14), Beth-Horon corresponds to the Arab village Beth Or of our time. Cf. also the *Encyclopedia Ivrit*, Vol. 8, pp. 606–607.

30. See the commentary of the Ran on Nedarim 48a, *s.v. ve-hayah mesi*.

31. Since one who is interdicted by a vow from enjoying any benefit from his neighbor may not enter his courtyard. See Nedarim 45b–46b.

32. The text in our Mishnah reads *be-rosho* which means literally "on his head," but the intended meaning is as though written *be-roshi* which means "on *my* head." When the subject discussed is an affliction, a curse, or a punishment, the tendency is to employ a euphemism and speak in the third person, rather than the first. Thus in the Talmud: ". . . and when his relatives saw this—that the crop of his field continues to diminish because he is disdainful of the commandment to contribute the tithes—they robed themselves in white, and came before him. He said to them: 'Did you come to rejoice because *this man* is under the ban?' . . ." (*Pesikta De-Rav Kahana*, ed. *Mekitzay Nirdamim*, 1868, p. 96a; it is also cited, with slight verbal changes, in the *Yalkut Shimoni* and the *Midrash Tanhuma, Re'eh*, on the verse "You shall tithe a tenth" [Deuteronomy 14:22]). [However, the Cambridge and Kaufmann manuscripts of the Mishnah have in the Mishnah text concerning the gift of Beth-Horon the term *be-roshi* which involves no euphemism but means explicitly "on my head."]

33. See note 25, *supra*.

34. "One who is interdicted from deriving a benefit from his neighbor and does not have what to eat, the maker of the vow may make a presentation to a third person and the interdicted person is

then permitted to use it." This is the opening clause of the Mishnah, Nedarim 48a.

35. Gittin 83a; see *ibid.*, 82a–b.

36. The commentary of the Ran on Gittin, Ch. *HaMegaresh.* What would be the law if the husband's condition were "that you do not enter a fully legal marriage with so-and-so"? In this instance, in my opinion, the divorce would be valid and the stipulation void. For the violation of the condition would usher in a vicious cycle which could never be ended—the violation will invalidate the divorce and the invalidation of the divorce will invalidate the violation and activate the divorce, and this would be repeated endlessly, and this is—analogically—like an impossible, positive condition ("on the condition that you ascend to heaven"), in which case we regard the person making the stipulation as "indulging in words in the spirit of humor and sport" (Gittin 84a; Maimonides, *Mishneh Torah, Hilkhot Ishut* 6:7), and the act remains valid as though no condition were attached to it.

37. Cf. the dictum "the verbal dedication to the Lord is the same as actual transfer to an ordinary person" (Kiddushin 28b, and many other sources elsewhere).

38. Buckland, *Manual of Roman Private Law,* 2nd ed., pp. 260–261.

39. Bava Kamma 70a; Maimonides, *Mishneh Torah, Hilkhot Sheluhin Ve-Shutafin* 3:1; *Shulhan Arukh, Hoshen Mishpat,* sec. 122, para. 4.

40. Bava Kamma, *ibid.;* Maimonides, *ibid.*

41. Bava Kamma, *ibid.*

42. Bava Kamma, *ibid.,* see Rashi, *ad loc., s.v. Rav Ashi palig.*

43. This is a striking expression used in the *Hidushay HaRashba* on Shevuot 33b (ed. Amsterdam, 1813, p. 16, 4th side, bottom).

44. *Hidushay HaRashba,* p. 16, 2nd side.

45. Sohm, *The Institutes of Roman Law,* 3rd ed., p. 63, note 15.

46. The English translation of the excerpt is not altogether exact. The German original states: "Der fiduziarische Vorbehalt hatte nicht bloss verpflichtende, sondern *dingliche* Wirkung. Es war ein anderes, *in sich beschraenktes Eigentum,* das Treuhaender-Eigentum, als das normale Eigentum" (Sohm, *Institutionen des Roemischen Rechts,* 14th ed., p. 75, note 15).

47. Cf. Jolowicz, *Historical Introduction to Roman Law* (Cambridge, 1932), p. 295, to note 5; Joers-Kunkel-Wenger, *Roemisches*

Recht, 3rd ed., p. 95; Kaser, *Das Roemische Privatrecht* (1955), pp. 42, 127; *aliter:* Sohm, cited by Jolowicz, *ibid.*

48. The Phoenician *maneh,* which is 25 *sela* or 100 *zuz* (see Bekhorot 49b–50a; Rashi, Bava Kamma 90b, *s.v. maneh zuri*).

49. Bava Metzia 62b.

50. Maimonides, *Mishneh Torah, Hilkhot Malveh Ve-Loveh* 5:15.

51. "You shall not give him your money on interest nor give him your food for profit" (Leviticus 25:37).

52. Quasi-interest is a transaction which does not involve real interest, and is therefore not forbidden by the Torah, but only by an enactment of the Rabbis. All interest—according to the well-known definition of Rabbi Nahman (Bava Metzia 63b)—involves "compensation for waiting," that is, the waiting of the creditor for the repayment of the debt, except that according to the Torah interest is forbidden only if the debt was contracted through a loan, and not through buying and selling or some other similar transaction; if the amount of interest was fixed initially; if it is definite or practically definite; if it was stipulated at the time of the loan and not later on. According to rabbinic enactment, however, interest is forbidden even where one of the above conditions was not met, as in the cases dealt with (on the basis of talmudic sources) in Maimonides, *ibid.,* 5:8, 11; 6:2, 3, 7; 7:5; 8:1. In the case dealt with here the view of Maimonides is that it does not involve even "quasi-interest" for it consists of a transaction in two parts, each of which is an ordinary sale. The Rashba shares the view of Maimonides (*Magid Mishneh* on Maimonides, *ibid.,* 5:15); and so does the *Bet Yosef* on the *Tur,* sec. 163, at end; *Shulhan Arukh, Yoreh De'ah,* sec. 163, para. 3 (see *Be'er HaGolah, ad loc.,* small para. 6). The words (in the *Shulhan Arukh, loc. cit.*) "it is forbidden to pay in money" mean, apparently, that it is forbidden to stipulate payment in money. Another explanation is found in *Tur, Yoreh De'ah,* sec. 163, end, in the name of the Ramban and the Rosh; Rama, *Shulhan Arukh, Yoreh De'ah,* sec. 163, para. 3.

53. Interest is forbidden both on the lender and the borrower (Bava Metzia 61a; Maimonides, *ibid.,* 4:2; *Shulhan Arukh, Yoreh De'ah,* sec. 160, para. 1).

54. "It is a precaution lest he came to accept the interest which is forbidden in the Torah" (Maimonides, *ibid.,* 6:1).

55. Bava Batra 82a.

56. Berakhot 17b.

57. See note 52, *supra.*

58. Cf. Bava Metzia 61b; Maimonides, *ibid.*, 4:6.

59. Sanhedrin 21b; see *infra*, Ch. 5, note 1.

60. If it is not "a law handed down to Moses at Sinai" in terms of the unique definition by Maimonides in the introduction to his commentary on the Mishnah; see Albeck, *Mavo LaMishnah*, pp. 26–27.

61. It may well be that this is the original meaning of the statement: "In all that the Sages ordained, they followed the parallel of the Torah"—all that the Sages ordained, they did so according to the law of the Torah—though as used in the Talmud, in all the eight cases where it is cited (Pesahim 30b; 39b; 116b; Yoma 31a; Yevamot 11a; Gittin 64b–65a; Bekhorot 54a) its meaning is that the laws of a rabbinic enactment were structured according to the characteristics of the laws of the Torah. This practical bond between the two reflects the deep inner connection between the laws of the Torah and the laws enacted by the Rabbis.

62. Mishnah, Sheviit 10:1, 3, 4. Cited with minor verbal modification in Gemara, Gittin 36a.

63. "And this is the manner of release: every creditor shall release that which he has lent his neighbor" (Deuteronomy 15:2); "it is a positive commandment to cancel the debt in the sabbatical year, for it is written 'every creditor shall release that which he has lent his neighbor'" (Maimonides, *Mishneh Torah, Hilkhot Shemitah Ve-Yovel* 9:1); "money due for a purchase in a shop is not cancelled in the sabbatical year, but if it was arranged in the form of a loan it is cancelled; wages due for a hired workman is not cancelled, but if it was arranged in the form of a loan it is cancelled" (Maimonides, *ibid.*, law 11). The source for these rulings is in Mishnah, Sheviit 10:1. "It is called 'arranged in the form of a loan' if he fixed a time for payment . . . and others say, 'at the time when the entire amount due was entered in the ledger'" (Rama, *Hoshen Mishpat*, sec. 67, para. 14).

64. Digest 46, 2, 6: *Novatio est prioris debiti in aliam obligationem vel civilem vel naturalem transfusio atque translatio.*

65. See Maimonides, *Mishneh Torah, ibid.*, 10:4; Rosh on Avodah Zarah, Ch. 1, sec. 6; see also the long responsum of the Ralbah, sec. 143 (ed. Lemberg, 1865, pp. 48a–52b, which deals with various calculations for fixing the sabbatical year).

66. *Sifre, Re'eh*; Arakhin 28b; Maimonides, *ibid.*, 9:4: "and at sunset in the evening of Rosh Hashanah at the conclusion of the sabbatical year the debt is voided."

67. Salo Baron, *A Social and Religious History of the Jews* (New

York, 1952), 2nd ed., Vol. II, Ch. XIV, p. 262; according to Klausner, *History of the Jews* (Hebrew), 5684, p. 76, the economic transformation began in the time of John Hyrcanus.

68. Cited in Baron, *op. cit.,* p. 417, note 39.

69. Tosafot, Gittin 36a, *s.v. mi ika.*

70. Mishnah, Sheviit 10:2, end; Makkot 3b; according to Rashi in Makkot, *ad loc.,* "the transfer of notes to the Court is the *prozbol* ordained by Hillel." But this is a minority view, and many challenge this. The Tosafot, *ad loc.,* demonstrated from the idiom employed in the Mishnah that this is not correct, but that "whoever transfers his notes to the Court—the debt will not be cancelled according to the law of the Torah." Moreover, the Yerushalmi, Sheviit 10:2, derives this position from the verse "but whatever of yours is with your brother, your hand shall release" (Deuteronomy 15:2). The *Sifre* on Deuteronomy—which is a much earlier source (see Sanhedrin 86b, and cf. Weiss, *Dor Dor Ve-Dorshav,* Vol. II, pp. 225–239)—derives the above law from the very same verse. It is thus clear that the law concerning the transfer of the notes to the Court predates the *prozbol.*

71. "And in the case of this one (that is, the one who transfers his notes), the Court makes the claim" (Maimonides, *ibid.,* 9:15); "for it is not you who collects, but the Court (*Penay Moshe* on Yerushalmi, *loc. cit.*).

72. See the texts of the *prozbol*—1, 2, 8, 9, 11, 14—cited in the supplement to the volume by Y. Z. Kahane, *Shemitat Kesafim* (Jerusalem, 5705), pp. 191–196. Note especially texts 2 and 14 in which the two-fold legal aims cited above come to full expression: the transfer of the debt to the Court, and the authorization to collect which the Court grants to the creditor.

73. Gittin 36b, and Rashi, *ad loc., s.v. ulbana.*

74. Gittin, *ibid.*

75. Tosafot, Gittin 36a, *s.v. mi ika.*

76. Exodus 16:29.

77. Jeremiah 17:21–22.

78. A talmudic *aggadah* (Eruvin 21b and Shabbat 14b) states: "When King Solomon established the *eruv* . . . a heavenly voice declared: 'My son, if your heart is wise, my heart too will rejoice.'" The profound thought which this statement implies is, in my view, that the Giver of the Torah Himself wanted that the Sages shall come later on with their ordinances and safeguard the observance of the Sabbath, that the "delight of Sabbath" shall not become an

"affliction." But from Rashi's comment (Eruvin, *loc. cit., s.v. Shlomoh tikayn*) and from the statement of Maimonides (*Mishneh Torah, Hilkhot Eruvin* 1:4, 5) it appears that King Solomon established simultaneously a preventive decree and a mitigating ordinance: he decreed against carrying an object [on the Sabbath] from a private to a public domain, which had been permitted in the Torah, and he established as a compensating measure the institution of the *eruv*. Cf. also Rashi, Shabbat, *loc. cit., s.v. eruvin,* and Maimonides, *op. cit.,* law 1. On the subject of the *"eruv* of the courts" and the "partnership in an alley," the "pole" [*lehi*] as a Sabbath marker, and the "form of the doorway"—see Maimonides, *ibid.,* laws 6, 7, 16, 17, and *Hilkhot Shabbat,* Ch. 17; *Shulhan Arukh, Orah Hayim,* sec. 362, para. 11; sec. 363; sec. 386; and elsewhere, *ibid.,* in the laws of the Sabbath.

79. Leviticus 25:37.

80. See *Nahalat Shivah,* sec. 40.

CHAPTER IV: QUANTIFICATION

1. M. Silberg, *Hok U-Musar BaMishpat HaIvri,* p. 23.

2. Although, in specific cases, the decision was in favor of an abstract principle, as: "If a person kindled a fire on his own premises, beyond what precautionary distance will the spread of the fire involve no culpability for the owner? . . . Rabbi Eliezer says: 'sixteen cubits, the equivalent of a road on a public thoroughfare.' Rabbi Akiba says: 'fifty cubits.' Rabbi Simeon says: 'it all depends on the height of the column of fire'" (Mishnah, Bava Kamma 61b). The law follows the latter opinion (Gemara, *loc. cit.;* Maimonides, *Mishneh Torah, Hilkhot Nizkay Mammon* 14:2; *Shulhan Arukh, Hoshen Mishpat,* sec. 418, para. 3).

3. Mishnah and Gemara, Bava Batra 23b. Rabbi Jeremiah was an expert questioner who loved to exasperate his teacher, Rabbi Zera, and to bring him to a point of laughing. It is told of him in the tractate Niddah, 23a: "Rabbi Jeremiah asked his teacher Rabbi Zera, 'According to Rabbi Meir (Mishnah, Niddah 21a) who holds that "a beast that was in a woman's body is a valid birth" (and the woman will require the usual rite of purification, forty days of impurity followed by purification in the case of a male, and eighty days in the case of a female) what if its father received for it a token of betrothal?' . . . Said Rav Aha bar Yakov: 'This is how far Rabbi Jeremiah sought to bring Rabbi Zera to laughter, but he did not

laugh.' " But Rabbi Jeremiah's question here about the bird seems to have been in greater earnestness, and bore a criticism on the fixation of precise measurements. Additional questions of this order by Rabbi Jeremiah are also found elsewhere, for instance in Rosh Hashanah 13a; Sotah 16b.

4. "A hopping bird" [*medadah*] is a bird that cannot fly but hops little by little (Rashi in Bava Batra, *loc. cit., s.v. hakha be-mai askinan*).

5. Mishnah and Gemara, Ketubot 104a.

6. Rashi, *ibid., s.v. va-hakhamim omrim*.

7. "Since she is not with the heirs, she cannot claim: 'I was embarrassed to make a claim against them as we are in the same household' " (Maimonides, *Mishneh Torah, Hilkhot Ishut* 16:23).

8. "If she did make a claim she resumes her original status, and has another span of twenty-five years to repeat her claim" (Gemara and Rashi, Ketubot 104a–b; *Shulhan Arukh, Hoshen Mishpat*, sec. 101, para. 1).

9. Leviticus 15:16.

10. Eruvin 4b; Pesahim 109a–b; cf. Maimonides, *Mishneh Torah, Hilkhot Mikvaot* 4:1.

11. ". . . that his entire body can get into it, which gives the appearance that he is totally covered by it" (Rashi, Pesahim, *loc. cit., s.v. kol besaro*).

12. *Se'ah* is a dry as well as a wet measure, and it is the equivalent of a third of an *ephah* (Menahot 76b) or of twenty-four *log* (Yerushalmi, Terumot 10:7). The *log* is approximately half a liter in weight (see Commentary on Mishnah by Hanoch Albeck, Menahot 9:2).

13. A *kurtuv* is "an eighth of an eighth" of a *log* or the sixty-fourth part of it. This is the reading in the text of the Talmud as we have it in Bava Batra 90a, and this is also the opinion of Rashi and Tosafot in Rosh Hashanah 13a, *s.v. haser kurtuv;* Maimonides, Commentary on Mishnah, Mikvaot 3:1, as well as others. But according to the Tosefta cited by the Rashbam in Bava Batra, *loc. cit., s.v. va-hazi sheminit,* a *kurtuv* is one sixteenth of a *log*. However, as far as the pool for ritual immersion "and not a *kurtuv* less" is really an imprecise statement, for "even less than this, even minus a drop, disqualifies it for ritual immersion" (Tosafot, Rosh Hashanah, *loc. cit.*).

14. Rashi, Ketubot, *loc. cit.*

15. Leviticus 25:4.

16. Rosh Hashanah 9a; Moed Katan 3b–4a; and elsewhere.

17. Rosh Hashanah 12b.

18. Rosh Hashanah 13a.

19. *Ibid.*

20. "A particle of food will not contaminate another particle of food . . . unless the contaminating particle is the size of an egg minus its shell": Maimonides, *Mishneh Torah, Hilkhot Tumat Okhalin* 4:1 (according to one opinion cited by Rashi in Pesahim 33b, *s.v. be-kebeza,* the food to be subject to contamination must also be the size of an egg). The source for this is Yoma 80a, where it is stated in the name of Rabbi Abbahu: " 'of every food that is eaten' (Leviticus 11:34), this implies that it must be of a size that can be eaten in one act of swallowing, and the Sages estimated that the swallowing organ cannot hold more than the size of the egg of a chicken." Rashi in Rosh Hashanah 13a alters the language somewhat and writes thus: "and the Sages have established that the swallowing organ cannot contain more or less than the egg of a chicken."

21. "Contaminates a seating area with ritual uncleanliness"—the latter becomes subject to the ritual uncleanliness of a seating area. "The impurity of a seating area" which results from sitting or lying by a man or woman who had an emission, or a menstruous woman, etc. is not applicable to garments of wool or flax unless their length and width were at least three cubits; the impurity contaminated by a dead body or other sources of impurity apply to them if they are three finger-lengths square. In the case of other garments, they become subject to impurity if they are three cubits square (Maimonides, *Mishneh Torah, Hilkhot Kelim* 22:1; Shabbat 26b–27a; Mishnah, Kelim 27:2). The reason for all this is that the Sages estimated that an area of these dimensions is suitable to sit on (Rashi, Rosh Hashanah 13a).

22. Here is an aggregate of various other illustrations culled at random, according to the order of tractates in the Talmud: "Two ears of grain dropped by the harvester is gleaning which belongs to the poor, but three is not" (Mishnah, Peah 6:5). "Whoever possesses two hundred *zuz* is not entitled to the poor man's perquisites of gleanings, forgotten sheaves, and the corner crop; if he had two hundred minus one, he may accept them even if a thousand farmers offer them simultaneously" (*ibid.,* 8:8). "If a person purchases two trees in his neighbor's field, he brings to the Temple the first fruits, but does not read the prescribed passage . . . but if he purchases three trees he brings the first fruits and reads the passage" (Mishnah, Bikkurim 1:6, 11, and cf. Bava Batra 27a and 81a–b). "What must be

the quantity of food used in the *eruv* which fixes the city limits for movement on the Sabbath? Food for two meals for each person in the community to be benefitted by the *eruv*. . . . Rabbi Simeon says: two-thirds of a loaf when three are made out of one *kav* of grain . . . the eating of half of such a loaf is the duration for a person to remain in a "leprous" house and become ritually impure, and half of this half is the quantity of ritually impure food which will communicate impurity to one who eats it" (Eruvin 82b). "The duration of seclusion with another man to give ground to the husband's suspicion and the duration of sexual intercourse" (Sotah 4a). "A goring ox resumes his status of innocence if he desists from goring for three days" (this is the opinion of Rabbi Judah, Bava Kamma 23b). Two estimates of the "duration of an utterance" (*ibid.*, 73b). A dab of fruit scattered over four ells (Bava Metzia 21a). "On finding the following he must make public proclamation . . . three coins one on top of the other . . . provided they are arranged as a pyramid" (*ibid.*, 24a–b). "An overcharge in the purchase, if it is less than a sixth the purchase remains valid; if more than a sixth it becomes invalid; if a sixth the purchase is valid but the amount overcharged is to be returned" (*ibid.*, 50b). "A nest of pigeons must be placed at least fifty ells from the city" (Bava Batra 23a). "The presumption of ownership of a house is established after uncontested occupancy for three years, from day to day" (*ibid.*, 28a, and cf. the discussion in the Gemara). "The placenta which emerges within three days after childbirth is assumed to be that of the child, but thereafter the possibility that there had been a second child in the womb to whom this placenta belonged must be considered" (Niddah 26b). "Intercourse as a means of betrothal is invalid if the girl is less than three years and a day old; such intercourse is deemed as putting the finger to the eye" (*ibid.*, 44b). Various additional examples might be cited.

23. See *supra*, note 13, end.

24. The concept "a statistical law of nature" has become well recognized in modern physics. This concept, for example, is invoked to explain the causes for the emergence of microscopic matter. In this realm and certainly in the sub-atomic realm, determinative causation means behavior patterns, approximate and not absolutely certain, which characterize the generality of things rather than the particular individuals. See Bohm, *Causality and Chance in Modern Physics,* 1957, pp. 22, 81ff.; Margenau, *Nature of Physical Reality,* 1950, Ch. 18; Lenzen, *Causality in Natural Science,* p. 98.

25. Ketubot 86a; Silberg, *Hok U-Musar BaMishpat HaIvri,* pp.

9–10. From the point of view of our thesis it would make no difference if the repayment of a debt is only a positive commandment or whether it also involves the negative commandments which caution against robbery and oppression. See *infra*, note 30.

26. Mishnah, Peah 1:1. Even performance of all the commandments of the Torah is not equal to the study of one item of Torah (Yerushalmi, Peah 1:1 and cf. the commentary *Penay Moshe*).

27. The term used in the Talmud is *piska de-dina* (Bava Batra 130b). The term *umai piska* (Ketubot 76b, 102b, and Nedarim 36b) does not mean a determination of the case involving two concrete litigants, but a general determination of the law. See *ibid*. On the other hand the term *pesak* occurs in the Talmud with a variety of other meanings.

28. Deuteronomy 17:8–10.

29. Exodus 18:20.

30. *Sefer HaHinukh*, Commandment 228: "that we must not retain what we hold which really belongs to another, through the use of force, or through evasion and deception as is done by iniquitous people who put off the claimant with the evasive suggestion to return another time so as to continue holding what they have which is not theirs . . . for whoever holds on to money belonging to another in this fashion is called an oppressor . . . and included in this category of oppression is the case of one who owes his neighbor money held by oppressive means, as the wages of hired workmen and the like, for this offense does not necessarily involve an actual transfer of funds from the oppressed to the oppressor . . . and although oppression and robbery and theft are all one, even though the action by which it is acquired differs, since our goal in dealing with each is to prevent a person from possessing what does not belong to him under any circumstances . . . the text, therefore, particularizes each separately and cautions against each separately." All that is stated here is equally applicable to money not acquired by actual "oppression"; thus we find in the *Responsa Darkhay Noam, Yoreh De'ah*, sec. 54 (note 40, *infra*), that non-payment of a debt to the lender is described as "robbery."

31. Decision of Justice Silberg in C.A. 248/53, *Rosenbaum v. Zager,* 9 *P.D.* 533, pp. 548 ff.

32. "The general principle of usury is that all compensation for waiting for one's money is forbidden" (Bava Metzia 63b; Rama, *Yoreh De'ah*, sec. 161, para. 1). Usury is payment for waiting for one's money.

33. Bava Metzia 44a–45a, Gemara and Rashi, *ad loc.;* Rif, Bava Metzia, beginning of chapter *HaZahav,* and *Nimukay Yosef, ibid.; Tur, Yoreh De'ah,* sec. 162; *Responsa Maharit Tzahalon,* sec. 33; *Shitah Mekubetzet,* Bava Metzia, beginning of chapter *Ezehu Neshekh,* citation in the name of the Ravad.

34. Bava Metzia 44b.

35. See Rashi, Bava Metzia, *ibid., s.v. iy amarat bishloma dahava* and *s.v. hava ley se'ah be-se'ah.*

36. *Bet Yosef* on *Tur Yoreh De'ah,* sec. 165; *Responsa Vayomer Yitzhak* on *Hoshen Mishpat,* sec. 154; *Responsa Shevut Ya'akov,* Vol. II, sec. 175; *Responsa Hatam Sofer,* on *Hoshen Mishpat,* sec. 58; cf. on the other hand the *Responsa of the Rashdam, Yoreh De'ah,* sec. 224; *Responsa Hikray Lev, Hoshen Mishpat,* sec. 154, in the name of the Ri Basan.

37. On the conception that the essence of a coin is its nominal value see Nussbaum, *Money in the Law,* 1950, pp. 17–18, 171–172, 350–351; Mann, *The Legal Aspect of Money,* 2nd ed., pp. 69–74, 103–104.

38. Bava Metzia, Mishnah and Gemara 65a; Maimonides, *Mishneh Torah, Hilkhot Malveh Ve-loveh* 7:8, 8:1; *Shulhan Arukh, Yoreh De'ah,* sec. 173, para. 1 and sec. 176, para. 6.

39. Bava Metzia 61a, 75b; Maimonides, *Mishneh Torah, Hilkhot Malveh Ve-Loveh* 4:2; *Shulhan Arukh, Yoreh De'ah,* sec. 160, para. 1, and cf. para. 4.

40. *Responsa Darkhay Noam, Yoreh De'ah,* sec. 54.

41. *Snook v. Grand Junction Waterworks Co. Ltd.* (1886), 2 T.L.R. 308; *Blyth v. Birmingham Waterworks Co.* (1856), 156 E.R. 1047.

42. *Bullock v. Bullock* (1886), 55 L.T. 703; *Stuart v. Stuart* (1897), 77 L.T. 128; *Dive v. Roebuck* (1909), 1 Ch. 328.

43. *Hobbs v. L. et S. W. Ry.* (1875), 32 L.T. 352; *Wyatt v. Great Western Ry. Co.* (1865), 122 E.R. 1356; *Sharp v. Powell* (1872), 26 L.T. 436.

44. See judgment of Justice Agranat, C.A. 406/46, *Perl v. Saltzman,* 1 *Pess.* 358; C.A. 59/43, 43 P.L.R. 203; C.A. 120/41, 41 Applebaum 350.

45. Paragraph 39 of the Magna Carta, 1215, provides that no free man shall be punished "nisi per legale judicium parium suorum vel per *legem terrae.*"

46. *Vide* Prof. S. Glaser, "Nullum Crimen Sine Lege," in *Journal of Comparative Legislation and International Law,* 3rd Series, Vol. 24,

Pt. 1, pp. 29–37; Jerome Hall, "Nulla Poena Sine Lege," in *Yale Law Journal*, Vol. 47, Dec. 1937, pp. 165–193.

47. A teacher taught: If they did not execute (the accused)—the witnesses against him who were refuted subsequently by other witnesses are themselves executed, but if they executed him, they are not executed. His father said to him: My son, but does it not follow *a fortiori*, that if the accused were executed, the witnesses against him who were refuted should be executed? He said to him: Master, you have taught us that we do not impose penalties on basis of law derived by logical inference. For it was taught: And if a man should wed his sister, the daughter of his father or his mother, that is, of his father but not his mother, or of his mother but not of his father . . . how do we know that the same law applies to a sister who is the daughter of his mother as well as his father? The text, therefore, declares categorically: he has uncovered the nakedness of his sister. But if he did not so derive it could we not infer it logically? If punishment is posited in the case of one who is his father's daughter, but not his mother's, or his mother's but not his father's, certainly penalty should be imposed in the case of one who is the daughter of both his father and mother! But from this you may derive that no penalty is imposed on the basis of inferences drawn by logic (Makkot 5b).

48. *E.g.*, Art. 4 of the *Code Pénal Français*, 1810; Art. 2 of the *Code Pénal Belge*, 1867; Art. 2 of the *German Penal Code*, 1871; Art. 1 of the *Turkish Penal Code*, 1926; Art. 1 of the *Danish Penal Code*, 1930; Art. 1 of the *Brazilian Penal Code*, 1940; Art. 2 of the *Yugoslav Penal Code*, 1951; Art. 29 of the *Argentine Constitucion de la Nacion* (cf. Mezger-Schoenke-Jescheck, *Das Auslaendische Strafrecht der Gegenwart*, Vol. 1, p. 23). Contra: Art. 16 of the *Soviet Penal Code*, 1926; the German Law of the 28th of June 1935; the *Corpus Juris Canonici*, 1917 (Glaser, *op. cit.*, p. 32). Cf. also Art. 2 of the *Danzig Code*, 1935, which was cited in the decision of Justice Silberg in Cr. A. 53/54, *Eshed v. Attorney General*, 8 *P.D.*, p. 830.

49. Unless the legislator—for special reasons—applied the norm retroactively.

50. The stand of British law toward the above principle is unprecedented and to some extent contradictory. On the one hand there is the opinion that the principle under consideration derives from ancient British law; on the other hand, it is well known that the major part of the British law on penalties has its source in the

common law, that is, in a law not formulated by legislators but created by the judges. Prof. Glaser, in the above-cited article (p. 31), touches on this question and declares that it would be erroneous to infer from this that the British judicial practice tends to create new offenses. "On the contrary, the characteristic spirit of judicial decisions in England is to regard only such acts as subject to punishment which, while not specifically covered by law, are fully in keeping with the conscience of the general law and traditional judicial practice." Certainly, in recent generations the tendency is not to increase punishable actions not in accordance with prior law, and the common law as it exists is deemed by English judges as the "written" law.

51. Prof. Glaser, *op. cit.*, p. 33.
52. Silberg, *Hok U-Musar*, p. 25.

CHAPTER V: THE LAW AND ITS RATIONALE

1. Sanhedrin 21b. "The greatest person in the world" is an allusion to King Solomon. The talmudic text continues thus: "It is written (Deuteronomy 17:17): 'And he shall not multiply for himself wives lest his heart turn away.' Said King Solomon, 'I shall multiply without turning my heart away'; but it is written (I Kings 11:4): 'And when Solomon became old, his wives led his heart astray.' It is likewise written (Deuteronomy 17:16): 'He shall not multiply for himself horses and he shall not return his people to Egypt to buy horses.' Said King Solomon, 'I shall multiply without returning'; but it is written (I Kings 10:29): 'A chariot would be imported from Egypt for six hundred shekels of silver and a horse for a hundred and fifty'. . . ."

2. The following commandments are cited with a reason: "If you take your neighbor's garment in pledge, you must return it to him before the sun sets; it is his only clothing, the sole covering of his skin. In what else shall he sleep?" (Exodus 22:25–26); "Do not take bribes, for bribes blind the clear-sighted and upset the pleas of the just" (Exodus 23:8); "Do not give your daughters to their sons or take their daughters for your sons; for they will turn your children away from me to worship other gods" (Deuteronomy 7:3–4); "When you build a new house you shall make a parapet for your roof, so that you do not bring bloodguilt on your house if anyone should fall from it" (Deuteronomy 22:8); "You should pay him his wages on the same day . . . for he is needy and depends on it" (Deuteronomy

24:15). Rashi, in his commentary on the above-cited passage in Sanhedrin, *s.v. lo nitgalu*, suggests that the question as to why the reasons for the commandments were not disclosed was directed solely at commandments known only through revelation [as opposed to those that might be inferred rationally], such as the prohibition of wearing a garment made of diverse materials [*shatnez*], or the prohibition of eating swine, and the like. But this is not congruent with the stumbling over the transgressions of King Solomon as cited in the Talmud. The matter bears further thought.

3. Thus: "Why did the Torah prescribe that a woman who gives birth brings a sacrifice offering? He said to them: 'When she is in labor, she vows to herself to avoid further marital relations with her husband. Therefore, did the Torah prescribe an atoning offering'" (Niddah 31b); "Why did the Torah ordain that circumcision occur on the eighth day? If it were on the seventh all the guests would rejoice in the festivities while the father and mother would be grieved because until the eighth day they are still forbidden to have marital relations" (Niddah, *loc. cit.,* and see Rashi *s.v. mipnay mah* and *s.v. shelo yiheyu*); "Why is earth used in the rite of testing a woman suspected by her husband of unfaithfulness? If she is proven innocent she will give birth to a son like Abraham who said of himself: 'Behold, I am but dust and ashes' (Genesis 18:27), but if she is not proven innocent—let her return to the earth" (Sotah 17a). Cf. Maimonides, *Guide to the Perplexed,* Pt. III, Chs. 26, 32, 33, 35, 36, 37, 39, 40, etc. where he expounds at length and in detail the reasons for the commandments. Cf. also the *Sefer HaHinukh* by Rabbi Aaron ben Yosef.

4. Sanhedrin 21a; Bava Metzia 115a; Kiddushin 68b; Gittin 49b; Sotah 8a; and elsewhere.

5. See Zechariah Frankel, *Darkhay HaMishnah* (Tel-Aviv, 1959), pp. 180–181.

6. *Warrender v. Warrender* (1835), 6 E.R. 1239; *Dolphin v. Robins* (1859), 11 E.R. 156; *Yelverton v. Yelverton* (1859), 164 E.R. 866.

7. "One court cannot annul the decisions of another court unless it exceeds it in wisdom and in numbers" (Mishnah, Eduyot 1:5; Gittin 36b; Maimonides, *Mishneh Torah, Hilkhot Mamrim* 2:2 and cf. the commentaries of *Kesef Mishneh* and *Lehem Mishneh, ad loc.;* cf. also Tosafot, Avodah Zarah 31a, *s.v. ve-hatenan.*

8. Chapter 3.

9. Ketubot 10a; Maimonides *Mishneh Torah, Hilkhot Ishut* 11:2, 4.

10. Ketubot 11a, 39b; Yevamot 89a; Bava Kamma 89a.

11. A rapist does not pay the *ketubah* settlement since "the reason the Sages ordained a settlement in the *ketubah* is to inhibit a man from divorcing his wife, but the rapist cannot divorce the woman he raped" and was forced to marry her (Ketubot 39b). The prohibition for a woman to sell her rights in the *ketubah* "follows the opinion of Rabbi Meir who holds that one may not live with his wife even a single hour without a *ketubah*. But what is his reasoning? Is it not so that he may not think lightly of divorcing her? But here he will not divorce her—for those who purchased the wife's rights in the *ketubah* can readily come and collect from him" (Bava Kamma 89a). "A raped woman whom the rapist is obligated to marry does not get a *ketubah*, for the Sages only ordained a *ketubah* so that it shall not be too easy for the husband to divorce her, but a rapist may not divorce the woman he raped and then married" (Maimonides, *Mishneh Torah, Hilkhot Na'arah Betulah* 1:4).

12. "The dinars of that time were not of pure silver, but of a current coin which was seven parts copper and one part silver, so that a *sela* contained half a *zuz* of silver. Thus two hundred dinars in a virgin's *ketubah* were only twenty-five *zuz* of pure silver, and the hundred dinars of a non-virgin were equivalent to twelve and a half silver *zuz*, and the weight of a *zuz* is the weight of ninety-six grains of barley, and a *dinar* is what is generally meant by a *zuz* whether of pure silver or of the current coinage (Maimonides, *Mishneh Torah, Hilkhot Ishut* 10:8). Joseph Karo, the author of the *Shulhan Arukh*, who lived till the latter half of his life in the Balkans, writes: "What is the amount stipulated in the *ketubah*? For a virgin two hundred *zuz* and for a widow one hundred, but in both cases in the coin of the realm, which means that the virgin's *ketubah* is thirty-seven and a half *drahma* of pure silver, and a widow's *ketubah* is half, which is eighteen and three quarter *drahma* of pure silver" (*Shulhan Arukh, Even HaEzer*, sec. 66, para. 6; the value of the *drahma* is estimated in the *Shulhan Arukh, Yoreh De'ah*, sec. 294, para. 6, and sec. 305, para. 1). Rabbi Moses Lima, author of *Helkat Mehokek* on the *Shulhan Arukh, Even HaEzer*, who lived in the seventeenth century and served as rabbi in Vilna and Brisk of Lithuania, estimates the value of the *ketubah* in Polish and Lithuanian currency, declaring: "The *ketubah* of a virgin is two and a gulden which are the equivalent of one Lithuanian *shuk* (*Helkat Mehokek, ibid.*, sec. 66, small para. 22).

13. "And when you reap the harvest of your land, you shall not

reap all the way to the edges of your field, or gather the gleanings of your harvest; you shall leave them for the poor and the stranger" (Leviticus 23:22); "when you reap the harvest in your field and overlook a sheaf in the field, do not turn back to get it; it shall go to the stranger, the fatherless, and the widow" (Deuteronomy 24:19). The gleanings, the forgotten sheaf, and the corner crop are the three gifts of the poor in the harvest (Hullin 131a), and the diverse rules which govern them are detailed in Mishnah Peah, and in Maimonides, *Mishneh Torah, Hilkhot Matnot Aniyim.* The student is invited to consult those discussions.

14. This is the special tithe assigned for the poor in the third and sixth year of every sabbatical (seven year) cycle: Rosh Hashanah 12b; Maimonides, *Mishneh Torah, Hilkhot Matnot Aniyim* 6:4. The basis for this is in Deuteronomy 26:12.

15. Commentary of Rabbi Samson of Sanz on Peah 8:8.

16. Cf. A. H. Freimann, "HaTakkanot HaHadashot Shel Ha-Rabbanut HaRashit Le-Eretz Yisrael Be-Dinay Ishut," *Sinai,* Adar-Nisan, 5704, p. 261.

17. See B. Shershevski, *Dinay Mishpahah,* 5718, p. 393.

18. Shershevski, *ibid.*

19. Additional illustrations may be found in other areas of law, alike or similar to the above, but the need for brevity and the fact that these are complicated themes does not permit us to deal with them here at length.

CHAPTER VI: LAW AND MORALITY

1. This chapter is taken from a lecture series I contributed to the lectures in memory of Judah Leib Magnes, and it was issued in pamphlet form under the title "Law and Morality in Jewish Jurisprudence" (Judah L. Magnes Press, Hebrew University, Jerusalem, 5712). Since the subject I dealt with in those lectures fits in well with the subjects treated here, I allowed myself to include it, as a separate chapter in this book, with some omissions and additions. The brief excerpts which I cited earlier, were, for technical reasons, cited according to the pagination in that (Hebrew) pamphlet.

2. M. Silberg, "HaMishpat BaMedinah HaIvrit," *HaPeraklit,* Iyar-Sivan, 5708.

3. Yerushalmi, Rosh Hashanah 1:3.

4. Bava Metzia 59a–b. "Akhnai" means a snake (see Bava Kamma 117b; Bava Metzia 84b). "Akhnai stove" means the stove (that is, the

question of the purity or impurity of the stove; see below) "which was encircled with arguments as a snake." "A snake tends to assume a circular position, holding its tail in its mouth" (Rashi, *ad loc.*).

5. "A stove made of tiles and baked in a furnace as pottery, the tiles were then connected by placing sand between the tiles" (Rashi, *ibid.*). Maimonides, *Mishneh Torah, Hilkhot Kelim* 16:5: "A stove cut into tiles and sand was placed between the tiles, and was then plastered over with cement on the outside."

6. The area of doubt is, whether the stove is now regarded as a vessel of pottery which is subject to ritual impurity if "it can hold another substance in it and was made for this purpose" (Maimonides, *ibid.*, 18:1; 2:1; and the source for it is in Mishnah, Kelim 17:15) or "it is not a pottery vessel but an edifice, like an object made of dung or earth which is not subject to impurity" (Rashi, Bava Metzia, *loc. cit.*).

7. Rabbi Eliezer referred to here is Rabbi Eliezer ben Hyrcanus, a disciple of Rabban Yohanan ben Zakkai, of whom it was said (Taanit 25b) that "he was not yielding in disposition," or, he was firm in his opinion, and was not easily intimidated.

8. Bava Metzia, *ibid.*

9. Rabbi Joshua mentioned here is Rabbi Joshua ben Hananyah, also a disciple of Rabban Yohanan ben Zakkai. Despite his bitter opposition to Rabbi Eliezer during his lifetime, he appears to have sought to appease him before his (Rabbi Eliezer's) death, as is suggested in a *baraita* (Sanhedrin 101a). He, moreover, sought to defend Rabbi Eliezer's honor after his death. "After his death four sages met to refute his teachings . . . but Rabbi Joshua said to them: 'We do not refute a lion after his death!' " (Gittin 83a).

10. Exodus 23:2.

11. This was apparently Nathan the Babylonian, the author of *Avot De-Rabbi Nathan,* who served in Usha as chief justice of the Sanhedrin under the presidency of Rabban Simeon ben Gamaliel. After he joined Rabbi Meir in revolt against the presidency of Rabban Simeon ben Gamaliel, it was ruled that his decisions not be quoted in his name but be cited as "some say" (cf. Horayot 13b).

12. Arakhin 22a.

13. Leviticus 19:36.

14. Rashi, Ketubot 86a, *s.v. periat.*

15. The last Rav Kahana, a Babylonian *Amora* of the fifth generation, was a pupil of Rava and a teacher of Rav Ashi (Berakhot 24a; Megillah 7b; Bava Kamma 95b). Rav Papa, one of the leading

Babylonian *Amoraim* of the fifth generation, was also a pupil of Rava (Bava Batra 126a; Nedarim 90b; Shabbat 93a, Tosafot *s.v. amar Rav Zevid*), and among the most prolific legal scholars in the Talmud.

16. This follows the text according to the version of Rashi in Ketubot, as cited previously. But Rashi in Hullin 110b, *s.v. kaftuhu,* cites another version of the text, and it should be consulted.

17. Ketubot 86a–b.

18. *Vide* Joers-Kunkel-Wenger, *Roemisches Recht,* 3rd ed., para. 103, and note 3 at p. 167; cf. Enneccerus-Kipp-Wolff, *Lehrbuch des Buergerlichen Rechts,* 15–17 eds., "Recht der Schuldverhaeltnisse," para. 227, II, 2.

19. On the dispute among the *Amoraim* whether the repayment of a debt is a commandment, and the practical implications derived from this, see the important study by M. Alon, *Kefiyat Hayav Le-Shem Geviyat Hov,* 1961 (unpublished doctoral dissertation), Ch. 2, pp. 32f.

20. The term "obligation on the person" [*shibud ha-guf*] is not mentioned in the Talmud. Rabbi Y. A. Herzog, in his book *Main Institutions of Jewish Law,* Vol. II, p. 4, declares: "To the extent that I can recollect it now, the term 'obligation on the person' does not occur in either Talmud (the reference is to both the Babylonian Talmud and the Palestinian Talmud)." This is indeed the case. The term is post-talmudic, late, and we first encounter it in the thought of Rabbenu Tam (Rabbi Jacob ben Meir, grandson of Rashi, 1100–1171, one of the leading Tosafists; see A. A. Urbach, *Baalay HaTosafot,* Ch. 3), in a citation of his opinion by the Ran (Rabbi Nisim Gerondi, 1320–1380) in a commentary on the Rif (Rabbi Isaac Alfasi, 1013–1103) in Ketubot 86b. We quote:

". . . A person who sells a note of indebtedness—though the sale is, according to the law of the Torah, valid—can forgive the debt, for the lender has two claims on the borrower: a claim on his person, since he is obligated to repay (and this is the primary obligation), and also a claim on the borrower's property if he should not repay— a derivative from the law of surety, as we say, 'a person's property is surety for him.' The claim on the person which the lender has on the borrower cannot be sold; all that may be sold is the claim on the property. Since the claim on the person which the lender has on the borrower cannot be sold, it remains unaffected, but when the lender proceeds to forgive the debt, the claim on the person comes to an end, and so automatically also the claim on the property which only derives its validity from the law of surety. . . ."

The term "a claim on the person" is somewhat misleading, especially when it is taken outside its context in the above citation. It suggests the impression that it is a claim on his body, in other words, on the flesh and blood of the obligated person, as was customary, in this or in another form, in ancient Babylonian law according to the code of Hammurabi, in ancient Greek law, and in ancient Roman law (see A. Gulak, *Toledot HaMishpat Be-Yisrael, Bi-Tekufat HaTalmud, (a) HaHiyuv Ve-Shibudav* (Jerusalem, 5699), Ch. 2, pp. 15–17). But this is not so, and M. Alon has noted correctly in his above-cited work, Ch. 2, p. 31, note 36, that " 'a claim on the person' means that the obligated individual is obligated to repay the debt as a personal commitment, in addition to the claim that the lender has on the property of the borrower, and this concept has no connection with a claim by the lender on the body of the borrower."

An analysis of the language used confirms this interpretation. The Hebrew term *gufo* [the term we translated as the "person"] means: he himself, he and no other, or the subject itself, and nothing outside it. "Any work on the Sabbath if completed by himself [*be-gufo*] calls for bringing a sin-offering—if shared with his neighbor, no sin-offering is required but the act itself remains forbidden" (Shabbat 153b); "work which is not needed for itself" [*le-gufah*] (*ibid.*, 94b); "whoever loves his wife as himself [*ke-gufo*] and honors her more than himself [*mi-gufo*] . . . of him did Scripture say (Job 5:24), 'and thou shalt know that thy tent is in peace' " (Yevamot 62b). "Obligation on the person" [*shibud ha-guf*] means then: an obligation on the person himself, and in this sense there is precedent for the use of the term in the Talmud, except that the talmudic form of it is Aramaic—*shibud nafshay* (Bava Metzia 13a); "in matters affecting his son a person obligates himself [*meshabed nafshay*] (Gittin 49b). The Aramaic term *nafshay* is synonymous with the Hebrew *atzmo* [himself]; thus, in the talmudic admonition, "Do not withdraw yourself beyond the law" (Sotah 16b), the Aramaic for *yourself, nafshakh,* is identical with the Hebrew term *atzmekha.*

21. The standard method for transferring a debt is as follows: If it is confirmed by a note—"writing and transmitting," that is, the transferor of the debt writes the purchaser, "acquire this note and all the obligations set forth in it," and he gives him the note (Maimonides, *Mishneh Torah, Hilkhot Mekhirah* 6:11) or transfer "incidental to the transfer of landed property" (Maimonides, *op. cit.,*

6:14). If the debt was a purely oral transaction—"in the presence of the three persons," which means: the person making the transfer declares to the person who owes him the debt in the presence of the purchaser, "the sum you owe me pay to this one" (Maimonides, *op. cit.*, 6:8). A debt effected orally cannot be transferred incidentally to the transferring of land (Maimonides, *op. cit.*, 6:7 and the commentary *Magid Mishneh, ad loc.;* cf. also Kiddushin 47b; Gittin 13b; *Shulhan Arukh, Hoshen Mishpat,* sec. 66).

22. The general principle is: a right of claim cannot derive from an inequitable cause. "One cannot simply say that every illegal act is absolutely devoid of validity and cannot occasion any legal consequences; at least one cannot draw on this principle to cancel all property rights. If a prostitute, for instance, received a house as the fee for her services, and it was registered in her name in the Registration Office, the house belongs to her, in all respects, and no other person—occupant, lessee or buyer—can challenge her right of ownership, although the payment of the fee—unless it was for a past obligation—is certainly an action contrary to law (from the standpoint of being immoral), and if the person had not hastened to transfer the ownership of the house, but had only obligated himself to transfer it, the woman could not claim in court a fulfillment of this obligation" (Decision by Justice Silberg, *Libman v. Lifshitz,* C.A. 87/50, 6 *P.D.* 57, p. 64).

23. In his well-known work on partnership, Lindley tells of a bizarre yet amusing incident—*Everet v. Williams*—which occurred in England in 1725. Two robbers, of experience and know-how, established a partnership for the purpose of robbing travelers and dividing the loot between them. After some time one of them, Williams, changed his mind, and began to rob independently. His aggrieved friend, Everet, went to the Court of Equity(!) and petitioned that his partner be obligated to give a detailed accounting of all the profits which belonged to the partnership and which he had pocketed from his "business" of robbing gold watches, rings, swords, hats, horses, saddles, bridles and the like. The end of the matter was: the claim was denied, both litigants were hanged, the attorneys for the claimant were fined, and one of them was banished (Lindley, *On Partnership,* 10th ed., p. 117, note (d); *The English and Empire Digest,* Vol. 3, no. 123).

24. *Ayerst v. Jenkins* (1873), 29 L.T. 126; *Pearce v. Brooks* (1866), 14 L.T. 288; *Cundell v. Dawson* (1847), 136 E.R. 552; *Re Mahmud & Ispahani* (1921), 2 K.B. 716; *Liverpool Borough Bank v. Turner*

(1860), 129 E.R. 172, 175; *Forster v. Taylor* (1834), 110 E.R. 1019; *Smith v. Mawhood* (1845), 153 E.R. 552; *Johnson v. Hudson* (1809), 103 E.R. 973; *Whetherell v. Jones* (1832), 110 E.R. 82; *Upfill v. Wright* (1911), 1 K.B. 506; *Shaw v. Director of Public Prosecutions* (1961), 2 W.L.R. 911.

25. *Gremaire v. Le Clerc Bois Valon* (1809), 170 E.R. 1110.

26. *Law v. Hodgson* (1809), 170 E.R. 1111.

27. Berakhot 10a, cited by Beruriah, the wife of Rabbi Meir.

28. Salmond-Williams, *Law of Contracts*, 2nd ed., p. 345; *Taylor v. Chester* (1869), 21 L.T. 359; *Alexander v. Rayson* (1936), 1 K.B. 169; cf. *Bowmaker v. Barnet* (1944), 2 All E.R. 579 and see Hamson, "Illegal Contracts and Limited Interests," in *Cambridge Law Journal*, Vol. 10 (1949), pp. 249 ff.

29. *Holman v. Johnson* (1775), 98 E.R. 1120.

30. *Bigos v. Boustead* (1951), 1 All E.R. 92.

31. "The oft-stated proposition that the courts 'will not assist an illegal transaction in any respect' (per Lord Ellenborough in *Edgar v. Fowler* . . .), is far from self-evident if what is sought is not enforcement of an illegal contract but quasicontractual recovery of money paid or property delivered under it. Here, it is the denial of relief which, in fact, perpetuates the effects of an illegal transaction. . . . The maxim *in pari delicto* cannot thus be explained and justified by reference to ethics. It is, indeed, amoral . . . they (the courts) can and should act as a social agency and, instead of remaining merely passive, be free to choose such course as would, in practice, best serve the public interest . . ." (J. K. Grodecki, "In Pari Delicto Potior Est Conditio Defendentis," *L.Q.R.*, Vol. 71, April 1955, pp. 265–266, 267, 273).

32. Temurah 4b–6b.

33. Two Babylonian *Amoraim* of the third generation, among the best known of all the *Amoraim*. The "discussions between Abaye and Rava" is a popular expression for the dialectic of the Talmud.

34. See the explanation posited, and its source, *supra*, Ch. 2, note 31.

35. The accepted principle is that wherever Abaye and Rava are in disagreement, the law follows the view of Rava, except for six specific cases in which the prevailing view is that of Abaye. A mnemonic reminds us of each of them: *yal k'gm,* compounded from the initial letters of the key words of each of the subjects disputed. *Y* stands for *yiush shelo mi-da'at* (Bava Metzia 21b); *A* stands for *ayd zomem le-mafrea hu nifsal* (Bava Kamma 72b); *L* stands for *lehi*

ha-omed me'elav (Eruvin 15a); *K* stands for *kiddushin shelo nimseru le-viah* (Kiddushin 51a); *G* stands for *giluy da'ata be-gita* (Gittin 34a); *M* stands for *mumar okhel nevelot le-hakhis* (Sanhedrin 27a). On the basis of this principle some codifiers have ruled that the law follows the view of Rava, and the action is invalid (*Teshuvot HaRosh,* principle 7; *Mordecai,* end of tractate Shevuot, in the name of the Ri bar Peretz).

36. *Mishneh LeMelekh* on Maimonides, *Mishneh Torah, Hilkhot Gerushin* 3:19; *Lehem Mishneh* on Maimonides, *Mishneh Torah, Hilkhot Bekhorot* 6:8; *Noda Bi-Yehudah Tinyana, Even HaEzer,* sec. 129; *Shemen Rokeah* on *Even HaEzer,* sec. 60.

37. Bava Metzia 65a.

38. Bava Metzia 61a; Maimonides, *Mishneh Torah, Hilkhot Malveh Ve-Loveh* 4:2.

39. Deuteronomy 23:20.

40. Bava Metzia 61b; Maimonides, *Mishneh Torah, Hilkhot Malveh Ve-Loveh* 6:5; *Shulhan Arukh, Yoreh De'ah,* sec. 161.

41. Bava Kamma 30b; Maimonides, *op. cit.,* 4:6; *Shulhan Arukh Yoreh De'ah, loc. cit.,* para. 11.

42. See *infra,* note 43.

43. Rashi, Bava Metzia 65a, *s.v. gelima.*

44. The Rosh on Bava Metzia, Ch. *Ezehu Neshekh.* The author is Asher ben Jehiel, 1250–1327, the father of Rabbi Jacob *Ba'al HaTurim.*

45. Rav Hai Gaon, the son of Rav Sherira Gaon, the last of the *Geonim,* 939–1038.

46. "The principle of what constitutes interest: all compensation for delay in payment is forbidden" (Bava Metzia 63b). This is the general rule about interest: any addition to the sum of a loan as compensation for waiting for repayment is forbidden.

47. Rabbi Yom Tov ibn Ishbili, born at the end of the thirteenth century and died in the beginning of the fourteenth (ca. 1329).

48. Rabbi Moses ben Nahman, 1194–1270.

49. Cited in *Shitah Mekubetzet* on Bava Metzia, Ch. *Ezehu Neshekh,* 65a, ed. Tel Aviv, 5714, p. 739a.

50. *Mishneh Torah, Hilkhot Mekhirah* 30:7.

51. See my decision, *Jacobs v. Cartuz,* C.A. 110/53, 9 *P.D.* 1401, p. 1413.

52. *Hilkhot HaRif* (Rabbi Isaac Alfasi) on Bezah, Ch. *Meshilin.*

53. *Shulhan Arukh, Hoshen Mishpat,* sec. 195, para. 11. As to the development of this law in later rabbinic literature, see my decision

in C.A. 110/53 cited *supra*, pp. 1414–1416. Various opinions are cited there on this question, among them: the view of the Sema (*Sefer Me'irat Enayim* by Rabbi Joshua Falk, 1550–1614), who holds that the invalidity of the action applies only when the offense pervades the full content of the action and not when the offense is only partial, as when the prohibition begins at a certain point in the action (Sema, *Hoshen Mishpat*, sec. 208, para. 1, small para. 3); the view of the Shakh (*Siftay Kohen* by Rabbi Shabtay ben Meir HaKohen, 1622–1663), who holds that the above principle applies only when the action necessarily must be done counter to law, but if it can also be carried out in accordance with law, it is efficacious (Shakh on *Hoshen Mishpat, loc. cit.*, small para. 2); the view of the Taz (*Turay Zahav* by Rabbi David HaLevi, 1586–1667), who sees as "sound advice" the following distinction: We say that the action is invalid when the violation is intrinsic to the action, but not when it derives from the circumstances "of the particular day when it occurs," or because "it violates an oath," or when "the violation is not in the fact of the sale itself but in the increase in the cost" (Taz, *Hoshen Mishpat*, beginning of sec. 208). All this points to the fact that even those who accept the view of Rava, that the action is invalid, have, however, surrounded the law with so many qualifications that it is almost wholly lost under the heap of refinements.

54. See *supra*, Ch. 4, sec. 2.

55. Makkot 3b; Maimonides, *Mishneh Torah, Hilkhot Malveh Ve-Loveh* 13:5; *Shulhan Arukh, Hoshen Mishpat*, sec. 73, para. 1.

56. See *infra*.

57. A Palestinian *Amora*, born in Babylonia, of the third and fourth generation.

58. Mishnah and Gemara, Bava Batra 23b.

59. Rashi, Bava Batra, *loc. cit., s.v. ve-al da afkuhu*.

60. See *supra*, Ch. 4, sec. 6.

61. Makkot 5b; cf. Sanhedrin 54a.

62. Deuteronomy 19:19.

63. Makkot 5b. See *supra*, Ch. 4, note 47.

CHAPTER VII: LAW AND EQUITY

1. An aphorism reminiscent of the statement in the Zohar: "Everything depends on good fortune, even a Torah scroll in the Ark." See *Otzar Leshon Hakhamim*, p. 141.

2. "Upright [*yishray, plural*] of heart" are referred to in Psalms

7:11, 11:2, 64:11, 97:11; "upright [*yosher*, singular] of heart," "up-rightness [*yishrat*] of heart" are referred to in Job 33:3, I Kings 3:6; "upright [*yesharim*] in their heart" is referred to in Psalms 125:4. All these allude to characteristics and dispositions which transcend the practical realm.

3. Here I include in the term "beyond the strict law" all types of *yosher*. For the various nuances, see *infra*, this chapter.

4. *E.g.*, equity follows the law.

5. It may well be that there exists a very fine distinction in nuance between "the spirit of the Sages is not pleased with him," and the "standard of saintliness."

6. Deuteronomy 6:18; and we find many biblical passages utilizing the word "the upright" by itself, in association with the verb "to do" (Exodus 15:26; Deuteronomy 12:25; I Kings 11:38). It is interesting and of considerable importance that the Talmud depends principally on the verse in Deuteronomy 6:18, cited above, where the combina-tion of "the upright and the good" is stressed, placing the accent on both aspects. Cf. *Kesef Mishneh* on Maimonides, *Mishneh Torah, Hilkhot Malveh Ve-Loveh* 22:17, where it is stated: "Since the action is demanded because of 'and you shall do what is upright and good,' if he should need to redeem it at more than what it was assessed for him, this would not be good for him."

7. *E.g.*, *Moses v. Mcferlan* (1760), 97 E.R. 676. Cf. dictum of Far-well J., in *Bradford Corporation v. Ferrand* (1902), 2 Ch. 655, p. 662, that "the conception of *aequum et bonum* and the rights flowing therefrom . . . are included in *jus naturale*" (*sic!*).

8. For we were not told by whom, where and when it was estab-lished, nor was it designated as a *takkanah*.

9. Bava Metzia 35a; see also Bava Metzia 16b.

10. The term "general mortgage" [*apotiki kelalit*] is not found in the Talmud nor in the talmudic and rabbinic literature of a later period. But the "commitment of property" [*shibud nekhasim*] in Jew-ish law hovers close to the zone of the general mortgage in Greek and Greco-Egyptian law, and of the Roman general mortgage, which was created after the early period of the Mishnah (see Gulak, *Toledot HaMishpat Be-Yisrael*, pp. 36, 37–41). An actual mortgage is, accord-ing to Jewish law, a commitment placed on a particular property, and this concept was conveyed by the linguistic interpretation of the term for mortgage, *apotiki:* (*apo tehe kai*), "here you take a stand" (Rashi, Bava Kamma 11b, *s.v. apotiki*; Rashbam, Bava Batra 44b, *s.v. ela afilu*). This is of course homiletics, and we find many others

of a similar nature, as *daytaki* (*da tehe lemekam ve-lihyot*, "with this you are to stand and to be," a *baraita* in Bava Batra 135b, and cf. the statement of Rashbam, *ad loc.*); *kapandria* (*admakifna adaray eyol beha*, "if you are blocked return and go up here," Berakhot 65b); *anfuria* (*en poh rayah*, "there is no proof here," Rashi, Bava Metzia 23b, *s.v. shelo sva'atan*); *afikoman* (*afiku man*, "remove your vessels," Rashi, Pesahim 86a, *s.v. ve'amar Rav*).

11. Bava Batra 175b.

12. Such as whether the first-born son receives a double share in the inheritance of a debt (Bava Batra 124b, 175b); whether a loan executed orally can be collected from heirs (*ibid.*, but see Tosafot, Kiddushin 13b, *s.v. amar Rav*).

13. In their time there were few people who knew how to write documents; this was apparently a specialized profession (allusion is made to a fee for the scribe in Bava Metzia 16b), so that the scribe, or the scribe together with the witnesses to the document, served as the source for publicizing loans made by a note executed in a particular city.

14. According to the Talmudist in the discussion in Bava Batra, *loc. cit.*, Ula did not cite his own opinion, but "he quoted the reason of the men in the west [Eretz Yisrael] but he himself did not entertain it."

15. Bava Batra 44b; Maimonides, *Mishneh Torah, Hilkhot Malveh Ve-Loveh* 18:2; *Shulhan Arukh, Hoshen Mishpat*, sec. 113, para. 1.

16. Kiddushin 26a.

17. Rashi, Kiddushin, *loc. cit., s.v. sheyesh lahem ahrayut*.

18. Bava Kamma 11b.

19. This, in my opinion, is the proper legal construction of "the commitment" [*shibud*] of movable property, though the sources are not altogether clear on this.

20. Rashbam, Bava Batra 169a, *s.v. ve-ha amar Rav Nahman*.

21. The assessment was made after a public announcement "morning and evening" over a thirty-day period that "whoever wished to buy may come and buy" (Mishnah, Arakhin 21b, and Rashi, *ibid., s.v. shum*), "and if this one (the debtor) came and bought it for more than what others assessed it, then we transfer it to him, after the end of the time set for the public announcement (Rashi, Bava Metzia 35b, *s.v. miki shalmu*). The public announcement for thirty days was made in connection with every creditor who sought to collect his debt with land from the debtor or those who purchased it from him (Tosafot, Arakhin 21b, *s.v. shum;* so it seems from the discussion in

the Talmud, Bava Metzia 35b, which see and infer). Another view is that of Maimonides, *Mishneh Torah, Hilkhot Malveh Ve-Loveh*, Ch. 22; cf. the distinction drawn there between law 6 and law 9, but he, too, does not differentiate between the property of orphans and other property.

The Rashbam, as we saw, constructs the term *adrakhta* from the term *dorekh*, "one who rules and *steps on*"; Rashi, on the other hand, constructs it from *rodef*, "one who *pursues* and attains (see Rashi, Bava Metzia 16b, *s.v. adrakhta*). This linguistic disagreement appears to have given rise to the variation in versions cited in note 22 *infra*.

22. The version found in our texts which were also those of the Rashbam is: "Every *tirpa* in which it is not written, 'We have torn up the note of indebtedness' is not a *tirpa* and every *adrakhta* on which it is not written, 'We have torn up the *tirpa*' is not an *adrakhta*. . . .'' The other version has in place of *tirpa—adrakhta*, and in place of *adrakhta—tirpa*.

23. *Shitah Mekubetzet* on Bava Batra 169a, in the name of the Ran (ed. Zioni Press, Tel Aviv, 5715, Bava Batra, Pt. II, p. 691a, top). See also the statement on the preceding page.

24. *Shetar Halitah* is a Hebrew translation, current among the early commentators on the Talmud [the *Rishonim*], for the talmudic term *halatatha* (Bava Metzia 16b). See the statement of the Rashba and the Ritba quoted in the *Shitah Mekubetzet* on Bava Metzia, edition cited *supra*, pp. 282–283.

25. *Nitraf* is a term coined by Maimonides to designate the purchaser, from whom the creditor seized the field in order to satisfy the debt due him from the debtor-seller. See Maimonides, *op. cit.*, law 16.

26. Maimonides, *ibid.*, law 11, but this *shetar halitah* is called by Maimonides *horadah* (see, *ibid.*, end of law 10, and infer). The nature of this *shetar halitah* is, in my opinion, constitutive and not declarative; that is to say, through this *shetar* the ownership is transferred from the debtor, or the one from whom it is seized, to the creditor. Evidence for this is: (1) in the very name *halatatha* or *halitah* (cf. the expression *huhlat ha-shor*, "the body of the ox is transferred to the plaintiff," in connection with an ox that is not presumed to gore but gored, in Bava Kamma 33a); (2) an analogy to the previous *shetar* where there is certainly a transfer of the right to exercise authority and take possession.

27. See the previous note.

28. Maimonides, *ibid.*, law 16; *Shulhan Arukh, Hoshen Mishpat,*

sec. 103, para. 9; another view is expounded by the *Tur* in *Hoshen Mishpat*, sec. 103, in the name of his father, the Rosh. The view of Maimonides has support in the Talmud, in the case of "two palaces," in Ketubot 91b (*Magid Mishneh* on Maimonides, *loc. cit.;* this view is shared by the *Bet Yosef* on the *Tur, op. cit.,* small para. 22, who declares: "and it is certain that this case—the reference is to the two palaces—so proves it").

29. *Kesef Mishneh* on Maimonides, *loc. cit.,* in the name of the Ramban; Shakh on *Shulhan Arukh, Hoshen Mishpat, op. cit.,* small para. 11, in the name of the Ritba; it appears to be similarly implied by Rashi, Bava Metzia, *loc. cit., s.v. de-medina,* and *me-resha,* check this and infer.

30. Bava Metzia 35a; Maimonides, *Mishneh Torah, loc. cit.;* *Shulhan Arukh, Hoshen Mishpat, op. cit.,* para. 10.

31. Rashi, Bava Metzia, *loc. cit., s.v. ada'ata de'ara.*

32. Bava Metzia 108a, and this is the law; Maimonides, *Mishneh Torah, Hilkhot Shekhenim* 22:5; *Shulhan Arukh, Hoshen Mishpat,* sec. 175, para. 6; the Rosh and the Ran, as quoted in the *Shitah Mekubetzet,* edition cited *supra,* p. 1061.

33. In the case of movable property there is no law of the neighbor with regard to purchase (*Shulhan Arukh, Hoshen Mishpat, op. cit.,* para. 53; the commentary of the Vilna Gaon, *op. cit.,* small para. 127: "and they issued a general rule to cover this: one who has a claim to land, but not slaves, for contiguous ownership applies only to something that is stationary," and the source for this is in the *Tur,* sec. 175, paras. 82–83, in the name of the Ri of Barcelona).

34. The law of returning assessed and seized property, which was explained previously.

35. A responsum of the Rif, cited in the *Shitah Mekubetzet,* edition cited *supra,* p. 1061. Cf. also Rashi, Bava Metzia 108b, *s.v. nokhri lav bar ve'asita.*

36. Ramban, cited in the *Shitah Mekubetzet,* edition cited *supra,* p. 1065.

37. Sema on *Shulhan Arukh, Hoshen Mishpat, op. cit.,* small para. 7; see also *Shulhan Arukh, Hoshen Mishpat, op. cit.,* end of para. 21.

38. *Teshuvot Maimoniyot, Sefer Kinyan,* sec. 32: "Also the statement made (by the rabbi who raised the question), that the case of the neighbor is to be directed not to the seller but to the buyer, is without substance. . . . And if the seller and the buyer entered into a private agreement to deny the land to the neighbor, by having the seller return the money to the buyer, they plunged into deep waters

only to bring up a potsherd, for they could not thereby deny the land to this neighbor for it had already become his property; the conclusion of the matter is that the seller must do for the neighbor all that he agreed to do for the buyer, and to establish it in his possession, both according to Jewish law as well as in the law of the nations. . . ."

39. For example, "if the coins of the person claiming the right of preemption are sealed in a package and those of the stranger are open, the law of preemption does not apply" (Bava Metzia 108b), and see the explanation of Rashi, *ad loc., s.v. hani zayri.*

40. This view is also suggested—if not actually proven—by the law quoted in Maimonides, *Mishneh Torah, op. cit.,* 14:1, and in the *Shulhan Arukh, Hoshen Mishpat, op. cit.,* para. 25. There it is stated: "One must wait for him," and the seller cannot say to the person claiming the right of preemption, "I will sell to the buyer and you then go and sue him!"

41. *Teshuvot HaRashba,* sec. 515 (Vienna, 1812), p. 104.

42. Cf. Maimonides, *op. cit.,* law 4; *Shulhan Arukh, Hoshen Mishpat, op. cit.,* paras. 6 and 23, end.

43. Rashi, Bava Metzia 108a, *s.v. ve'asita;* Rosh, *Shitah Mekubetzet* on Bava Metzia, *op. cit.,* p. 1061. It stands to reason, and there is no need to cite proof for this, that in later generations and in countries of the diaspora outside of Babylonia, land was not readily available for purchase by Jews and therefore the law of preemption was either abrogated by the action of the communities, or—on the contrary—this law had become altogether obsolete but was reintroduced in certain places through the action of the communities. See the *Responsa of the Rashdam, Hoshen Mishpat,* sec. 299, where two contradictory statements appear. At first he declares: "It is true that here in Salonica the law of preemption is not current, for so did the early sages agree. . . ."; and several lines below this he adds: "but in the great city—great in population and quality—of Constantinople, it appears that they have the consent to practice the law of preemption. . . ." Since then many responsa were written concerning the law of preemption in connection with seating in the synagogue, which was "under Jewish jurisdiction."

44. "If he sold all his property to the same person" (Bava Metzia 108b).

45. "To sell a far-lying field and redeem one nearby" (*ibid.*).

46. Rashi, Bava Metzia, *loc. cit., s.v. limkor be-rahok,* and *eyn bah;* Rama, *Hoshen Mishpat, op. cit.,* para. 23; *Teshuvot HaRalbah,* sec.

61. Note that the Ralbah does not say "a loss to the seller," but "a loss," without further specification. This is indeed how this principle should be qualified, that it may also serve as the basis for all those disadvantaged—that is, purchasers such as women, orphans, and the like—who, because of the difficulties created for them, are not required to withdraw and transfer the land they bought to the person with the right of preemption (see Bava Metzia, *loc. cit.;* Maimonides, *op. cit.,* laws 13 and 14; *Shulhan Arukh, Hoshen Mishpat, op. cit.,* para. 47; cf. also the Rosh in Bava Metzia, Ch. *HaMekabel,* sec. 25).

47. Yevamot 88a.

48. *Teshuvot Maimoniyot, Sefer Kinyan,* sec. 32.

49. Bava Metzia 108a: "I sent you to improve. . . ."

50. Maimonides, *op. cit.,* law 5; 13:7; *Hilkhot HaRif,* Bava Metzia, Ch. *HaMekabel,* on the theme of the person with the right of preemption; *Tur, Hoshen Mishpat,* sec. 175, paras. 7, 8; *Shulhan Arukh, Hoshen Mishpat, op. cit.,* para. 6; the commentary of the Vilna Gaon on *Shulhan Arukh, Hoshen Mishpat, op. cit.,* small para. 18, where it is written: "as he wrote later in sec. 190, para. 4," and his reference is to the following: "Some say that the law is the same if one said to his neighbor, 'Here is a hundred *zuz* and let your field be sold to so-and-so,' once he accepted it from him, the field was acquired by so-and-so." But the Rama adds there "provided that so-and-so wants this"; but we forego this condition in connection with the purchaser and the person with the right of preemption.

51. As in the conception that "whoever betrothes a woman does so on the assumed consent of the Sages," which turns every case of betrothal into a betrothal on the condition that the Sages will consent, and thereby makes possible the revocation of the betrothal (Gittin 33a and elsewhere); or regarding the husband as the "first purchaser" in his wife's private property (see Bava Kamma 88b and Rashi, *ad. loc., s.v. be-Usha hitkinu;* and Bava Metzia 96b and Rashi, *ad. loc., s.v. ha-ba'al motzi),* in order to gain through the elegance of law the effect of the ordinance adopted at Usha which establishes that "if the wife sold her private property in her husband's lifetime and she died, the husband can reclaim the property from the purchaser" (Ketubot 78b; Bava Kamma, *loc. cit.,* and many places elsewhere).

52. So these laws are designated in the *Tur* and the *Shulhan Arukh, Hoshen Mishpat,* sec. 272. Maimonides cites these laws in his book on damages, *Mishneh Torah, Hilkhot Rotzeah U-Shemirat Nefesh,* Ch. 13. In practice these laws are a "branch" of the commandment to return a lost object, for the general conception behind them is the duty to be concerned and to act for the preserva-

tion of a neighbor's property. For this reason they compared the law of loading to the law of returning a lost object in connection with the exemption of an "elder and it is not in keeping with his dignity," as it appears from the discussion in Bava Metzia 30b, though in a formal sense the cases are different (see the enumeration of the commandments by Maimonides, commandments 203, 204; *Sefer HaHinukh,* commandments 538, 541).

53. Bava Metzia, *loc. cit.;* see Maimonides, *Hilkhot Gezelah Va-Avedah* 11:13, 17; *Hilkhot Rotzeah U-Shemirat Nefesh* 13:3, 4; *Shulhan Arukh, Hoshen Mishpat* 263:1, 3; 272:3.

54. *Zaken*—an important and honored person. "Only he is called *zaken* who has acquired wisdom" (*zaken* may be seen as an abbreviation for *zeh kanah,* the one who acquired: *Sifra De-Be Rav, Kedoshim,* sec. 3, Ch. 7, 12). Rabbi Ishmael ben R. Yose was a *Tanna* of the fifth generation, "the head of Sephoris" after the death of his father, Rabbi Yose ben Halafta (see Eruvin 86b, and Rashi, *ad. loc., s.v. al pi mi na'aseh*), and a great expert in knowledge of the Bible. Thus Rabbi Ishmael ben Rabbi Yose said, "I could write out the entire Bible by heart" (Yerushalmi, Megillah, Ch. 4, ed. *Torah LeAm,* Jerusalem 5720, Seder Moed, p. 74b).

55. "You shall not see your brother's ass or his ox fallen down on the road and hide yourself from them; you shall surely help him lift them up again" (Deuteronomy 22:4). "For we were commanded to help our brothers when they should require to place the load on the animal or the person . . . and concerning this it is written, 'You shall surely help him lift them up,' and the Sages called this *te'inah,* loading" (*Sefer HaHinukh,* commandment 541). See Bava Metzia 31a, and Rashi, *ad. loc., s.v. hakem takim,* and cf. *Mekhilta De-Rabbi Ishmael, Mishpatim,* Ch. 20, ed. Bamberger and Wahrman, Jerusalem 5720, p. 326.

56. Cf. the leading judgment of Justice Agranat in connection with false declarations offered through negligence by an expert, according to English and Israeli law: Mot. 106/54, *Weinstein v. Kadimah,* 8 *P.D.* 1317. Cf. B.G.B., 676.

57. Danko and Isur are the names of two famous moneychangers, who were great experts in this field.

58. Bava Kamma 99b.

59. The reason is that in the case of so great an expert we look upon the error as totally accidental, or at least as something non-deliberate. See *ibid.* in the Talmud and the commentaries, and probe carefully.

60. Bava Metzia, Ch. *Elu Metziot,* in many places. "Despair" is an

indication by the loser that he no longer hopes to find the lost object or to have it returned, as in the case where he was heard to say, "Alas for the monetary loss" (Bava Metzia 23a). If the lost object is without an identifying mark, we assume that he despaired of it immediately on losing it. This despair, whether explicitly indicated, or assumed by inference, puts it in the class of "ownerless property" [*hefker*] or it will result in its becoming ownerless property, and for this reason the finder is not obligated to return it and he may keep it for himself (cf. Rashi, Bava Metzia 21a, *s.v. ma'ot mefuzarot*).

61. Bava Metzia 24b.

62. The reference is to the father of Samuel, the great *Amora* of the first generation. The name of Samuel's father was Abba bar Abba (see Prof. M. Margaliot, *Encyclopediah Le-Hakhmay HaTalmud Ve-HaGeonim*, Vol. I, pp. 5–7; *Seder HaDorot, s.v. Shmuel HaKohen*).

63. He "saw them at the beginning of the year and he saw them at the end of the year" (*Shitah Mekubetzet* on Bava Metzia, *loc. cit.*, p. 371, in the name of the Ravad). Thus is removed the difficulty raised in the Tosafot, Bava Metzia, *ibid., s.v. l'vatar*.

64. "And there is proof that owners despair of regaining a lost object after twelve months, for it is written (Psalms 31:13): 'I have been forgotten as a dead man from the heart, I have become as a lost vessel,' and they decreed that a dead person be forgotten from the heart after twelve months. The comparison is drawn between a lost vessel and a dead person: as a dead person is despaired of after twelve months, so is a lost vessel." (*Tosafot Hitzoniyot*, cited in *Shitah Mekubetzet* on Bava Metzia, *loc. cit.*).

65. Among the well-known "presumptions" in the Talmud, whether they are preceded by the word *hazakah* or not, are the following: "There is a presumption that a person does not trouble himself to prepare a feast and then spoil it" (Ketubot 10a; on the basis of this presumption a husband is believed so as to invalidate his wife's *ketubah* with the claim that he found her not to be a virgin); "there is a presumption that a person does not pay within the time allowed for a loan" (Bava Batra 5b; on the basis of this presumption that a person does not pay a loan within the time allotted for it, a creditor can collect, in this instance, his debt from orphans, without taking an oath, and we are not concerned with the possibility that their father may have paid the debt); "a person does not put aside what is permitted, to eat in its place that which is forbidden" (Gittin 37b and many other places); this presumption is the basis for the well-known presumption that "a person does not

turn his act of coitus into immorality" (Ketubot 73a and cf. *Shulhan Arukh, Even HaEzer*, sec. 149, para. 1), and this leads to the result that the act of cohabitation between a man and a woman are customarily regarded as an act of betrothal through cohabitation which is acknowledged in the Torah, and the woman would require a divorce if the union were to be dissolved. The assumption of "despair" after twelve months is also a "presumption" in the above sense, even though it was not explicitly designated by this term.

66. Kiddushin 49b, 50a; Nedarim 28a; Meilah 21a.

67. Kiddushin 49b; Maimonides, *Mishneh Torah, Hilkhot Mekhirah* 11:9; *Shulhan Arukh, Hoshen Mishpat*, sec. 207, para. 4.

68. Maimonides, *loc. cit.; Shulhan Arukh, Hoshen Mishpat, loc. cit.;* cf. the decision of Justice Silberg, C.A. 130/50, *Amal v. Shindler,* 6 *P.D.* 710.

69. A parallel to the expression "you did not leave a daughter of father Abraham . . ." (Gittin 89a).

70. "And there are matters that do not even require an open indication because there is a supportive conjecture and even if he did not disclose what was in his mind at the time of the action, this is not deemed to be 'words in the heart,' for without an open indication we ourselves bear witness that this was his intention. . . . All these are supportive conjectures, and therefore we do not require an explicit indication, neither at the time of the action nor at the time preceding it" (Rosh on Ketubot, Ch. *Almanah Nizonet*, sec. 9). Cf. Tosafot, Kiddushin 49b, *s.v. devarim shebelev* and Tosafot, Ketubot 97a, *s.v. zavin.*

71. The concept that a supportive conjecture has the same effect as an explicitly declared condition and as a condition which meets all legal requirements for a condition ("as the condition of the children of Gad and the children of Reuben," mentioned in Mishnah and Gemara, Kiddushin 61b–62a), is made manifest by many *halakhot,* such as: "If a person's son went overseas and he heard that his son had died, and he proceeded and willed his property to another, and subsequently his son returned . . . , Rabbi Simeon ben Menasya says that his gift is not a valid gift, for had he known that his son was alive—he would not have made it" (Bava Batra 132a, and the law follows the view of Rabbi Simeon ben Menasya: Maimonides, *Mishneh Torah, Hilkhot Zekhiah U-Matanah* 6:1; *Shulhan Arukh, Hoshen Mishpat,* sec. 246, para. 1); "if he did not leave himself any land his gift is not a valid gift," "and if he recovered his health he can have a change of heart, even if others had purchased the land

from the beneficiary, for it appears clear that he made the gift because he expected to die and with the understanding that if he did not die—the gift shall not be validated" (Mishnah Bava Batra, 146b, and Rashbam, *ad loc., s.v. lo shiyayr*): "if he died after the engagement a virgin collects only two hundred *zuz* of the *ketubah* allowance, and a widow a hundred, for he only wrote (the supplement to the *ketubah*) because he had expected to consummate the marriage" (Ketubot 54b, and see 56a); see also the subject of supportive conjectures mentioned by the Rosh on Ketubot, *ibid.*, though they are not all in the category of equivalents for a valid condition.

72. Cf. *Tosefot Ri HaZaken*, Kiddushin 49b–50a.

73. Ketubot 97a.

74. The explanation here offered follows the view of the Tosafot (Ketubot, *ibid., s.v. zavin*), in contradistinction to the interpretation of Rashi (*ibid., s.v. zavin*), for the explanation of the Tosafot was supported by almost all the codifiers (see Maimonides, *Mishneh Torah, Hilkhot Mekhirah* 11:8; *Tur, Hoshen Mishpat*, sec. 207, paras. 6, 7; *Shulhan Arukh, Hoshen Mishpat*, sec. 207, para. 3; the Rif on Ketubot, Ch. *Almanah Nizonet;* the Rosh on Ketubot, *ibid.;* agreeing with Rashi's interpretation is the Ritva on Ketubot, Ch. *Almanah Nizonet,* ed. Amsterdam 1709, p. 59a).

75. Ketubot, *ibid.*

76. Ketubot, *ibid.*

77. Ketubot, *ibid.*

78. Mar Shmuel is Samuel, and the incident on which he based himself in his reply to Rav Judah was the action carried out by his father, the father of Samuel.

79. Bava Metzia 24b.

80. Mishnah, Bava Batra 133b.

81. Rashbam, Bava Batra, *loc. cit., s.v. eyn ruah hakhamim.*

82. But he could not do this when in a state of health (Maimonides, *Mishneh Torah, Hilkhot Zekhiah U-Matanah* 12:2; *Hilkhot Nehalot* 6:4; *Shulhan Arukh, Hoshen Mishpat*, sec. 281, para. 5. Cf. Bava Batra 131a and Rashbam, *ad loc., s.v. be-vari haykh* and *bar oroti*).

83. Bava Batra 130a.

84. Mishnah, Bava Batra, *loc. cit.*, in the name of Rabbi Yohanan ben Beroka, and this is the law: Maimonides, *Mishneh Torah, Hilkhot Nehalot, loc. cit.*, laws 1, 2, 3; *Shulhan Arukh, Hoshen Mishpat,* sec. 281, probe there and infer.

85. Mishnah, Bava Batra 126b and Rashbam, *ad loc.:* "for a person

is empowered to make a gift of his property to anyone he wants";
Maimonides, *Mishneh Torah, Hilkhot Nehalot, loc. cit.*, law 5;
Shulhan Arukh, Hoshen Mishpat, loc. cit., para. 7.

86. The definition of *shekhiv mera* is: " a sick person whose body
has become weakened and who has lost his strength owing to illness,
so that he can no longer walk about and is confined to bed—such a
one is called *shekhiv mera*" (Maimonides, *Mishneh Torah, Hilkhot
Zekhiah U-Matanah* 8:2; see Bava Batra 153b, bot.).

87. "The oral instructions of a *shekhiv mera* are as though written
and transmitted" (Bava Batra 151a and elsewhere; Maimonides, *loc.
cit.*, law 1; *Shulhan Arukh, Hoshen Mishpat,* sec. 250, para. 1). This is a
takkanah ordained by the Sages "lest he lose consciousness" (Bava
Batra 147b), "for if his oral instructions did not take effect we fear
that he might lose his reason because of distress, knowing that
his children will not carry out his will" (Rashbam, *loc. cit., s.v. matnat
shekhiv mera*). The *Amoraim* Abaye and Rava disagreed as to when
the recipient acquires the property: "upon the onset of death" or
"after the onset of death" (Bava Batra 137a); it makes a difference in
connection with a specific matter, and the law is—after the onset of
death (Maimonides, *Mishneh Torah, Hilkhot Zekhiah U-Matanah*
12:10; *Shulhan Arukh, Hoshen Mishpat,* sec. 248, para. 4).

88. Not necessarily total disinheritance, but also discrimination
among the heirs by increasing the portion of one and decreasing the
portion of another (Rashbam, Bava Batra 133b, *s.v. ki avuray
ahsanta*).

89. This may be inferred from Maimonides, *Mishneh Torah,
Hilkhot Nehalot* 6:11.

90. Bava Kamma 97b.

91. See *supra*, Ch. 6, note 38.

92. Bava Kamma, *loc. cit.*

93. Maimonides, *Mishneh Torah, Hilkhot Gezelah Va-Avedah* 1:13.

94. "We do not accept from robbers and those who lend money on
interest who made voluntary restitution, . . . for the Sages made the
takkanah for penitents, they did not make a *takkanah* for robbers
who persist in their rebelliousness" (the Ramah, cited in *Shitah
Mekubetzet* on Bava Kamma Ch. 9, *loc. cit.*, p. 651). Maimonides
wrote similarly in the *Mishneh Torah, Hilkhot Gezelah Va-Avedah,
loc. cit.*): "and the robber sought to do penance, and came of his own
free will and returned the money he had robbed."

95. Maimonides, *ibid.*

96. The meaning is: after the sabbatical year had passed, for the

sabbatical year does not cancel a debt until its end (Rashi, Gittin 37b, *s.v. ha-mahazir*).

97. Sheviit, Ch. 10, *mishnah* 9.

98. Arakhin 28b; *Sifre,* Deuteronomy, sec. *Re'eh.*

99. Sheviit, *loc. cit., mishnah* 1, and elsewhere.

100. Sheviit, *loc. cit., mishnah* 8; Gittin 37b; Maimonides, *Mishneh Torah, Hilkhot Shemitah Ve-Yovel* 9:28, 29.

101. The reference here is to "objects that are not ordinarily lifted," for in the case of objects which are ordinarily lifted, the token of acquisition is lifting and not pulling (Bava Batra 86a; Maimonides, *Mishneh Torah, Hilkhot Mekhirah* 3:1). As far as the substantive conception of the Mishnah is concerned, it is of no consequence which is the efficacious token of acquisition.

102. Sheviit, *loc. cit., mishnah* 9.

103. Except for certain matters in which no formal token of acquisition is required, such as "writs of specification" [of dowry] (" 'How much do you give your son?' 'So much and so much.' 'And how much do you give your daughter?' 'So much and so much.' If they proceeded and effected a betrothal, the transaction is consummated; these are matters which are acquired orally": Kiddushin 9b); or the obligation of one who stands as surety for another in certain instances (see Bava Batra 173b, 176a and b; Maimonides, *Mishneh Torah, Hilkhot Malveh Ve-Loveh* 25:2; *Shulhan Arukh, Hoshen Mishpat,* sec. 129, para. 2).

104. For instance: acquisition through pulling, transfer and lifting, in the case of movable property and living things (Kiddushin 26a and 25b); entry into one's courtyard (Bava Metzia 11a–12a); incidental to the acquisition of land (Kiddushin 26a–27a; Bava Kamma 12a and b); money, writ, token of use, in connection with landed property (Kiddushin 26a); exchange or pulling at a garment which is efficacious to acquire every property (except coins) and to establish every form of obligation (Bava Metzia 47a and b); writing and transferring as acquisition of "letters," that is to say bills (Bava Batra 76a–77a); in the presence of the three, for the transfer of a debt (Gittin 13b); admission (Bava Batra 149a).

105. As the acquisition through pulling a garment (see note 104).

106. Yerushalmi Sheviit, Ch. 10, end.

107. Yerushalmi Sheviit, *loc. cit.*

108. I stated in note 5 *supra* that conceivably there may be a very fine distinction in nuance between "the spirit of the Sages is not pleased with him" and "the standard of saintliness." There is room

to argue that the call to keep the standard of saintliness (*midat hasidut*) is directed to the *hasidim* only, to one who is truly a *hasid* in all his ways. Proof for this, when we probe carefully, is to be found in the words of Maimonides, *Mishneh Torah, Hilkhot Nehalot* 6:11:

> Whoever bestows his property upon others and disinherits his children—even though they do not behave as they should—the spirit of the Sages is not pleased with him but those others acquire whatever he gave them. It is within the standard of saintliness that a *hasid* shall not serve as a witness to a will in which an heir is disinherited from his inheritance.

The term *midat hasidut*, the standard of saintliness, means in essence: the standard by which *hasidim* guide themselves—a category established by experience, as it were. It bears a kernel of the imperative: seek to be a *hasid* and in the end you will act like them! As long as you have not yet reached to the measure of saintliness, it is not for you to pursue saintly actions, for your actions will be unrelated actions, out of character, that will not fit in with your spiritual state. This concept—that there is not much merit to the good deed when it is detached from the general moral stature of the doer—received much stress in the "moralistic yeshivot" of Lithuania, and it found support in the statement of the *Mesilat Yesharim* by Rabbi Moshe Hayim Luzzatto, Ch. 14, on the dictum of Mar Ukba in the chapter *Kol HaBasar* (Hullin 105a). Mar Ukba stated there: "In respect to this matter I am, in comparison to my father, 'vinegar, the child of wine.' If my father ate meat now, he would not eat cheese until the next day at the same time; although I would not eat it at the same meal, I would eat it at the next meal." And why did not Mar Ukba act like his father? One must say, because his general moral stature was lower than that of his father, "because he did not practice as much abstinence as he."

109. It is my impression that there are no more in the Babylonian Talmud, but I may be mistaken. It is interesting—and I do not know if others have noted it—that the author of the statement "a standard of saintliness is referred to here" is in every instance the *Amora* Rav Hisda, in accordance with the statement: "You are Hisda and your words are kindly [*hisda'in*] (Gittin 7a).

110. The *sela* is four *dinarim* (*zuzim*) and the *dinar* is six silver *ma'ot* (cf. Mishnah, Bava Batra 165b; Bekhorot 50a). The coin *isar* mentioned here is a silver *ma'ah* (see Rashi, Bava Metzia 51b, *s.v. isar le-dinar*).

111. Bava Metzia 51b–52a.

112. *Ibid.*, 52b.

113. See the discussion in the Gemara, Bava Metzia 52a, in the beginning of the discussion.

114. Shabbat 120a.

115. *Ibid.*

116. Hanoch Albeck, *Shishah Sidray Mishnah, Seder Moed*, tractate Shabbat 16:3.

117. *Shulhan Arukh, Orah Hayim*, sec. 334, para. 9. Concerning the items that may be salvaged from the fire on the Sabbath and the extent of salvaging, see Mishnah and Gemara, Shabbat, Ch. *Kol Kitvay*.

118. The interpretation adopted here conforms to the views of most commentators, except for the matter of the "wisdom" of the rescuer which I have explained according to Albeck's interpretation, which appears to me to be basic, for it tends to resolve many difficulties in this theme.

119. Here, apparently, there is no supportive conjecture for the intention of the owner of the house, for only "a wise one" understands this, and therefore it falls into the category of "words in the heart," which diminish nothing from the legal status of ownerless property.

120. According to the second view in the discussion of the Talmud, Rava's view, as explained by Rashi (Shabbat, *loc. cit., s.v. hakha*), only a person who is "God-fearing but not a *hasid*," will claim compensation for his rescue, for a *hasid* is accustomed to "forego his own." According to this view, the law as expounded in the Mishnah is in contradiction to the standard of saintliness.

121. Hullin 130b.

122. See *supra*, Ch. 5, notes 13, 14.

123. Rashi, Hullin, *loc. cit., s.v. ve-tzarikh litol.*

124. Hullin, *ibid.*, beginning of side b. There is an alternative explanation for this law; probe there.

125. Rashi, Hullin, *ibid., s.v. she'en lo tov'eim.*

126. This becomes apparent from the challenge of Rava, *loc. cit.*: "The *Tanna* taught, 'He must pay,' and you say that we are dealing here with the standard of saintliness!"

127. Probe and infer from Tosafot, Hullin, *loc. cit., s.v. tanna tani yeshalem.*

128. The Rif and the Rosh on Bava Metzia, Ch. *HaSokher et HaUmanin.*

129. Bava Metzia 83a.

130. The use of the plural term (*tavrayn*) indicates, in my opinion, that the reference is to the pots and not to the potter, and therefore we must render the term "they were broken" rather than "he broke them" as is explained by the author of *HaPerush HaKatzar* on the Yerushalmi.

131. *Gulta* refers, it seems, to an outer garment. Cf. Bava Metzia 85a: "a wise craftsman made you and they spread over you a *gulta* of gold"; Shabbat 77b: "unroll your *gulta* and sit down," and the commentary of Rashi, *ad loc.*

132. Yerushalmi, Bava Metzia, Ch. 6, end (*HaSokher et HaUmanin*).

133. Sanhedrin 17b: "They sent from there (from *Eretz Yisrael*) Rabbi Yose bar Haninah."

134. Rashi, Bava Metzia 83a, *s.v. shkulai:* "and they broke it, not in a sloping place and in gross negligence, or on a pole [*digla*]," and cf. Gemara, *ibid.*, 82b and 83a. *Digla*—a pole split at the top with the loads of two people suspended on it, and he placed his neck between the two splits and bore the load which was on his shoulders . . ." (Rashi, *ad loc., s.v. dedaro be-digla*), and see Maimonides, *Mishneh Torah, Hilkhot Sekhirut* 3:2; *Tur, Hoshen Mishpat*, sec. 304, para. 3; *Shulhan Arukh, Hoshen Mishpat*, sec. 304, para. 2.

135. The view of the Ramakh, cited in the *Shitah Mekubetzet* on Bava Metzia, *loc. cit.*, p. 904.

136. Shabbat 128a; *Seder HaDorot, s.v. Rav Huna*, letter *vav*, probe it.

137. Bava Batra 136b; Margaliot, *Encyclopediah LeHakhmay HaTalmud Ve-HaGeonim, s.v. Rabbah bar Rav Huna.*

138. See *infra*, note 139.

139. Sanhedrin 19b.

140. Mishnah, Bava Metzia 33a.

141. Rosh Hashanah 25b.

142. Shevuot 18a.

143. Sanhedrin 110a.

144. Mishnah, Bekhorot 28b; Bava Kamma 100a; Sanhedrin 33a. There are many distinctions and differences of opinion with reference to this, such as: a distinction between one who is an expert and one who is not, or between one who erred with regard to something written in the Mishnah and something which is in his discretion, and others (see the discussion in Sanhedrin, *ibid.;* the discussion in Bava

Kamma, *loc. cit.*; Maimonides, *Mishneh Torah, Hilkhot Sanhedrin,* Ch. 6; *Shulhan Arukh, Hoshen Mishpat,* sec. 25), but it is conceivable that under certain circumstances Rav would have been obligated to pay the damage.

145. We do not derive a new law from what is said in the Prophets and the Hagiographa; see Bava Kamma 2b, and Rashi, *ad loc., s.v. divray kabbalah;* Hagigah 10b.

146. Some support for this may be found in the *Tur, Hoshen Mishpat,* sec. 304, para. 1, and *Sema, Shulhan Arukh, Hoshen Mishpat,* sec. 304, para. 1, small para. 1. Incidentally, the *Tur* and the *Sema,* following Rashi (Bava Metzia 83a, *s.v. be-derekh tovim*), place the obligation which Rav placed on the employer in the category of "beyond the strict law," which is to say, an obligation from the laws of *yosher.* It appears to me that this is not so, and the proof herefor is: Maimonides and the *Shulhan Arukh* did not include in their writings this law of *yosher.* See *infra,* section 7 of this chapter.

147. Though there are at times certain specified cases on whom the obligation of *yosher* does not fall, such as a woman and orphans in connection with the law of prior right for a neighbor to buy land contiguous to his own (Bava Metzia 108b).

148. Under discussion here is "beyond the strict law" in the "technical" sense, as exemplified practically in the cases cited in the Talmud. In a general way, and in the free "literary" sense, the commentators and codifiers used this term to designate all those actions which are done "outside the law." It is conceivable that it is in this general sense also that Rashi, the *Tur,* and the *Sema* used the term in connection with the incident reported in "those porters" (see note 146 *supra*). Also the expression the "standard of saintliness," or the "way of saintliness" is to be found in post-talmudic literature as a general designation for the laws of *yosher* (see, for example, Maimonides, *Mishneh Torah, Hilkhot Shekhenim* 14:5).

149. Maimonides, *Mishneh Torah, Hilkhot Gezelah Va-Avedah* 11:7; *Tur, Hoshen Mishpat,* sec. 259, para. 10; *Shulhan Arukh, Hoshen Mishpat,* sec. 259, para. 5; Maimonides, *Mishneh Torah, Hilkhot Rotzeah U-Shemirat Nefesh* 13:4; *Bet Yosef* on the *Tur, Hoshen Mishpat,* sec. 12, small para. 5, in the name of R. Yeruham, in the name of the Rosh; *Rama, Hoshen Mishpat,* sec. 12, para. 2; otherwise in *Hagahot Maimoniyot* on Maimonides, *Mishneh Torah, Hilkhot Gezelah Va-Avedah,* Ch. 11, in the name of the Raviah, in

the name of Rabenu [Samson] of Chinon; *Rama, Hoshen Mishpat*, sec. 12, para. 2, in the name of the *Mordecai*.

150. See Bava Batra, 133b; Maimonides, *Mishneh Torah, Hilkhot Nehalot* 6:11, end; *Shulhan Arukh, Hoshen Mishpat*, sec. 282, para. 1.

151. See Kiddushin 49b. Rabbi Elazar ben Azariah was a very wealthy person, and the tithe from his flock amounted to 12,000 calves each year (Shabbat 54b).

152. Snell, *Principles of Equity*, 22nd ed., p. 2.

153. *I.e.*, King's Bench, Common Pleas and Exchequer.

154. Tout, *Place of Edward II in English History*, cited by Holdsworth, *History of English Law*, 7th ed., Vol. 1, p. 395.

155. Hanbury, *Modern Equity*, 7th ed., p. 6.

156. *Vide* Kerly, *History of Equity*, p. 28.

157. Hanbury, *op. cit.*, p. 6.

158. Hanbury, *op. cit.*, p. 13; cf. Holdsworth, *op cit.*, p. 457.

159. Hanbury, *op. cit.*, p. 14.

160. Cf. Holdsworth, *op. cit.*, at 454: ". . . the Chancellor so developed the duties . . . of the persons to whom property had been conveyed on trust, that the interest of the cestui-que use, that is the person for whose benefit the property was conveyed, became a form of *equitable ownership* of a sort *which has no parallel in any other system of law.*"

161. *Vide* Hanbury, *op. cit.*, p. 15.

162. Halsbury-Hailsham, *Laws of England*, Vol. 13, p. 11, para. 4; *Bennet v. Davis* (1725), 24 E.R. 746.

163. Holdsworth, *op. cit.*, p. 458.

164. See note 160 *supra*.

165. See *supra*, Ch. 3, end of section 2.

166. See above, Ch. 3, note 43.

167. For the *takkanot* of Usha see Ketubot 78b; cf. Bava Kamma 89b, and Rashi, *ad loc., s.v. savruha*.

168. Mishnah and Gemara, Nedarim 88a; Maimonides, *Mishneh Torah, Hilkhot Nedarim* 7:17; *Hilkhot Zekhiah U-Matanah* 3:14; *Shulhan Arukh, Yoreh De'ah*, sec. 222, para. 1; *Shulhan Arukh, Even HaEzer*, sec. 85, para. 11, and compare the variant readings there.

169. There exist one or two other forms of acquisition which are capable of creating an obligation, but the matter is fraught with controversy and this is not the place to elaborate.

170. Cf. and probe well in Tosafot, Ketubot 54b, *s.v. af al pi;* the Rosh, *ad loc.; Tur, Hoshen Mishpat*, sec. 60, para. 10; *Shulhan Arukh, Hoshen Mishpat*, sec. 60, para. 6; see Z. Warhaftig, "Specific Per-

formance in Hebrew Law," *Scripta Hierosolymitana,* Vol. 5, *Studies in Law,* pp. 195–218.

171. Bava Kamma 37a, and see Rashi *ad loc., s.v. eyn tzerikhin.*

172. Cf. *Teshuvot HaRosh,* principle 85, secs. 5, 6; *Responsa of the Rashdam,* division *Hoshen Mishpat,* sec. 434.

CHAPTER VIII: AT THE CROSSROADS

1. *Hasan Hamad v. Beralsina,* L.A. 1/36, 3 P.L.R. 178; *Kuri v. Slavsky,* C.A. 132/38, 5 P.L.R. 378.

2. *Faruki v. Ayoub,* P.C.A. 1/35, 2 P.L.R. 390; C. A. 191/37, 2 Lebanon 169.

3. See L.A. 1/36, mentioned in note 1 *supra.*

4. Such as the need for corroboration to single evidence in the case of sexual offenses, or to single evidence of a partner to the offense; laws concerning "estoppels," including matters of "res judicata," which are, as is well known, also "rules of evidence."

5. Like the Criminal Code Ordinance 1936, sec. 4; Civil Wrongs Ordinance 1944, sec. 2.

6. *Sherman et al. v. Danovitz,* C.A. 113/40, 8 Lebanon 17.

7. *London Society for the Advancement of Christianity v. Or,* C.A. 29/47, 14 P.L.R. 218.

8. *"Shimshon" v. Attorney General,* Motion 41/49, 4 *P.D.* 143; *Fingold et al. v. the General Guardian et al.,* C.A. 55/49, 5 *P.D.* 1180; the decision of Justice Cheshin, *"Peles" Ltd. v. Office of Transportation,* C.A. 28/52, 9 *P.D.* 436, pp. 440–441; my decision, *ibid.,* pp. 443–444.

9. *Jakobovitz v. Attorney General,* Cr. A. 125/50, 6 *P.D.* 514.

10. *Ibid.,* pp. 564–565.

11. *Eshed, Temporary Center for Transportation v. Attorney General,* Cr. A. 53/54, 8 *P.D.* 785.

12. The reference is to the English decision in the case of *R. v. Newland* (1954), 37 Cr. App. R. 154.

13. 8 *P.D., op. cit.,* p. 796.

14. See note 12 *supra.*

15. *Kokhavi v. Becker et al.,* C.A. 81/55; 84/55; 91/55; 92/55, 11 *P.D.* 225.

16. The reference is to my separate decision in the case of *Eshed,* 8 *P.D., op. cit.,* pp. 828–829.

17. 11 *P.D., op. cit.,* p. 244.

18. *Supra,* note 15.

19. This is the age which is regarded as the time of retirement from work, and until then the courts customarily obligate the one who caused the damage to pay for the loss of his capacity to earn, or at least the reduction in the capacity to earn, on the part of the damaged person. This is also the age of male retirement from work, for purposes of receiving old-age pension, according to para. 5 (1) of the National Insurance Law, 5714–1953. See the decision of Justice Landau, *Tanenbaum v. Nahum*, C.A. 94/56, 10 *P.D.* 1602, p. 1608, but cf. the decision of Justice Bernson, *Wolfovitz v. Fisher*, C.A. 286/55, 11 *P.D.* 379, pp. 388–391.

20. *Grossman v. Roth*, C.A. 70/52, 6 *P.D.* 1242.

21. 6 *P.D., ibid.*, p. 1252.

22. Paragraph 33 (b) of the Law of the Courts, 5717–1957, which provides: "A decision rendered by the Supreme Court obligates every court, except the Supreme Court." But cf. my decision, *Balan v. the Executors of the Will of Raymond Litvinsky*, F.H. 23/60, 15 *P.D.* 71, pp. 75–76.

23. *Romm v. the Minister of the Treasury*, H.C. 287/51; 34/52; 324/52, 8 *P.D.* 494.

24. (1955), 3 All E.R. 796.

25. 11 *P.D., op. cit.*, p. 244.

26. *Ibid.*, p. 236.

27. *Ibid.*, p. 246.

28. See the statement of Justice Vitcon, *ibid.*, p. 236, before the sentences cited here, and the statement of Justice Landau, *ibid.*, p. 237, at the opening of his decision.

29. Cf. Allen, *Law in the Making*, 5th ed., p. 281 *et seq.*

30. Avot 2:7.

31. Kaunitz, *History of Philosophy*, p. 13.

32. *Cavendish v. Middleton* (1628), 79 E.R. 725; *Thorpe v. Thorpe* (1701) 92 E.R. 980; *Davis v. Morgan* (1825), 107 E.R. 962. Cf. *etiam* Holmes, *The Common Law*, 40th ed., p. 274 *et seq.*

33. *Nicholson v. Chapman* (1793), 126 E.R. 536; *The Great Northern Railway Co. v. Swaffield* (1874), 30 L.T. 562; *Sims and Co. v. Midland Railway Co.* (1913), 1 K.B. 103, 112; *Springer v. Great Western Railway Co.* (1921), 1 K.B. 257, 268; McCardie J., in *Prager v. Blatspiel* (1924), 1 K.B. 566, 568–570; but cf. Scrutton L.J., in *Jebara v. Ottoman Bank* (1927), 2 K.B. 254, 270–271.

34. *Ridley v. Blacket* (1795), 170 E.R. 195; *Crapp v. East Soonehous Local Board* (1889), 5 T.L.R. 501; *Metropolitan Railway Co. v. Jackson* (1877), 37 L.T. 679; *Hobbs v. L. & S. W. Ry. Co.* (1875), 32

L.T. 352; *Smith v. London & S.W. Ry. Co.* (1870), 23 L.T. 678; *In re Polemis v. Furness, Withy & Co.* (1921) 3 K.B. 560; *Overseas Tankship (U.K.) Ltd. v. Morts Dock & Engineering Co., Ltd.* (1961) 1 All E.R. 404; see my decision in *Malkah v. Attorney General,* Cr. A. 47/56, 10 *P.D.* 1543.

35. Note 33 *supra,* the decision in the case of *Prager v. Blatspiel.*

36. Cited in my decision, *Shapiro v. Posnansky,* C.A. 46/53, 10 *P.D.* 461, p. 471.

37. See *supra,* section 3 of this chapter.

38. *Supra,* note 12.

39. Cf. the decision of Justice Cheshin, *Eshed v. Attorney General,* Cr.A. 53/54, 8 *P.D.* 785, cited *supra* (note 11), and especially the beginning of section 9 of the decision, p. 796, *ibid.*

40. M. Silberg, "Lashon—Zu Signon," *Leshonenu La-Am,* 5721, pp. 166–167.

41. M. Silberg, "HaMishpat BaMedinah HaIvrit," in *HaPeraklit,* Iyar-Sivan 5708, p. 105.

42. M. Silberg, "Li-She'elat Arikhat Kodex Ivri," *HaPeraklit,* Tishre 5708, pp. 262–264.

43. In my essay, *HaPeraklit, ibid.,* p. 264, it is written erroneously: the *Tur.*

44. See the general rules followed by the Deciders [*poskim*] as drawn up by the author of *Keneset HaGedolah,* sec. 25, in the name of Rabbi Moses Galante, in the name of the *Bet Yosef.*

45. As in the cases of: *Agushevitz v. Futerman,* C.A. 47/48, 5 *P.D.* 4; *Danokh v. Attorney General,* Cr.A. 10/50, 5 *P.D.* 81; *Wolfson v. Spinnes,* C.A. 25/50, 5 *P.D.* 265; *Dvik v. Lalo,* C.A. 99/49, 5 *P.D.* 625; *Engelmayer v. Linderman,* C.A. 90/51, 6 *P.D.* 426; *Rappaport v. the Mayor of Netanyah,* H.C. 59/52, 6 *P.D.* 492; *Amal v. Shindler,* C.A. 130/50, 6 *P.D.* 710; *Pesahovitz v. the Chairman and Members of the Council of Bat Yam,* H.C. 172/52, 6 *P.D.* 934; *"Eged" v. Brandes,* C.A. 207/51, 6 *P.D.* 1089; *Rotenstreich v. Attorney General,* Cr.A. 35/52, 7 *P.D.* 58; *Mashchensky v. Michalitz,* C.A. 64/50, 7 *P.D.* 324; *Solomon v. Attorney General,* Cr.A. 106/53, 7 *P.D.* 824; *Hecker v. Barash ("Arizona"),* C.A. 208/51, 8 *P.D.* 566; *Eshed v. Attorney General,* Cr.A. 53/54, 8 *P.D.* 785; *Rosenbaum v. Zager,* C.A. 248/53, 9 *P.D.* 533; *Jacobs v. Cartuz,* C.A. 110/53, 9 *P.D.* 1401; *Malkah v. Attorney General,* Cr.A. 47/56, 10 *P.D.* 1543; *Lubin v. Township of Tel Aviv,* H.C. 163/57, 12 *P.D.* 1042; *Township of Tel Aviv v. Lubin,* F.H. 13/58, 13 *P.D.* 118; *Tribish v. Attorney General,* Cr.A. 141/59, 13 *P.D.* 1793; *Padva v. Friedman,* C.A. 260/57, 14 *P.D.* 427;

Kizis v. Shapushnik, C.A. 551/59, 14 *P.D.* 1380; *Shmuel v. Yisrael,* C.A. 99/60, 14 *P.D.* 1642; *Dagay Doar Ltd. v. the Director of Taxes and Farmer's Produce,* C.A. 20/60, 14 *P.D.* 1933; *Rabbi Solomon Abudi v. the Minister of Religions,* H.C. 205 + 210/60, 14 *P.D.* 2020; *Rabbi Solomon Abudi v. the Minister of Religions,* F.H. 21/60, 14 *P.D.* 2045; *Finkelstein v. Frusteir,* C.A. 459/59, 14 *P.D.* 2327; *The Director of Inheritance Tax v. the Estate of Sociano,* C.A. 376/60, 14 *P.D.* 2475; *Attorney General v. So-and-So and So-and-So,* Cr.A. 222/60, 14 *P.D.* 2511; *Kleiner v. the Director of Inheritance Tax,* C.A. 263/60, 14 *P.D.* 2521; *Rehani v. Tzidki,* C.A. 335/59, 15 *P.D.* 159; *So-and-So v. So-and-So,* C.A. 407/60, 15 *P.D.* 212; *Sahar v. Attorney General,* Cr.A. 20/61, 15 *P.D.* 561; and others.

46. M. Silberg, "Tehiyat HaMishpat HaIvri Ke-Mishpat Ha-Medinah Be-Yisrael—Kaytzad?" *Sura,* Vol. III, pp. 459 ff.

47. Mishnah, Eduyot 1:5; Gittin 36b, and cf. *ibid.*

Index